UNTOLD STORIES
HONG KONG ARCHITECTURE

RAYMOND FUNG

UNICORN

Amidst a departure from the mainstream,
these humble tributaries shall persist in their eternal flow.

Everyone should have ideals while they dream.
Being an architect with ideals is a promise to Hong Kong.
My promise to Hong Kong is writing a story about this city.

Preface

From a tender age, I harboured a steadfast dream of becoming an architect. Through the labyrinthine path that life presented, that dream transformed into a tangible reality. However, as the sun began to set on my professional journey, a new aspiration took hold: to bring forth a retrospective book infused with the flair of the 'literary youth' that draws upon my experience as an architect. In the year 2016, I unveiled the culmination of this ambition and published *The Untold Story of Raymond Fung*, adorned with the captivating subtitle – *Untold Stories: Hong Kong Architecture*. Yet, even as the ink dried on its pages, an unspoken yearning lingered within me – an intangible sense that there remained untrodden paths awaiting exploration, beckoning me to continue my creative odyssey.

The result is this publication – a book that expounds the stories behind local works of architecture and design: *Untold Stories: Hong Kong Architecture*. The content has been centred around specific architecture selected by our team, as well as the stories and heartfelt dialogues with the respective architect or designer so that these unknown stories could be told. The team has divided the city of Hong Kong into seven regions and seeks to lead readers on a journey to understand and appreciate these masterpieces so painstakingly designed by their creators.

The theme of this book is 'Amidst a departure from the mainstream, these humble tributaries shall persist in their eternal flow.' The 'non-mainstream' architectural works being introduced here are not confined to the most outstanding or grand, nor are they the most familiar local landmarks. The basis of consideration while the team went through the process of selecting around seventy architectural projects focused on creating a holistic experience for the reader – leading them on a walk through the streets and alleyways of the city, whether in real life or solely through the pages of this book.

Partitioning a region is quite a challenge. If partitioning were carried out according to the traditional Hong Kong, Kowloon and New Territories areas, some areas would have been unevenly represented. However, referencing all eighteen districts would have been too cumbersome, as well. Therefore, a final compromise was made to divide the city into seven districts: Island North, Island South, Kowloon East, West Kowloon, New Territories East, New Territories West and the Outlying Islands, with six to ten interviews allocated to each district. From a purely design-focused perspective, there are more than one hundred architects, landscape architects and designers being covered in this book. Some of the projects covered here were also done in collaboration with other project teams including their respective 'Authorised Persons'; to this end, we hope readers will be understanding if some of the details of such projects are not comprehensively covered. We look forward to supplementing this book with more content in the future with the introduction of a new generation of beautiful architecture to make up for any deficiencies in this present edition.

Selection of Works

It should be noted that the team are all admirers of fair-faced concrete architecture, which has had a long history in Hong Kong. In the 1960s, the late Mr Szeto Wai was the architect in charge of the then new campus of The Chinese University of Hong Kong. The foundation of this fondness for fair-faced concrete was thus later laid in its masterplan. The Japanese modern architecture style that was widely popular amongst the youth in Hong Kong, from the brutalism of the Kenzo Tange style to the minimalistic style of Tadao Ando, has flourished and continues to be visible in abundance on the campus of The Chinese University of Hong Kong today.

Concerns of the Team

Throughout the various chapters of this book, we have often expressed our concerns on the redevelopment of the old districts. While there are those who yearn to break the old and establish anew, there are others who reminisce about the past and are worried about losing the simple folk customs and harmony which characterise the old neighbourhoods – a sentiment that resonates with me, personally. New developments have brought forth large-scale buildings and generic shopping malls that impact on the original texture of this city as well as the social fabric attached to it; such phenomena may well trigger contemplation of the original intention of creating 'people-oriented' spaces.

Land scarcity is severe in Hong Kong, so shouldn't we cherish every available inch of space? The people of this city have resorted to travelling overseas to seek out the simple and natural garden parks in foreign lands. If large-scale greeneries could be preserved by our local parks, wouldn't that provide the beautiful and unrestrained visual enjoyment that the people of this city have long dreamed of? Mies van der Rohe once presented his golden proposal of 'Less is More', to which I propose 'Building Less for More'. While the former is about simplicity, the latter is about restraining the scale of architecture, and leaving more breathing space for the people.

Raymond Fung
Spring 2022
Archivilla

Table of Contents

	Preface	4
Island North	Reading Guidance	14
	TUVE Hotel | Why Be High-Profile If You Can Stay Low-Key?	22
	H Queen's | The Colourful World Shall Come to You	28
	ACTS Rednaxela Serviced Apartments | The Song of a Wanderer	34
	The Oi! Phase II · Eastern Community Green Station | Urban Respite	40
	Transforming Star Street | The Study of a Storyteller	48
	Blue House | Continuation of a Splash of Blue	54
	Hong Kong Waterfront Promenade · Central Market | Seventy-Three Kilometres	60
	Hong Kong Museum of Coastal Defence · Fireboat Alexander Grantham Exhibition Gallery | Guarding the Memory of Hong Kong	68
	Aldrich Bay Park | Further, Wider, Deeper	74
Island South	Reading Guidance	80
	University of Chicago Booth School of Business, Hong Kong | Born Here, Honoured Here	84
	St Stephen's College Preparatory School · The Béthanie | Bringing History Into Life	88
	Victoria Peak Garden | Guardians	94
	Stanley Promenade · Stanley Municipal Services Building | Coming to a Small Town by the Sea	100
	Graduate House, The University of Hong Kong | Undaunted by the Highest of Mountains and the Deepest of Valleys	108

Kowloon East	Reading Guidance	114
	Bridged House | Rhythm in the Upstream	122
	Diamond Hill Crematorium | Ponder Deeply, Move on Gently	128
	Kwun Tong Promenade · Energizing Kowloon East · InPARK · Hoi Bun Road Park | The Secret That Lies in Patience and Perseverance	134
	Concert Hall of the Alliance Primary School, Kowloon Tong, Oootopia | Pyrophoric	146
	Morse Park · P.L.K. Stanley Ho Sau Nan Primary School | Miniature Community	152
	Cattle Depot Art Park | First Step to an Interesting Path	158
	Zero Carbon Building | Beauty out of Thrifty	162
	La Villa De La Salle | Frozen Zeal	168
West Kowloon	Reading Guidance	174
	The Hong Kong Palace Museum | Every Cloud Has a Silver Lining	180
	Hong Kong Museum of Art | A New Cubic Look	188
	West Kowloon Mediation Centre · Long Mei Beach · Shing Kai Road Refuse Collection Point | A Minimalistic Temperature	192
	Jao Tsung-I Academy | A Refined and Silent Nurture	198
	Jockey Club Creative Arts Centre | It All Starts Here	202
	Tsim Sha Tsui Promenade | Strolling by the Sea	206

New Territories East	Reading Guidance	212
	Hoi Ha Visitor Centre · Che Kung Temple Sports Centre | Picking Chrysanthemums Under the Eastern Hedge	216
	Wo Hop Shek Crematorium · Pak Shek Kok Promenade | The Art Museum at the End	224
	Wo Hop Shek Columbarium | The Land of Reminiscence	230
	French International School · Shaw Auditorium, Hong Kong University of Science and Technology | No Going Back	234
	Lai Chi Wo Hakka Life Experience Village | Mr Reclusive	240
	Archivilla · The Flower Box | House of the Rising Sun	244
	Learning Garden, The Chinese University of Hong Kong University Library | The Difficulty of Determination Lies in Challenging Yourself	250
	The Lee Shau Kee Architecture Building, Chinese University of Hong Kong | Isn't it Delightful to Roam Within	256
	Morningside College, Chinese University of Hong Kong | Runway	260
	Sai Kung Visual Corridor | Not Just the Rear Garden of Hong Kong	264

New Territories West	Reading Guidance	274
	The Hong Kong Wetland Park | Building Less for More	278
	Chu Hai College of Higher Education | Though the Sparrow Is Small	286
	The Mills | A Place for Sharing Inspirations	292
	Tsing Yi Southwest Sports Centre | Between Strength and Gentleness	298
	The Community College at Lingnan University | Revitalising the Siheyuan	302
	Vice Versa House | As Within, So Without	306

Outlying Islands	Reading Guidance	312
	OOAK LAMMA | Unwilling to Wait Ten Years for the Applause	316
	The Wisdom Path | Behind the Contentment	322
	Jockey Club Mong Tung Wan Hostel | You Gotta Dance	326
	Christian Zheng Sheng College | The Path of Return is Always Longer	332
	Tai O Heritage Hotel | Big City, Small Scene	338
	Ham Tin Villas | An Immersive Moment	342

Giving Young Architects a Chance	346
Epilogue: The Whys and Wherefores of this Book	352
Acknowledgements	354
List of Interviewed and Mentioned Architects	355
Citation	356

New Territories West

39 The Hong Kong Wetland Park
40 Chu Hai College of Higher Education
41 The Mills
42 Tsing Yi Southwest Sports Centre
43 The Community College at Lingnan University
44 Vice Versa House

New Territories East

29 Hoi Ha Visitor Centre
30 Wo Hop Shek Crematorium
31 Wo Hop Shek Columbarium
32 French International School
33 Lai Chi Wo Hakka Life Experience Village
34 Archivilla
35 Learning Garden, The Chinese University of Hong Kong University Library
36 The Lee Shau Kee Architecture Building, Chinese University of Hong Kong
37 Morningside College, Chinese University of Hong Kong
38 Sai Kung Visual Corridor

West Kowloon

23 The Hong Kong Palace Museum
24 Hong Kong Museum of Art
25 West Kowloon Mediation Centre
26 Jao Tsung-I Academy
27 Jockey Club Creative Arts Centre
28 Tsim Sha Tsui Promenade

Kowloon East

15 Bridged House
16 Diamond Hill Crematorium
17 Kwun Tong Promenade
18 Concert Hall of the Alliance Primary School, Kowloon Tong
19 Morse Park
20 Cattle Depot Art Park
21 Zero Carbon Building
22 La Villa De La Salle

Island North

1 TUVE Hotel
2 H Queen's
3 ACTS Rednaxela | ACTS Rednaxela Serviced Apartments
4 The Oi! Phase II
5 Star Street
6 Blue House
7 Hong Kong Waterfront Promenade
8 Hong Kong Museum of Coastal Defence
9 Aldrich Bay Park

Outlying Islands

45 OOAK LAMMA
46 The Wisdom Path
47 Jockey Club Mong Tung Wan Hostel
48 Christian Zheng Sheng College
49 Tai O Heritage Hotel
50 Ham Tin Villas

Island South

10 University of Chicago Booth School of Business, Hong Kong
11 St Stephen's College Preparatory School
12 Victoria Peak Garden
13 Stanley Promenade
14 Graduate House, The University of Hong Kong

Island North

The general public does not usually find Hong Kong's architecture to be all that appealing. Perhaps this is due to the people of this city having an acquired taste for antique buildings, the best of which have unfortunately disappeared during the last century in the 1960s and 1970s. This has resulted in a common perception that much of modern architecture looks and feels aesthetically unpleasing, like square boxes that are neither gigantic nor unconventional enough to be iconic. Thus, this has often given Hong Kong a bad name for lacking architecture with soul and substance.

Fortunately, Hong Kong Doesn't Have Many Super-High-Rise Buildings

I think it best that Hong Kong's architecture does not have the so-called iconic elements, especially in light of the world's increasingly irrational obsession with taller and bigger buildings. With the continuous advancement of engineering technology, competing in the height category of a building is no longer a meaningful or difficult feat. Take the current tallest building in the world, for example, the Burj Khalifa at 828 metres, whose title will soon be claimed by the 1,008-metre-tall Jeddah Tower; and the fourth tallest building in the world, the 601-metre Makkah Clock Royal Tower, an overtly gigantic building unbefitting of its surroundings. The frenzy of the skyscraper boom that originated in New York over a hundred years ago has travelled across to Asia in the last twenty years. As a result, Asia is now home to ten of the tallest buildings in the world scattered across its major cities. However, such mindless and numb pursuit in the representation of technological and economic powers is gradually becoming meaningless.

Many of the world's strange yet proud buildings have become the laughing stock of the cities in which they reside. In Chinese Mainland, for example, in order to raise the standard of the ordinary citizen's appreciation in the art of architectural design, competitions are held for both the most beautiful and ugliest buildings in the country. The Central Government also recognises that flamboyant buildings not only impair a city's visual harmony but can also cause serious damage and waste in energy; as such, policies have been put in place to prohibit the construction of skyscrapers above 500 metres. Fortunately, no such exaggerated building yet exists in Hong Kong, as the residents of this city do not have such a height obsession when it comes to architecture. As an example, construction of the 88-storey International Finance Centre attracted considerable controversy. At that time, Ms Christine Loh, who was against the idea of building such a behemoth along the central waterfront thought such a structure would be incoherent to the overall cityscape. She later assembled several hundred architects at the Designing Hong Kong[1] consultation forum and proposed an alternative plan for a complex of buildings. Through my participation at the forum, I was deeply moved by the love shown by the community of local architects towards the city, as well as their shared awareness of the importance of coherence for our cityscape. Although the forum did not manage to alter the outcome, the whole episode sent a clear message to the authorities that the people of this city would not be proud of architecture based merely on its height alone. Currently, the two tallest buildings are the 415-metre, 88-storey high International Finance Centre and the 484-metre, 108-storey high International Commerce Centre; positioned on either side of the Victoria Harbour, they act as the 'Doorway to Hong Kong.'

Island North – A Great Place to Appreciate Modern Architecture

To appreciate modern architecture in Hong Kong, one can begin this journey of appreciation from the Hong Kong Island. Taking the central mountain range of the Hong Kong Island as a dividing point, the island can be divided into the southern and northern parts. This chapter covers the northern part of the Hong Kong Island from Sai Wan (Western district) to Chai Wan (Eastern district), and along the coastline there is the world-famous and beautiful Victoria Harbour, which is located in the section from Central to Admiralty where many landmark buildings stand: the HSBC headquarters building designed by Norman Foster[2], the Bank of China headquarters building designed by I.M. Pei[3], Phases 1 and 2 of the Hong Kong International Financial Centre designed by César Pelli[4], the Henderson designed by Zaha Hadid[5], the Hong Kong Club Building designed by Harry Seidler[6], Lippo Centre designed by Paul Rudolph[7], the AIA Central designed by SOM[8], the Asia Society Hong Kong Centre designed by Tod Williams[9] and Billie Tsien[10], and the British Consulate General Hong Kong designed by Terry Farrell[11]; these are famous buildings designed by world-renowned architects as well as many local

master architects. Together they have turned Hong Kong into an international architecture expo and a great place for admiring modern architecture.

Walking along the Island North, it is easy to gain a perspective on Hong Kong's historical pulses, as it was the earliest sector of the city to be developed. It is home to the traditional salted fish and seafood stores in Sai Ying Pun, the longstanding ginseng shop of Nam Pei Hong in Sheung Wan and Central, which itself is the embodiment of the 'Central Values' (a term coined by Ms Lung Ying-tai) due to its historical legacy of being both a political and financial district.

The Central District (now known as the Central and Western District) of the Hong Kong Island was the starting point of development by the British and in the 1930s, Central was metaphorically referred to as the 'Little London of the East'. With rapid economic development in the 1970s, many of the classic buildings in Central were demolished due to the lure of redevelopment. The youth of today often indulge in a misguided reverie when it comes to British-governed Hong Kong. It is indeed a beautiful misunderstanding to assume that the cultured people of Britain would cherish British-styled architecture in Hong Kong. Elegant and classical buildings have been disappearing due to economic reasons for the past hundred years, and all that remains now are buildings that have been preserved either for special historical reasons or due to unintended administrative outcomes. However, they are certainly not the most spectacular historic buildings Hong Kong has to offer.

It is conceivable that, whether they be art installation or one of the non-mainstream buildings featured in this book, they will all gradually become history with the passage of time. For instance, the bright orange installation designed by Mr Gary Chang named *The Cascade* next to the stone steps on Wyndham Street, Central, was quietly dismantled. His works have gained much attention both in the Mainland and also within the international communities, yet his works in Hong Kong are rarely seen. One of his more recent works – the ACTS Rednaxela – has been featured in this book.

Hong Kong – A Convergence of Eastern and Western Cultures

The historical background of Hong Kong has given birth to its unique DNA, a fusion of East and West. Having preserved and honoured traditional Chinese cultures and festivities while also absorbing certain lifestyle elements from the West, there has been a blossoming of various trends and styles throughout different districts. This in turn has led to the city harbouring perfectly compatible elements of two different cultures. Beginning in the early days for Lan

Kwai Fong, followed by Soho South, Soho North, Sheung Wan, Sai Wan, Wan Chai and Tai Hang are all tasteful districts that exude a sense of romance due to each being a unique community. Such developments would not have been possible without the enthusiasm of certain individuals and their collaboration with the communities. Take the Starstreet Precinct and Blue House Cluster revitalisation programme, for example; it would not have been possible without the consistent effort of Mr Christopher Law, whose contributions must be given due credit. Mr Kenneth Tse, too, whose unwavering dedication and intelligent design has led to the succes of the Blue House Cluster revitalisation programme.

Having grown up on Hollywood Road, I have always taken a personal interest in its development. Its wonderful array of antique shops, cafés, galleries and street stalls have become highly rated tourist attractions. Although antiques are gaining traction in the Mainland, the younger generation in Hong Kong has lost interest in traditional Chinese culture. This, coupled with the hidden concern that these antique shops may have no successors, has led to the industry facing a contraction. Meanwhile, fluctuations in rental rates have made operations difficult for cafés and galleries. The cultural ambience that has taken form over recent years along Tai Ping Shan Street is an almost direct result of the low rents in the area. If this trend is to continue, it may well be dependent on the will and determination of the local residents as well as the government to promote cultural endeavours.

For example, while redeveloping the Former Police Married Quarters on Hollywood Road, the HKSAR government repurposed it to give young designers a retail spot, thus giving birth to PMQ. Next to PMQ are the Hong Kong News-Expo and the Central

Police Station Compound, the revitalisation of which brought forth the cultural melting pot of Tai Kwun. The original design for Tai Kwun consisted of a bamboo-shed structure made of glass material. Rising to a height of 160 metres, it was supposed to look from a distance like a gothic church sculpted out of ice. The design, however, was shelved as it was deemed to be 'too tall' and 'incompatible' with the surrounding historic buildings. The Central Market, co-managed by the Urban Redevelopment Authority and the Chinachem Group, embodies the synergistic effect of revitalised historic building, making it the new cultural hub in Central. Mr Donald Choi, who represented Chinachem Group, brought in old and new brands alike that are meaningful to the local communities. His dedication to serve was instrumental in ensuring that the historical continuity of the market managed to live on, at the same time recreating a heartwarming cultural landmark filled with local customs. Today it is a popular hangout spot for the Central patrons and, coupled with the presence of a sizeable bookstore and the architectural marvel of the H Queen's (designed by Mr William Lim), they collectively bring out the cosmopolitan charm of Central's symbiosis between the West and the local communities.

An Architect With a Soul

Admiralty used to be a quiet British military barracks Today, it has been transformed into an extension of Central as a commercial and financial centre. Many real estate conglomerates have taken root in the area, leading to the rise of prosperity in the Wan Chai district. The Hong Kong Arts Centre along the Wan Chai waterfront was the first non-government arts centre in Hong Kong, created through the hard work of the late Mr Tao Ho. In recognition of Mr Ho's contribution, a permanent exhibition curated by Ms Chan Lai-kiu, known for her passion for promoting architectural and cultural activities, has been set up at the lower entrance of the arts centre. Her involvement in the *Bi-City Biennale of Urbanism/Architecture* and other exhibitions of different themes has provided young architects with new opportunities to shine. The personal stories of Mr Ho have been published in many books and periodicals, the details of which this book shall not reiterate. However, Mr Ho has repeatedly been referred to as the 'Renaissance Man' by the architecture community; in today's terms, perhaps he would be called a cultural connoisseur. I had the opportunity to work with Mr Ho for a year, and in that short period of time I was deeply moved by his passion, erudition and perseverance. Later, Mr Ho unfortunately suffered from a stroke whilst in the Mainland and he was sent for treatment in Beijing by the Central Government. Coincidentally, I was teaching at the Central Academy of Fine Arts at the time and was therefore able to visit him. Sadly, Mr Ho passed away in 2019.

In the 1970s, Mr Ho was a pioneer in promoting the architectural and cultural scene in Hong Kong. Instrumental in nurturing many in these

fields, he was recognised as a spiritual mentor for many young and talented professionals. It was Mr Ho's example that inspired Mr Charles Lai to apply for the Design Trust Feature Grant funding scheme to support his in-depth and comprehensive research into the life and work of Mr Tao Ho. Mr Charles Lai is a young architecture academic who focuses on the history of local architecture with the aim of raising awareness and appreciation amongst the younger generations. The aforementioned Design Trust is a non-profit architectural and cultural platform co-founded by Ms Marisa Yiu. The aim of the platform is to provide funding for the research and cultural activities both in Hong Kong and the Greater Bay Area, and at the same time supporting and curating community projects and workshops for those with the potential talents to further build on their expertise.

Speaking of the enthusiasm of young architects promoting architecture-related events, I cannot help but recall the indefatigable Mr Joshua Lau and his righteous voice of justice which has brought forth an alternative, healthy image for the architecture industry. I remember the late Mr Joshua Lau as a young and promising individual, especially in the area of design. Always able to deliver exceptional designs that yield results wherever he worked, his greatest strength lay in his ability to shine a light on social justice. His tireless work to expose the fraudulent bid-rigging conduct amongst contractors not only successfully recovered fair compensations for minority owners, but has also given society a better understanding of the true meaning of professional ethics. Unfortunately, while he was successful in triumphing against such injustice, he was unable to overcome the damage brought about by cancer. Sadly, he passed away at the age of thirty-six and was unable to continue shining for Hong Kong.

When looking at the highlights of the Wan Chai district, one cannot neglect to mention the Hong Kong Convention and Exhibition Centre. In order to increase capacity for hosting international flagship exhibitions including the *Business of Design Week, Art Basel, Fine Art Asia, Art Central* and the *Affordable Art Fair*, the Hong Kong Convention and Exhibition Centre has expanded into its third phase. Since the tax regime in Hong Kong favours the art market, visual arts activities have become increasingly vibrant. In recent years, Hong Kong has become the second-largest trading centre for visual arts globally and has attracted many sizeable galleries and auction houses from around the world to settle in the city.

In the eyes of tourists, Hong Kong is an international, modern and efficient city filled with dynamism. That explains why it is also a favourite amongst young westerners looking for work. The city of Hong Kong is named as one of the three most important metropolises in the world with the acronymical term of 'Nylonkong' coined by *TIME* Magazine. Although other Asian cities are picking up the pace, Hong Kong still retains its inherent advantages; especially in light of its alignment with the national policy set out in the '14th Five-Year Plan', which has positioned the city as a pivotal hub for both Chinese and Western cultures.

Reflections on the Reclamation of Victoria Harbour

Victoria Harbour, with its brand-new look and a view full of colours and dynamism, is one of the most fascinating places on the Island North. The new promenade took ten years of reclamation work and is a worthy topic of reflection for the general public of Hong Kong. The discussion should begin with the controversy over its reclamation.

The reclamation project of Victoria Harbour caused much controversy in the city. At that time, Mr Winston Chu[12] and Ms Christine Lok had gained much public support in their opposition to the reclamation project under the organisational banner of the Society for Protection of the Harbour. It was thought that the reclamation would cause Victoria Harbour to become too narrow and thus risk turning it into the 'Victoria river', causing irreparable damage. My understanding is that the aim of the reclamation project was to connect an underground tunnel from the Eastern Corridor to Central. The government also guaranteed that, post reclamation, there would not be any high-density projects on the reclaimed area. As per my observation, the area that is reclaimed from the sea has indeed narrowed the harbour, but what has been achieved in return is more land area and

public space for more family-friendly, water-based activities. This in turn has benefited the general public. In addition, the Society for Protection of the Harbour had successfully pushed for the Protection of the Harbour Ordinance[13], which came into force on the 30 June 1997, and effectively banned any further reclamation work along the Victoria Harbour. Thus, I do believe that the aforementioned reclamation work was indeed the last one for Victoria Harbour.

The new waterfront today has been the result of the supervision and guidance by the Harbour Front Commission. The Chairman of the Commission, Mr Vincent Ng's advocacy of the 'first connect, then improve upon' approach has been critical to the success of this endeavour. The greatest feature of this lies in the seamless connection of previously segmented waterfront areas, as well as the creation of distinct designs and water facilities for each section. Along the way, one gets to admire art installations by different young architects, including the works by Mr Stanley Siu and Ms Sarah Mui, which have helped to create a waterfront for the people, bringing in new perspectives and allowing them to be closer to the sea.

Along the area from the Central Star Ferry Pier to Admiralty, large green spaces have been created to cater for facilities that promote beneficial activities for the general public. These facilities include the Hong Kong Observation Wheel & AIA Vitality Park, Formula-E, Art Central and theme parks, providing non-stop, all year-round, large-scale outdoor activities.

I believe that those who have participated in these activities will no longer complain about the previous administration's decision on the reclamation initiative. Instead they should enjoy the fruits of the labour brought forth by the reclamation project.

On this piece of newly created land there will be a new, huge but low-lying building nicknamed the 'Land Scrapper'. The idea behind this building is to provide for sufficient commercial retail space to balance out the rental cost, and at the same time to create a brand-new space to connect the old and the new alongside the waterfront. This will allow visitors to casually stroll towards the new Star Ferry Pier and admire the scenery along the way. This brand-new facility is expected to become a new landmark in Central that includes a large area of outdoor green space, resting platforms and the redesigned Hong Kong General Post Office and clock tower of the Star Ferry Pier. For this reason, the government had, for the first time, introduced an additional requirement of 'design elements' for the Conditions of Sale for this lot of land. In the end, the proposal and collective design from Wong & Ouyang HK Ltd and Lead8 was selected with the hope that it would deliver on all levels.

If one were to pick a classic architecture in Central, it would be the Hong Kong City Hall. Built in 1962 and a rarity in Hong Kong for its Bauhaus-styled architecture, the Hong Kong City Hall is also the youngest declared monument in the city. It was an architectural breakthrough for Hong Kong brought about by a bold design from Mr Alan Fitch[14] and Mr Ron Phillips[15]. The building has since become a place of collective memory for generations of people growing up in Hong Kong and it is also a cultural palace from which many of Hong Kong's master artists have been cultivated. I was placed in charge of the extensive renovation works, carried out in 1992 and 2002, specifically for the City Hall Memorial Garden and Edinburgh Place. The former aimed to create the harmonious yin and yang relationship between the dynamic and static zones, with the Memorial Shrine serving as the central axis as a form of respect. The latter is a series of silhouettes depicting life in Hong Kong, which, in conjunction with the century-old streetlights of the Hong Kong Electric Company Limited, enriches the local characteristics of the square.

a wooden colonnade to create a horseshoe-shaped building, his design presents a row of bright lines and a sense of rhythm derived from light projection effects. His works focus on public architecture, and I have always appreciated his participation in the public art scene that very much reflects the enthusiasm of the younger generation of architects to include, where possible, artistic elements in their designs.

When passing through the Canal Road Flyover, one will notice a commercial building that emphasises the lines of the rhombus yet has a flowing façade that creates the effect of sparkling diamonds. The building, named V Point, was designed by Mr William Liu. Liu did not initially intend to stay in Hong Kong for long, but he later found himself unable to leave the Pearl of the Orient. In addition to V Point, he also designed the Iceberg along Kimberley Road in Tsim Sha Tsui. However, my personal favourite is the little village he designed in Ham Tin on Lantau Island, which will be introduced with more detail in a later chapter.

won praise for their combination of Eastern and Western elements, together with their use of natural ventilation and innovative materials.

Three decades have gone by and although the design of the aforementioned public lavatory has undergone many changes, the core design and the deliberate effort of the past is still visible. Surprisingly, the design that won second place in that same competition has also been realised as a physical structure. It is located next to the Carpenter Road Park and continues to be in use today. Designed by Ms Wailee Chow, it is an incredibly avant-garde public lavatory, often referred to as having a high-tech architectural style with its appearance resembling that of a spaceship. Another untold story of Victoria Park is that every year it leases the venue to the Hong Kong Tourism Board for the annual Mid-Autumn Lantern Carnivals. This event has indirectly nurtured many up-and-coming architects, amongst them Mr William Lim and Mr Stanley Siu. The former utilised the flexibility of bamboo to construct a colourful structure resembling a firmament, while the latter constructed ball-shaped structures with changing colours, made from plastic bottles. These pieces certainly left a lasting impression on the audience.

Moving Eastward from Island North

There is a community recycling facility – the Wan Chai Community Green Station – along the Island North Wan Chai promenade. It is a masterpiece designed by Mr Benny Lee for one of the projects under the government's 'Community Green Station'[16] initiative. Using

Originally built in 1957, the Victoria Park in Causeway Bay was once ridiculed by councillors at an Urban Council meeting as a dilapidated Third-World facility look-alike. Thereafter, it was rebuilt and the structure we see today is a refurbished version of the 2002 design. The design team included Ms Elva Tang, Ms Sofia Lau, landscape architect Mr Tony Mui and myself. Prior to the renovation, situated at the east side of the park stood a public lavatory on Hing Fat Street, which had been the winner of a lavatory design competition held by the Urban Council in 1992. The designers involved – Mr Wallace Chang, Mr Lo Chi-sing and Mr Adrian Lo – had

In Tin Hau, the work that has surprised me the most is a very simple, dark-coloured building next to the flyover on Tsing Fung Street. With a pair of tall rusted iron gates at the storefront and no signboard in sight, this very quirky and stylish hotel – TUVE – is a 'product' created by designer Mr Lam Wai Ming. Why is it called a product? That's because every facility – every piece of furniture, component, appliance and product, no matter its shape or size – has been designed and produced by the designer himself. This speaks volumes about the level of confidence the owner has in his designer, without which this unique and quirky hotel would never have come to life. Near the hotel, on Tin Hau Temple Road, is a high-end residence named Pavilia Hill. The most notable feature worthy of admiration is the garden designed by Japanese Zen master Shunmyo Masuno, who adopted Japanese design elements and emphasised integration with nature. Since the garden is made of natural boulders that had to be carved and arranged by hand, its design is truly one of a kind. Anyone who visits Pavilia Hill must also be sure to visit and admire this exquisite and rare Japanese garden.

The careful preservation of the former State Theatre in North Point by its new owner was a major breakthrough brought about by Hong Kong's belated conservation culture. At the same time, this has also reawakened the regrets of the people in the city for losing the Lee Theatre. The Lee Theatre would have been preserved had it still existed in the present era, now that more emphasis is being placed on conservation. Lee Theatre would have been the most elegant opera house in Hong Kong. Comparatively more fortunate was the 'Oil Street Art Space', which sat on the original site of the Royal Hong Kong Yacht Club. After its relocation, the old club site was revitalised several times until it became the home of the Leisure and

Cultural Services Department's Art Promotion Office, an art platform that interacts and works with non-governmental organisations. It holds many design competitions for large-scale sculptures, art installations and garden seats in the park. It has indirectly cultivated many young architects, whether through small-scale works or large-scale buildings, by providing them with opportunities to put their talents to good use. Mr Stanley Siu, Ms Sarah Mui, Mr Benny Lee, Mr Paul Mui and Mr Karr Yip are young professionals who have focused on participating in outdoor art installation projects. I have an appreciation for their creativity and perseverance, as many of their works are wonderful examples of active participation of public architecture.

I volunteered to assist in the renovation of the first phase of the Oil Street Art Space. The building itself was designed in the British Arts and Crafts Movement style. The main purpose had been to retain this original style, including the beautiful red brick walls and the arched porches, and to make full use of the retired wooden railway sleepers donated by MTR Corporation Limited for laying down the outdoor platforms; in addition, the original boat storage space had also been converted into an arts café, adding a people-friendly and 'literary youth' ambience to the area. The second phase was a newly constructed section with a modern exhibition space, co-designed by Mr Peter Lau and Mr Thomas Wan. Another advantage of this cultural exhibition venue is its outdoor art space which enables larger-scale outdoor exhibitions to be staged, by providing more space and flexibility for artists to showcase their talents. At the bottom of the Eastern Corridor and opposite the Oil Street Art Space, a unique boardwalk and opening bridge will be built to connect with the new Island North promenade. Upon its completion, it will no doubt become a new experience and a popular new spot amongst locals.

The Aldrich Bay Park in Shau Kei Wan is a masterpiece from landscape architect Mr Lin Wai-tung. Reflecting his own personal fondness for the art of architecture, he included a traditional wooden Chinese junk boat as a homage to Hong Kong's past as a fishing village – a bygone time not lost to history. Under the flyover near the park, there is the beautifully designed Eastern Community Green Station, a collection point for recycled materials under the 'Community Green Station' initiative. Walking along the coast to Shau Kei Wan Main Street East, there is an outdoor performance theatre which is a minor project built using the HKD100 million funding allocated to each district.

The Lei Yue Mun Barracks in Chai Wan is the place where most British-styled buildings were left behind after the withdrawal of the British army. Today, it has been converted into Lei Yue Mun Park. To one side of the barracks is the Hong Kong Museum of Coastal Defence. While Mr Jason Yuen was responsible for overseeing the delivery of this project behind the scenes, Mr Kenneth Tam was the soul of its design. It features a canvas which covers the original sunken fortress like a military tent. It is a structure filled with historical legacy and at the same time a masterpieces of public architecture in the fair-faced concrete era. Along the waterfront of Quarry Bay Park in

Taikoo Shing, there is the almost unknown exhibition hall which is also another project by Mr Kenneth Tam – the Fireboat Alexander Grantham Exhibition Gallery[17]. It is common practice around the world for retired warships to be moored for use as exhibition space. Here lies a fireboat that has served Hong Kong for many years, and the exhibition hall within proudly displays its past great achievements.

Since we have arrived in Chai Wan, I would suggest continuing a little further to the Sai Wan War Cemetery, not far from the Chinese Permanent Cemetery. There is a green grassy slope with 1,578 neatly arranged tombstones; the most notable is the granite memorial pavilion designed by Colin St Clair Oakes[18] which highlights an hollowed-out granite cross with the simple inscriptions '1939' and '1945', marking the beginning and end of the Second World War. Carrying the weight of war history and religious symbolism, along with powerful messages and the sophisticated masonry work, it is a distinguished piece of architecture with a profound sense of solemnity rarely seen in Hong Kong.

Notes

1 Designing Hong Kong: Designing Hong Kong is a non-profit organization that pays special attention to local urban planning and design from the overall to district level in Hong Kong with the aim of raising public awareness and building a sustainable, beautiful city with a high quality of life.

2 Norman Foster: British architect who won the design competition for the HSBC Headquarters. He created one of the most advanced buildings in the world; with a price tag of HKD5.2 billion, it was also the most expensive. Built in 1985, the HSBC Headquarters has since become known as one of the defining works of Foster's career.

3 I.M. Pei: Chinese-American architect. The Bank of China Tower is the headquarters for the Bank of China in Hong Kong, I.M. Pei began his design of the building towards the end of 1982. When completed in 1989, it was the tallest building in Hong Kong and the fifth tallest building in the world.

4 César Pelli: Argentinian architect who won a design competition for the International Finance Centre. The first phase was completed in 1998 and the second phase in 2003. It is the second-tallest building in Hong Kong after the International Commerce Centre.

5 Zaha Hadid: Iraqi-British architect who became the first woman to win the Pritzker Architecture Prize. The Henderson was designed by Zaha Hadid Architects for the Henderson Land Development Company.

6 Harry Seidler: Australian architect who is a main advocate of modernism. The current third-generation Hong Kong Club Building was built in 1984.

7 Paul Rudolph: American architect. He has been hailed as one of the most important American modernist architects and is a former chair of the Yale School of Architecture. The Lippo Centre was designed jointly by Mr Paul Rudolph and Wong & Ouyang (HK) Ltd. Completed in 1988, it sits on the former site of the Bond Centre.

8 Skidomore, Owings & Merrill (SOM): An architecture firm founded in 1963 by Louis Skidmore and Nathaniel Owings in Chicago, USA. John Merrill officially joined the firm in 1939. The AIA Central was designed jointly by SOM and Aedas Architects in 2005.

9 Tod Williams: American architect. The Asia Society Hong Kong Centre was built in 2012 on the former site of the Explosives Magazine of the Victoria Barracks.

10 Billie Tsien: Chinese-American architect who started working with Tod Williams in 1977. They later married and founded the Tod Billie Tsien Architects. The couple has received the National Medal of Arts awarded by Barack Obama and was later selected by the Obama Foundation as the chief architect for the Obama Presidential Library in Chicago.

11 Terry Farrell: British architect and town planner. He and his friend Sir Nicolas Grimshaw, they co-founded Farrell-Grimshaw. The firm was renamed Farrells in 1980 when they went their separate ways. Terry Farrell won the design competition for the British Consulate General in Admiralty and later set up TFP, Farrells' Hong Kong office.

12 Mr Winston Ka-Sun Chu: A Hong Kong Lawyer who is the Founder and Chairman of the Society for Protection of the Harbour. He authored the Protection of the Harbour Ordinance. His effort was instrumental in curtailing the government's extensive harbour reclamation plans.

13 Protection of the Harbour Ordinance: Prior to the Handover of Hong Kong in 1997, the ordinance was proposed in 1996 in the form of a private draft by Ms Christine Lok, a member of the then Hong Kong Legislative Council. The aim of the ordinance was to prohibit reclamation of the Victoria Harbour in order to protect and preserve the harbour. The draft won a large majority and was adopted, and entered into force on 30 June,1997.

14 Alan Fitch: British architect who used to work for the Public Works Department.

15 Ron Phillips: British architect who used to work for the Public Works Department.

16 Community Green Station: The Environmental Protection Department has set up recycling stations in 18 districts to receive common recyclables such as plastics, glass bottles, small electrical appliances, electronics, fluorescent tubes, rechargeable batteries, as well as wastepaper and metals.

17 Fireboat Alexander Grantham Exhibition Gallery: The fireboat *Alexander Grantham* entered service in 1953 and was decommissioned in 2002. It was later handed over to the Leisure and Cultural Services Department and was subsequently set up as a small exhibition hall in Quarry Bay Park, serving to introduce the history of the fireboat.

18 Colin St Clair Oakes: Architect of the Commonwealth War Cemeteries Commission, responsible for designing war cemeteries and memorials across Asia after the Second World War including the Kranji War Memorial in Singapore.

TUVE Hotel

Why Be High-Profile If You Can Stay Low-key?

In the corner of Tsing Fung Street, Tin Hau, there is a humble hotel that can easily be missed the first time one looks for it. However, once you do find it, this place is as unforgettable as it gets, just like its designer.

I made an appointment with Mr Lam Wai Ming at his office in Lai Chi Kok at 9 am, and once I was out of the elevator, I knew I was at the right place. A large metal wall at the front door brought a stark contrast to this ordinary building. Lam sat quietly in his office, patiently waiting for the doorbell to ring.

At 9 am on a Saturday morning, the office was particularly quiet. Although Lam didn't have a drowsy look on him, let's just say that he wouldn't normally be there at this hour. He lit up the screen in front of him, and as it turned out, he had prepared a briefing for our interview.

Lam graduated in interior design from the Hong Kong Polytechnic University and subsequently joined a British architecture firm for seven years, working mainly on infrastructure projects for the Hong Kong International Airport and its surrounding area. He did not delve into specific details, but did recall contemplating on several directions upon the completion of said projects – working for another design firm in Hong Kong, venturing abroad for a few years, or seizing the opportunity to test his mettle by starting out on his own. 'In fact, it wasn't all that difficult to decide back then. It was shortly after Hong Kong's return to China and things were headed towards a fresh start. I had this feeling that I should give it a try instead of spending time building someone else's career.'

Lam founded Design Systems in 1999. 'It wasn't all that difficult to start a business, especially when there was only one person doing it. Taking up two projects would already be sustainable.' However, as the saying goes, maintaining a business is more difficult than starting one. 'The difficulty lies in its maintenance.' Lam unhurriedly uttered those few words. 'For the first ten years we were basically doing commercial projects, but after that, doubts arose in my mind and it felt like it wouldn't work going forward.' 'What wouldn't work?' 'It was hard. For example, you would be working on five different stores at the same time and the hardest part was not knowing what it was all for.'

Lam often chatted with his colleagues, not so much as from the position of their boss, but as he hoped to grow with them in the process, as a peer. For his firm's projects, he was not the sole-decision maker; 'I didn't name the firm after myself because I did not want it to be personalised'. He even laughed at the fact that he didn't conceive the name of the firm himself. 'I often tell them that I would love for them to take away something useful when they walk out of this door, and to think about what they truly have a liking for.'

Lam decided to let go of the projects in the commercial space and started looking for other possibilities. A few years ago, someone came to his office with a picture taken by Danish photographer Kim Høltermand. It was an image of Lake Tuvesjöen (TUVE) in Sweden. In the photograph, there was a light mist floating on the lake and it was so surreal that it gave off a sense of tranquillity that was hazy yet beautiful. 'We wanted to convert a building into a small to medium-sized hotel.'

'When did art begin?' Lam suddenly asked, and upon hearing no response, he continued sharing. Lam once went on a business trip to France to help out Hermès with a visual merchandising project and it was there he met with Hermès's creative director, Pierre Hardy. 'The first time we met, I thought we were going to talk business, who knew that would be the first question he would ask me'.

1. Hotel entrance corridor design concept. The hotel does not have an ornate lobby, only a narrow zigzag corridor. The design focuses on the creation of an ambience by omitting decoration and using only geometry, material texture, as well as the application of lighting.
2. The design of the hotel's main entrance is of a streamlined and minimalistic style.
3. At the entrance of the hotel, the space is reduced to only walls and ground, with light shining up from the ground instead of down onto it. From the moment the door is pushed open, visitors are aware they are in a different kind of space.
4. Behind the sleek and minimalistic concrete front desk, there lies a ceiling and walls adorned with hints of starlight, reminiscent of a starry night sky.

'Of course, I said I had no idea.' Pierre then went on to elaborate, beginning from the primitive age. 'When we were hairy all over, we had to hunt in the morning and climb up onto the trees to rest at night. However, one day, this group of people decided to head up to the mountain and enjoy the sunset after a day of hunting.' He went on to quote from Pierre, 'It was then that you learnt to appreciate beauty, and so art began.'

When Lam walked to Tsing Fung Street, looking at the messy, yet authentic, scenery of the street, he remembered what Pierre had said. He began to ponder the meaning of a hotel. What was its essence? He opened up the dictionary and looked up its definition: 'a place providing travellers with accommodation'.

'My understanding was also very simple: a settlement, and an adventure.' However, hotels are the exact opposite, you first travel for adventures and then you settle in. If, according to Lam, the essence of a hotel was to rest and adventure, how should it be presented? 'The surprise of an unprecedented experience.' Lam said.

The hotel was called TUVE. It not only shared the same name as the lake in Sweden, but it also had a slight resemblance to its atmosphere. For the first time, the hotel presented its signboard in a low-key manner that if you didn't look carefully enough, you would probably miss it. It could have been under your feet. Lam had this to say about its design: 'Having no signboard is a signboard in itself.'

The large iron door opened onto a space where dim lights emanated from ground level. Moving through the curved zigzag corridor, the space reduced to one of only material texture, light and shadow. Such a dimly lit environment could very well give patrons the sense that they are entering into a game in an escape room. The hotel lobby was located on the first floor, with no expensive decorations but only a huge concrete table for guest reception, as this is not a place where guests would stay for any length of time.

Once I arrived at the door to my room, it very much felt like that there was this square box placed right in front of me, and the only way to find out what kinds of furniture laid within was to open it. As I pushed open its door, the strong contrast between the simplicity and brightness of the space invoked a sense of the old saying about silver linings. Even the furniture and cabinets in the room adhere to the concept of 'hidden and revealed'. Upon entering the bathroom, a different ambience is felt. The ink-like stone walls and a brass mirror seemed to be saying, 'The bathroom may not be a place to stay the longest, so it doesn't hurt to be more intense.'

From the colour palette and design to the atmosphere created by this space, TUVE Hotel was, like the illusionary lake in Kim Høltermand's photograph, hazy with mystery and poetry, and always inspiring patrons to a closer and deeper exploration. The seemingly simplified elements and designs were actually the result of Lam's condensation and refinement, and those unexpected textures would slowly emerge once you took the time to appreciate them.

1. In the concept design for the reception, only a counter and two small benches are being depicted. The intention behind this is to avoid creating a barrier with guests having to communicate with hotel staff over a reception counter. Instead, the illustration portrays a scene of staff and guests conversing side by side by the corner of said counter, emphasising the importance human interaction in this space.
2. A bathroom within the room. Serving as the culmination of a journey, the atmosphere of the room should be calm and comfortable. Hence there is a softer use of light compared to that of the communal space. The texture has become more delicate, as well. These design elements reflect the designer's understanding of a 'good rest'.
3. The ink-like textured walls provide a strong visual effect. Inside the bathroom, the brass fittings that are frequently touched by users have been polished to be as smooth as a mirror.

Untold Stories

H Queen's

The Colourful World Shall Come to You

Walking into William Lim's office didn't feel much like walking into an architect's office. How should one describe it? Well, paintings of various sizes, sculptures that stood densely against the wall; in fact, that was a polite way of putting it. Literally every available inch of space was occupied by his collection, and there was only one pathway for you to walk through.

On his desk, to the right-hand side of the entrance (though in the most conspicuous spot), laid an unfinished painting and a palette with half-dried paint. The working computer had been squeezed into the far corner of the desk and had minimal presence. As for the large white wall that faced directly towards the entance, he reserved it for an oil painting – *Abandoned* (2014) by Hong Kong artist Mr Lewis Lau. The painting depicted a red swing placed quietly in a vast clearing, and it was impossible to tell where it was, though there was an inexplicable melancholy in that quietness.

Looking at the dazzling array of gadgets in front of him, Lim said, 'The studio in Wong Chuk Hang is what I would call being filled with collections.' I raised my eyebrows slightly thinking that what I saw in front of me must be just the tip of the iceberg, 'I want to move the firm into the Wong Chuk Hang area. It is not as dense as it is in the city.'

Lim and his wife Lavina began focusing on contemporary art works since the early millennium. Over the years, they have collected more than ninety pieces for their 'Living Collection'. It certainly does not lack works by Hong Kong artists and has essentially documented the development of contemporary art in Hong Kong. On the opening of the M+ Museum, the couple donated most of their collection to the museum.

The Russian materialist philosopher Nikolay Chernyshevsky once said, 'Art comes from life and is higher than life.' The couple's collecting journey began with the purchase of small items during their trips together, which seemingly served as a record of memories and moods of each trip, and these are the pieces upon which the 'Living Collection' is based on. Their understanding of art and its collection was, as the name suggested, 'from life'. Lim not only loved collecting, but also began to focus on creating in recent years. Even for his main job – architecture – he did not want to leave the word 'art' out of it. Speaking of his works, we cannot omit mentioning the H Queen's, built in 2018.

H Queen's is a 24-storey building shaped like a transparent glass box that sits in the hustle and bustle of Queen's Road and right at the junction of Stanley Street. Its simple and modern architectural style exudes the temperament of Central. If the last thing high-rise Central needed was another tall building, then what should H Queen's existence stand for in this context?

Walking into H Queen's, the elevator floor is marked with signs of galleries from around the world, including Zwirner Gallery, Hauser & Wirth Gallery, Whitestone Gallery and Pace Gallery. The building also hosts a number of international artists and their exhibitions throughout the year.

Globally, this self-styled 'vertical art space' is not a common form of architecture. The fact that Hong Kong has become a favourite spot amongst galleries is inseparable from its being a densely populated, cosmopolitan city. These factors have led to the city in recent years becoming one of the world's top three art markets.

1 The floors are illuminated with LED lights, and, from a distance, H Queen's creates a strong contrast with nearby buildings.
2 The curtain wall of H Queen's uses three layers of Low-E ultra-clear glass to block ultraviolet light. White 'frits' have been added to the glass to brighten the light indoors.
3 The colour temperature is close to that of sunlight, which is conducive to the display of artworks. A large patio has been added to the top floor so the restaurant can be completely outdoors.

In 2013, Art Basel acquired ARTHK, renaming it Art Basel HK that same year.

Except during the pandemic, Art Basel HK has held an exhibition annually lasting several days. This annual exhibition has attracted galleries, artists, collectors and art lovers from all over the world. Lim, who had always paid close attention to the art-collecting scene, came up with this bold idea once he had realised the impact of Art Basel's arrival on the local art ecosystem, its impact on Hong Kong artists, and the subsequent transformation it brought to the Hong Kong art market.

Originally an old commercial building, H Queen's was acquired by Henderson Land in 2013. The initial idea was simply to construct yet another office building in this area that is already filled with office spaces. Speaking of Central, Lim often lamented that it was far too commercial. 'It's not somewhere I would visit over the weekend. Besides, the last thing Central needs is another office building.'

However, Central is not just about commercial buildings. It is actually the home of many galleries, but they are scattered in different places; some are set up in the Pedder Building, some on Hollywood Road, while some have been set up elsewhere. 'But on the weekends, most of the commercial buildings have their entrances closed with metal gates, so whenever visitors did visit these galleries, they would have to sneak in, and this has indeed created an obvious barrier.' Thus, during the concept and design stage, in addition to its appearance, Lim paid special attention to what the building could do as well as what it could bring to the table. 'We are in the service industry, so in addition to satisfying customers, architects can sometimes take the initiative to take one step further. For instance, how does one turn an ordinary site into something more interesting?'

Not far from H Queen's, the Pedder Building was also home to several galleries, but there are certainly some differences. 'The essence of Pedder's business does not cater primarily for galleries, so it will be inconvenient when placing large-scale artworks.' Drawing on this experience, H Queen's was designed with high ceiling spaces on the ground floor with devices like high-altitude booms and curtain walls installed to facilitate the transportation and placement of large-scale artworks by galleries. At the same time, the glass curtain wall was chosen so that under warm sunlight, the interior space would appear more spacious, thus making this a space that is truly tailored for galleries.

The galleries on different floors also feel different in terms of their spatial experience, as they have been created by different designers. For instance, the Zwirner Gallery and Hauser & Wirth Gallery have been designed by American Architect Annabelle Selldorf. Pace Gallery was designed by Italian architects Enrico Benetti and Dominic Kozerski, while the Whitestone Gallery was designed by Japanese architect Kengo Kuma. 'When people visit H Queen's they won't just get to admire the art pieces from within, but they will also get to experience its well-designed space.'

Architects and artists alike have the ability to create works with much thunder but little rain. Especially in this era of 'fifteen minutes of fame', it was no difficult task stirring up the conversations. However, H Queen's

The glass boxes design and their combination has filled the space with transparency.

did not follow the path of the bizarrely designed. Instead, it sat quietly and towered over the bustling corner of Central. 'A good building can influence, enhance and even contribute to its surrounding environment.' Lim bluntly said that he was very resistant towards architecture that has nothing to do with its surroundings, and was even more afraid of designs that served only to kick up clouds of dust.

Lim had an easy-going personality and, with constant laughter between his words, he spoke of how he got involved in architecture. 'I seemed to have entered the architecture school in a muddle.' Lim grew up in Hong Kong and furthered his studies in the United States in his last year of high school. Drawing was something he had always loved ever since he was a child, 'There is nothing else that can make me sit quietly for two to three hours.' The influence of the conservative school of thought often stereotyped art as something that carried no future. 'Today's society is very different. So long as you like it, just do it. But it wasn't like that back in the day.' Lim's father was in real estate and often dealt with architects. 'Architecture is also called architectural drawing, and it seems to be closer to the idea of "drawing".' Thus, with the encouragement of his father, he chose architecture.

'I actually quite enjoyed it, but I basically failed during my first semester because I had no concept of architecture at all.' He recalled with a smile, 'I still remember having fun after school, but what I didn't know was that the other students had stayed late in the studio and worked really hard'. He also added with a laugh, 'My professor actually suggested that I should change my course of study.' It was only then that he realised he ought to begin serious work.

In his second year at Cornell University, Lim met with a professor who was particularly fond of oriental art, 'I was starting to understand that many architects, including Frank Lloyd Wright and Ludwig Mies van der Rohe were influenced by oriental culture; and ever since then I started paying special attention to how I could apply oriental culture to my work.' This touch of oriental cultural sentiment is evident in some of his large-scale art installations showcased at the Victoria Park during the Mid-Autumn Festival, such as the *Lantern Wonderland 2003*, *Lantern Wonderland 2011* and *Mooncake Pagoda*. During the *Venice Architecture Biennale 2006*, Lim put his inspiration from bamboo to good use and combined it with the art of bamboo scaffolding to create his masterpiece: *Ladders*. Then there was the art installation in the Nishimura Restaurant, Beijing, the design concept of which sought to infuse the contrast of yin and yang. 'Looking back at some of the sketches and designs that I drew, they were actually very similar to what I was taught in university and especially so with my graduation thesis; so, actually, my education has indeed influenced my entire career path.'

'However, not all influences have come from textbooks; surely you can learn a lot from friends, too.' During his time in university, Lim had a good friend from South America who, unlike Lim's restrained and conservative ways, had a more straightforward personality with an unreserved way of expressing his emotions. This impacted his views on how people should communicate with each other and how they should treat each other. 'All these years, he would call me on my birthday...' At this point, Lim sniffled and was unable to speak. Those simple words were light on the ears, and yet they carried much weight. Lim continued after a pause. 'Whether between friends or dealing with work, how you express yourself is actually very important. This industry is not all about having good designs; treating others and things right is also very critical.'

After graduation, Lim worked in Boston, while his friend went to Dallas. They later crossed paths again due to work when the company his friend was working for had a project to transform an old warehouse into a design centre. 'He found our firm and specifically appointed me to do it.' The whole project took five full years, equivalent to Lim's time in Boston. 'The final outcome of this project is actually quite similar to H Queen's.' As a result of his work on this project, Lim began to pay more attention to the relationship between architecture and interior design. 'Perhaps many architects often have this line of thought: why would I bother with interior design when I am in architecture? In reality, however, there are many famous architects who would not be content with just completing an outer shell and would rather have their own interior designs, too. The two actually influence each other.'

The project ended in 1987, after which Lim returned to Hong Kong to further his career. After working at Nelson Chen Architects Ltd for half a year, he realised the architecture scene in Hong Kong was very different to that of the United States. Thus, he chose instead to work for a real estate developer thereafter, Paliburg Holdings Limited, for six years. As fate would have it, Lim later went on to join CL3 Architects Limited in 1992 and became one of its four founders, 'Years later however, I was the only one left at CL3.'

Upon looking at the unfinished paintings on his desk, Lim's earlier mention of his current schedule came to my mind: 'Work in the morning, draw in the afternoon.' In fact, it did not matter who was left in CL3, because what he had wanted in his heart, whether it be architecture or art, would not be too far away after all.

Photo Credit: Carlo Lavatori, Archivio Alessi

ACTS Rednaxela

The Song of a Wanderer

It took a while to make sense of my interview with Gary Chang. Not because I was completely without a clue, but because everything that was said was a key point through and through. As I began writing, looking through my interview notes that were scribbled with starred remarks, a particularly profound sentence jumped out at me: 'You must write down what I am about to say!'

On rereading these words, I paused to allow time to resonate, as if in slow-motion. What followed, was a short history of Gary's achievements, but as the handwriting on the notes became more scribbled, I had an increasingly hard time deciphering it.

Adjectives are a great way to quickly sketch out a person's character, but how would I describe Gary? In my mind, words began to run in a panic like ants on a hot griddle. The starred remarks I had put in my notes were of no help; it was difficult and time consuming to decide on the words, let alone to clarify them.

Gary combed his oily hair and started to speak, very quietly. His eyes were unnerving, as he stared with a real intensity, but I soon realised that he wasn't so scary. He spoke quickly, about one-and-half times the usual speed. An interview with him was really just listening, as there was little chance to ask questions. And even if one did manage to ask something, he would continue saying what he had wanted to say anyway.

Some of Gary's best works were prominently displayed at the entrance to his Quarry Bay office, and as he walked me through, he began introducing them. 'I have more books than the Eslite bookshop... My office is bigger than my residence.' I cannot recall all of the details, as his two-storey office was stuffed with his trophies. I followed him to the second floor, where we began the interview with a toast, and the lights were dim to create the mood he had intended to set. It was no wonder that my notes became more illegible as the interview progressed.

Gary founded Edge Design Institute Ltd in 1994. On the occasion of Edge's twenty-fifth anniversary, he celebrated it by splitting it in half and creating Mini Edge and Super Edge. 'I used to have a lucky number – twenty. The company then had more than twenty staff and the end result was that I had to be involved in any project that came my way, which was just not suitable for me.' Mini Edge now consists only of six staff members, providing quality over quantity. 'We are a bit like the Shaolin Temple here – all of them are trained in the eighteen forms of martial arts.' Gary is like the abbot of a temple to his staff. Once in a blue moon, while he travels around, he comes in to provide them with guidance. On the other hand, Super Edge is like a kung-fu tournament, where masters gather, but the tournament itself is about cooperation, not competition. Enraptured, Gary continued in such a way that I was totally captivated and unable to interrupt. There were pauses in between his words which no doubt would have given anyone the impression that he was finished speaking, but whenever I tried to ask a question, he would say, 'I am not done yet!' and would return to the main topic again. 'That's my grand plan. The trend in the world now is about cooperation. We should all help one another out; the scale of the project does not matter, and this is how flexible it is.'

When he was a child, Gary had three younger sisters with whom he lived in a 334-square-feet flat in Sai Wan Ho. 'I spent a lot of time thinking how I could transform the flat because of its limited area.' As an older brother

1   A 4-metre-long multifunctional desk placed in the 24-square-metre triangular space. The enlarged glass on the inside cleverly makes the space look incredibly spacious.

2   A 19-storey serviced apartment located in the Mid-Levels West, Hong Kong. The exterior walls of the building have been decorated with a note of bright orange, together with large windows designed to expand the limited interior space.

3   The units have a usable area of 24-square-metre, which is less than the combined area of the communal spaces (lift, lobby and a pair of emergency staircases).

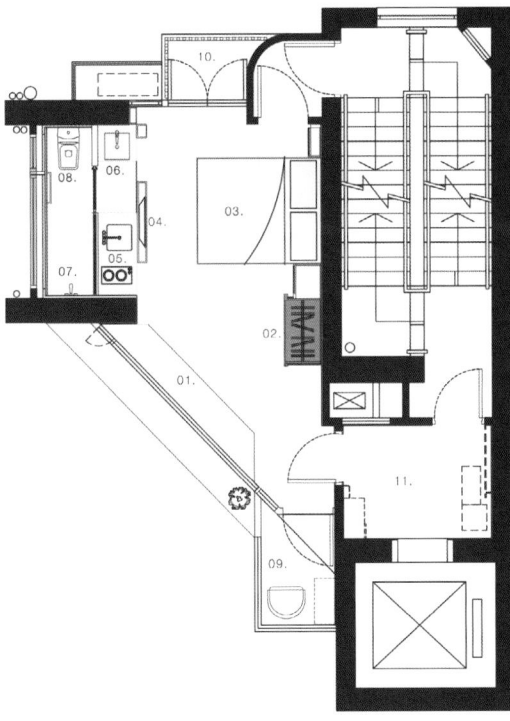

and also the master of the living room, he recalled that even whilst in high school, he had been drawing up plans for his residence. 'If my aunt had come to live with us, I would have given her the whole attic, and put my three sisters in the darkest corner...' He couldn't help but laugh at his own evil remarks. 'So, for me, architecture is not necessarily an interest but rather a solution to a very practical problem.'

Gary attended Queen's College for high school and was the typical well-behaved student with his grades amongst the very best. 'I was afraid of being late on a daily basis.' His public examination results were also outstanding and should have allowed him entry into the Faculty of Architecture of the University of Hong Kong. 'Who would have known? I failed the interview because of my introverted character!' It was hard to imagine someone as talkative and prone to laughter as Gary was once a quiet and bashful individual.

The first thing Gary did once he entered university was to find ways to change his course of study. He was busy running around offices, arranging meetings with professors and student counsellors. 'There was no precedent at that time. To put it in an old-fashioned way, you ought to persist and not be resigned to your fate.' It should have been inspirational, but coming from him, it indeed sounded a little old-fashioned. During his university years, Gary was actually quite a popular figure, not because of his excellent grades but because they were mediocre. After getting into the Faculty of Architecture as he had wished, he released whatever had been suppressed within him during the previous five years in high school. 'I was very rebellious and was going all out; and how could you blame yourself for the bad grades? Of course, you would blame the teachers and your classmates.' After laughing at his own words yet again, he added, 'It was actually useless blaming others. What was needed was self-reflection.'

Gary described how enlightenment really came to him in his fourth year in university. 'When I saw a poster for the *Milan Design Exhibition* in school, I decided that I would take part in it with my classmates. I even made a promise there and then that I was going to win.' It was the 17th International Student Competition at the *International Architecture Triennale* of Milan, open to all but with only ten winners. 'And we really did win.' His eyes widened even at the mention of it today. 'Once I set my eyes on a prize, I will get it.'

Gary's participation in the competition was, to a certain extent, a sign of his rebellion and nonconformity; by winning it, he proved that having mediocre grades did not stop him from attaining an award. He vividly recalled the theme of the competition was 'office of the future.' 'Wouldn't you say it was quite a coincidence? We set our eyes on the prize, standing right in front of the poster, and it was indeed wonderful that we won.' He was young and exuberant, with an award under his belt. In his fifth year, Gary essentially ignored all his homework and instead became focused on writing complaint letters. 'I made a big fuss out of everything and everyone knew whom I disliked.'

Speaking of awards, there was a milestone achievement that had already been underlined in my notes without needing a reminder from the man himself. Gary received the Young Architect Award from the Hong Kong Institute of Architects in 1996. 'But did you know that I was not a young architect at all?' His widened eyes turned into a crescent moon as he laughed.

He was certainly young enough, but just not an architect. After he had won the award, the Hong Kong Institute of Architects received a complaint, requesting that the rules be changed. Now, one must be a qualified architect in order to be eligible for the Young Architect Award. Although, as Gary said wittily, 'I'm not an architect, and yet I won the Young Architect Award! Surely that's an even greater achievement!' It sounded a little ironic, but this is Gary, the man who laughingly said that 'master of architecture' sounded better than 'architect'.

Gary had never written a cover letter; nevertheless, he had already been recruited by an architecture firm before his graduation. After graduating in 1987, he went straight to P&T Group, where he stayed for seven years. When he left, he handed in a letter that consisted of seven pages, four of which were used to express his dissatisfaction with the company. The last three were about his salary trends over the past seven years. Thereafter, Edge Design was founded.

Not only was Gary dashing and free but he was also a complete hedonist. 'Money is only yours after you have spent it, and you have to spend it before it disappears.' Gary once had a special travel agent to arrange his travel itineraries. 'It doesn't matter where I am going, I just want to leave.' *Aren't you tired, always travelling around?* 'No, I am most creative when I am not at the office.' He smiled and continued, 'When I am in Hong Kong, I often set my phone to flight mode. I don't like calls. That's pretty conservative, right?'

Anyone who knows Gary probably knows of his obsession with hotels. His obsession has even extended from staying in them to wanting to publish a book about them; from experiencing them to designing them. 'I want to publish a book on the most hated hotels in Hong Kong once I retire. Don't write that down, I haven't retired yet.' Gary attributes his fondness for staying in hotels to having grown up in his small home, and also his love for freshness. 'There is a very special phenomenon in Hong Kong: high density and yet everything is possible. My definition of home is that it is actually an extension from your home to your neighbours and subsequently to the entirety of your city, and all that – it's actually your home.' Choosing between a home or a hotel for his sense of belonging, he would actually pick the latter simply because of the freshness it provided. 'I calculated that if you were to buy a one thousand-square-feet home in Hong Kong, you could instead stay in a hotel for 10 nights a month with a budget of three thousand dollars per night, and this lifestyle would be sustainable for 20 to 30 years. In that case, why not?'

Looking at the books and the countless trophies on his bookshelf was like looking at his rebellions once again. 'In fact, I was quite down for a few years, because I couldn't be an architect, at least not in name. So I kept on participating in competitions, and I kept winning them.' And what made him famous overnight turned out to be that little home he used to grow up in.

He really did realise his childhood idea of transforming the 334-square-feet residence into a *'Domestic Transformer'*. Inspired by movable mechanisms and intervals, his design realised a spatial experience that well exceeded the flat's nominal area. Upon its completion in 2007, he had already anticipated incoming interviews, 'but I didn't expect that people would still be discussing it.' In addition to interviews and books, one of the episodes of Apple TV+'s documentary – *'Home'* was titled 'Domestic Transformer' and was aired in 2020. Time and again, he stressed, 'You must watch it!'

'Domestic Transformer' brought him some follow-up projects, including ACTS Rednaxela. It was a 'one household per floor' project with a very high degree of privacy. Although it wasn't spacious, as he did with his deformed dwelling, he injected a kaleidoscope of possibilities with plenty of surprises. 'After talking about this for more than ten years, I realised I had actually nailed down a global phenomenon – our homes are now smaller.' However, this is what makes Gary magical – making full use of the possibilities of any given small space – and he does so to his heart's content. In addition to the spaces being changeable, Gary has also given much thought to details such as furniture: in front of the floor-to-ceiling glass window was a tailor-made marble workbench, paired with a bright orange chair from the Italian brand Arper, which added a touch of embellishment to the simple space.

Speaking of products, he mentioned in the interview that the homeware brand Alessi had produced a 'Kung Fu' tea set. Made of silver and purple granulated clay, the designer of which was, of course, the man himself. Unabashedly, he said, 'I think it should be in the Hong Kong Museum of Tea Ware.' However, the most impressive aspect was the price of the tea set, 'Li Ka-shing sent his secretary, who, after learning of its five-hundred-thousand-dollar price tag, never returned for follow-up discussions!' He added, 'I am counting on you now, Raymond, to help me close this deal!' And all that was needed from me was an awkward but polite smile.

Before I left, he did not forget to show me the two models placed at the front door. They were models of the Domestic Transformer and the ACTS Rednaxela to be collected by the M+ Museum. 'You will see them at the museum!' As I was preparing my camera, he jokingly tilted his head over in a deliberate manner. *Click!* the shutter froze on his unfocused and unprepared expression. Being vain as he is, he probably would have wanted to delete that picture, if he were ever to lay eyes on it.

1 The exterior design of the building breaks away from of the usual narrow window design derived from most residential properties in Hong Kong that seeks to meet the minimum requirements of the Building Ordinance. In addition, the terrace is painted in orange, creating a contrasting effect of the terrace adhering to the dark exterior.
2 The apartment is designed to explore the possibilities of the 'Toothpick Flat' in Hong Kong, even an area of 100 square metres can be developed into a high-rise building.

The Oi! Phase II
Eastern Community Green Station

Urban Respite

Oil Street Art Space (Oi!) is a public art space on the former site of the Royal Hong Kong Yacht Club. A historic English-style building rated as a Grade II historic building, it is located in the downtown area of Fortress Hill and North Point on Hong Kong Island. The architectural environment is both culturally rich and livelihood-oriented and is surrounded by an ambience of the 'literary youth'. The revitalisation work has been completed, and it now serves to connect the community with art while being mainly responsible for promoting exhibitions and activity centres of the visual arts. The second phase of Oi! uses an open square and exhibition hall to explore ideas on the symbiosis between city and nature, as well as on providing a healthy and secure ecological platform.

To provide a broader space to display artistic creations, the second phase of Oi! was expanded in 2019 and integrated with the adjacent public open space. The aim of the expansion was to bring artistic elements into the dense environment of high-rise buildings so that the public could appreciate works of art while undertaking leisure actitvities, thus further promoting public interaction. At the same time, through their architectural design, the new exhibition halls would provide a contemporary and artistic echo of the historic buildings.

The newly added site can accommodate large-scale outdoor art installations, as well as community screening platforms, art performances, symposiums, workshops and other activities to allow for more public participation. The main building features a long, sloping handrailed ramp that interweaves with the overall design, forming an iconic architectural feature. Above this structure sits an exhibition space that sparkles and gleams. The pavement is largely made of cobblestones, which collide with the surrounding green foliage to form a print-like pattern while also serving as a landscaped space for the public to rest.

The architect in charge of the project, Peter Lau, who also took charge of the renovation project for the Court of Final Appeal, was deeply touched by the beauty and value of the historic buildings. 'Architecture is not about complying with regulations or to fill up a given space; it is about creating an excellent space for the public.' Looking back at the first and second phases of the Oi! project, it was about utilising a historic building to present a new scene through the combination of old and new, so that a seemingly closed space could contain infinite possibilities and endless variations from one form to another.

Environmental issues are closely related to the future of mankind, and the Community Green Station initiative was put forward during the Government Policy Address in 2014. Its aim is to set up facilities to assist communities in recycling resources in the eighteen districts of Hong Kong while integrating environmental education. The project was opened for bidding and would be run by a number of NGOs.

According to Edward Wong, choosing the right locations for each district would first require two sets of models to be built and to which the designs for the remaining sites could refer. The project was spearheaded by the Sha Tin and Eastern districts, with the architect choosing the most ideal site for development. The Eastern Community Green Station is located at the bottom of a flyover which was originally a parking lot and also a passageway for the public to travel between the north and the south areas. The architects decided to preserve this passageway, so that it might serve to connect the old district with the new. Although there were challenges arising from this location, it is nevertheless an interesting place.

The Eastern Green Community Station creates an impression different from that of the usual waste recycling centre. Employing different

The new main exhibition hall and various outdoor exhibition spaces form a museum that is open 24 hours. The design uses concrete screens to frame the art space, forming different activity spaces both inside and outside the frames. The main exhibition hall, located on the first floor, is a glass box that resembles an elevated stage.

1. The main exhibition hall uses glass and glass bricks as the main materials for the exterior wall, thus enhancing the transparency of the space and visually connecting the public square with the relatively quiet and private courtyard.
2. The main exhibition hall is of a visually open design that creates a lantern effect at night, becoming the focal point in this concrete forest. (*'Floating Monkey'* art installation by Dylan Kwok).

45 Island North

A hidden yet beautiful spot, the Eastern Green Community Station has brought green architecture under the bridge. Perhaps this may even afford the dismantled cargo containers a different personality.

types of recycled materials together with cargo containers, which form its basic element, it is of a minimalistic, green and innovative design, making abundant usage of steel and wood. Due to the presence of randomly placed glass panels, the interior of the structure is exposed to an ample amount of sunlight. When describing the design of the Eastern Green Community Station, Thomas Wan had this to say: 'It is in line with oriental elements, with the incorporation of layered expressionism of traditional Chinese art.' Despite being a recycling centre, the structure with its surrounding ambience is remarkably serene. Bamboo screens have been incorporated within the facility to aid in cooling, and various cargo containers have been transformed to evoke a garden-like atmosphere, elevating both its practicality and sensory appeal. The building can also be used for educational purposes, mainly through community education and by encouraging the public to participate in recycling activities so that they may understand the importance of environmental protection, cultivate environmental awareness and ultimately change their habits accordingly.

1. The design uses modern building techniques and materials to interpret traditional Chinese gardens. From outdoor to indoor, cloisters to pavilions, it seeks to bring out the traditional ethos of creating harmonious unity between nature and man, which is in line with the modern emphasis on environmental protection.
2. Shatin Community Green Station, designed by Thomas Wan, is located in the heart of the industrial estate, creating an oasis that can be integrated into the community.
3. The complex is converted from old cargo containers. The garden and passageway are like pavilions and corridors, interpreting the transition from indoor to outdoor, public to private space, and bringing out the layered expressionism of Chinese gardens.

Transforming Star Street

The Study of a Storyteller

How should one go about describing Christopher Law? An architect whose ultimate goal was not about the creation of architecture but, rather, the study of storytelling. Not believing in hearsay, I typed the words 'Christopher Law architecture' into my internet search engine. The results were not unexpected. I came across articles with keywords such as 'Narrating Community Stories', 'Very Hong Kong', 'Urban Diary', 'Revitalising Historic Buildings Through Partnership Scheme', 'Urban Planning' and 'Bottom-up'.

On the day of the interview, Law was wearing his suit as usual and a pair of frameless glasses. He spoke slowly and rationally. The volume of his voice was at the perfect level to exude a sense of gentleness and elegance that would certainly have made him a storyteller in ancient times. The Oval Partnership, a firm co-founded by Law and his partner Patrick Bruce in 1992, made no mention of architecture at all, not because they weren't engaged in architecture, but because architecture was not everything to them.

'Many of our colleagues are academics and teachers.' Law took a quick look at the office outside the conference room, and then continued to share his understanding of architectural practice. 'Architectural practice is not confined only to the construction of buildings. Using your knowledge of architecture to improve the life of a city and to enhance the level of happiness for the city folk is also a solid form of architecture.'

In 2009, the HKSAR Government collaborated with Swire Properties to revitalise the old neighbourhoods of Wan Chai, including the current Starstreet Precinct. Law, who loved old neighbourhoods and public spaces, had always been on the lookout for opportunities to do something with the fabric of public spaces for the city. 'The general approach of revitalisation usually involves improving the space within a building, but we hope instead to improve the quality of life in the neighbourhood.'

Initially, the project began cautiously, and deliberately so, to allow for a time of consultation. A pop-up-store was set up on Sun Street to display the possibilities of the Starstreet Precinct. Next to it was a wishing wall that allowed people to express their ideas for the 'ideal Star Street'. Several rounds of focus group consultations were held to learn as much as possible about the proposed ideas for the neighbourhood. In the end, between eight and nine hundred responses were collected.

'It was really interesting, because, as it turned out, most people were very happy with the current Star Street and wanted to keep its existing atmosphere. They didn't want it to become Pacific Place.' That was an unexpected answer for Law. However, preservation of its original atmosphere did not mean it had to be static. The neighbourhood of Star Street consisted of people from all walks of life and different age groups, including the elderly and children. To reflect this, the team made some changes to details such as stairs, handrails, pedestrians' pathways and lights. 'It turns out that these little things were more important than a having a new look.'

The 'Starstreet Precinct' is a neighbourhood consisting of Sun Street, Moon Street, Star Street, Saint Francis Street and Wing Fung Street; the names 'Sun', 'Moon' and 'Star' evoked 'the three luminaries' from the *Three Character Classic*, echoing the location of Hong Kong's first power plant built here in 1889.

1	
2	4
3	

1. Standalone stores, cafés and speciality restaurants have successively entered the scene in Sun, Moon and Star Streets, lending this Wan Chai back garden a cool vibe of the 'literary youth'.
2. A street concert in Dominion Garden. Very Hong Kong organised a series of place-making events in the Starstreet Precinct in 2013.
3. Graffiti and murals created spontaneously by users add a touch of art to Star Street.
4. The shade created by the original trees preserved in Dominion Garden make it a good spot for passers-by to cool down.

Ever since Hong Kong began international trading activities in the 1840s, Star Street had been home to many Portuguese and Catholic communities from Macau. They had established seminaries, orphanages, churches, and in the area of Star Street and Saint Francis Street was also the first resting place for Catholics in Hong Kong. History had added a Western flavour with a southern European ambience to the Starstreet Precinct.

Along the streets and alleys where the warmth of the sun radiated through gaps in the swaying branches, one could smell the aroma of coffee wafting in the breeze, and hear the clashing sound of a wok and an iron pot in a food stall. On a bench under a tree, an old man was attending to his grandson who had just finished school and was having a little snack; there was a sense of tranquillity and an almost languid laziness in the air.

'There is laziness, and there is also yin energy.' Law smiled. Even after being baptised for one hundred and fifty years, that kind of atmosphere was still in the air. 'What we are seeking to protect is not just certain individual buildings, but to preserve this psychogeography so that the history, people and things of the past, and even ghosts, can continue to stay on Star Street.' Undoubtedly, this line of thought was very different from a typical architect's subjective way of thinking on architecture. These histories and stories were very important values to local residents, 'or rather, in line with the values they have come to expect'.

Generally, upon the completion of a project, an architect will hope that the finished product will be both recognisable and recognised. 'However, on the contrary, one would want the Starstreet Precinct project to feel as though nothing has changed (for the neighbourhood) even after its completion.' Law smiled heartily. 'For me, this is a great revelation.'

After the Starstreet Precinct project, Law and Ms Margaret Brooke co-founded the Very Hong Kong Foundation in 2013 to organise various community-led creative and cultural activities. Very Hong Kong works effectively as a middleman by listing vacant government sites for residents to apply to use them as community public spaces; one of its major projects, Collaborate HK, sought to help different groups find suitable sites and apply to the government for various place-making projects. These include the current Tsuen Lung Community Photography Centre, Tin Library – Tin Shui Wai House of Stories and Prince Edward Carer Support Centre.

In the same year that Very Hong Kong was founded, there was a street carnival for the Star Street community – 'Very Star Street'. There were indie bands, exhibitions and workshops, and Moon Street was transformed into a catwalk for design students from the Hong Kong Polytechnic University to showcase their costume designs. The festivities were made even more merry thanks to a sponsor providing champagne.

'I was very glad that not only had we received no complaints from our neighbours, but we had also managed to secure assistance from the shops nearby for the event.' Law recalled that joyful carnival, but he also recalled some of the worries he had. Before organising the event, he was planning to proceed the same way he had when launching the Starstreet Precinct project, by making many home visits to test the water. 'In fact,

The renovated pavement makes the restaurant a great spot for outdoor dining

Untold Stories

the whole process was about building dialogue and understanding amongst everyone, and on this basis, everyone helped one another out and tried to resolve problems rather than going right ahead based on any wishful thinking.'

During the interview, Law repeatedly mentioned how the knowledge gap affected the outcome. Could this be the reason for his obsession with community participation? 'Architects have ideals, but they don't necessarily have the know-how, so often they will feel very frustrated after completing a project.'

Long before the Starstreet Precinct project, Law collaborated with St. James' Settlement to turn part of a vacant site on Lun Fat Street in Wan Chai into the Bauhinia Garden, a public sitting area. Now known as Lun Fat Street Sitting-out Area, it was the first public space in Hong Kong to be designed by the community and, as such, a fine example of the bottom-up principle. Similar examples that followed included the Tai Wong Street East Sitting-out Area and the Blue House Cluster revitalisation project, which also injected the concept of 'retaining both the house and the occupants'.

Rather than being concerned with constructing a piece of architecture, Law was more committed to place-making that would improve the quality of life and sense of belonging to the neighbourhood. He also believed that the most straightforward way of finding an on-the-ground solution was to get the local community involved in the planning and development of public spaces and the city. 'Without community participation, the mark will be missed. Even with lots of research and investigation being done, the solution they (architects) come up with may not be what the neighbourhood wants.'

If you were to ask him during his secondary school years what architecture was, perhaps he would have already then been able to give you the answer. 'Back then, I would regularly visit the Swindon at the Ocean Terminal with my family during the weekends, and that was where I came across a book.' *An Outline of European Architecture by Nikolaus Pevsner* gave him an initial understanding of architecture. 'When I was in secondary school in England, I would also read books and papers written by Charles Jencks.' 'You studied Charles Jencks's works in secondary school?' I caught a smile from Law. 'I was in boarding school back then, and there wasn't much to do. It just so happened that the library carried it, and so I read it.'

He understood what architecture was, and he gradually came to understand what architectural practice and architectural culture were once he entered university. However, as to how the existing education system could train up an architect, he had always had his doubts.

'In those days, as long as they thought it was a good piece of architecture, it would be right for you to just follow along. It wasn't difficult, since they would teach you; and in those years you would learn from their ways and would have gained something in the process.' Law's tone was flat with a trace of resignation as he spoke. 'If you wanted to participate in competitions, win awards and get high scores, then follow their ways, but this practice is actually...' Law paused before unconsciously repeating himself. 'I gave in; I really did give in.' 'That is why I am not Rem Koolhaas.

He was just going about it his own way. What others thought didn't matter to him, and he had this attitude of "If you don't like it then fail me". I conformed and submitted to their power.' He couldn't help but emphasise again that, 'I ended up getting an A for everything I did.'

Law often used 'them' and 'these things' to describe educators and products under the system, respectively, and although his tone was always flat, he still could not hide his confusion. 'How can an architect's professional culture, professional practice and architectural know-how contribute more to society? Such contribution creates values, although such values may not necessarily be monetary...' He had carried this question with him since day one and was still searching for the answer.

Unlike other architects, on the day of my interview with him, it was not architectural models that sat on his desk but stacks of *Urban Diary*. On its website, *Urban Diary* describes itself as follows: 'We promote sustainability through narrating community stories, building digital databases, and organizing community events. Cities are multilayered and multifaceted, and we use text, audio, illustrations and moving images to capture their complexity. In Urban Diary, we believe that people's everyday tales are pivotal to comprehending cities and to building a sustainable future.'

He flipped through one of them, and within it was one story after another about the city of Hong Kong and its people. So what did storytelling have to do with architecture? 'Most of our work involves social research. We utilise big data for our social research and urban design initiatives, and then communicate through narratives to help people understand it.' Which could be summarised as 'research first, then design'. Law then added, 'Since 5,000 years ago, the most effective method of communication has always been storytelling. You can't communicate by writing reports.'

From studying the art of storytelling to engaging in urban design through storytelling, he described it as 'pushing the boundaries of architectural practice', while looking back at the statement 'people's everyday tales are pivotal to comprehending cities and to building a sustainable future.' It was simple yet intriguing. He was not unengaged with architecture; he was just doing it differently.

Blue House

Continuation of a Splash of Blue

Looking back at the history of the Blue House, it was an unassuming civil architecture not representative of glamour. 'But civil architecture is also representative of a side of Hong Kong,' said Kenneth Tse, the architect responsible for the revitalisation of the Blue House. 'It represents the collective memory of a certain era in Hong Kong.'

The Blue House was actually a tenement house built in the 1920s with a living-above-store design. It was one of the remaining hundred tenement houses in Hong Kong that was relatively intact and well known. Tse's initial impression of the Blue House had come from him passing through the place when he was in school. 'My memory of it had stayed the same since then. However, it was only when I started working and revisited the place that I realised it had turned blue.'

Participating in a guided tour of the Shek Kip Mei Estate, he had a chance meeting with two social workers from St. James' Settlement. 'At that time, they wanted to apply for a ground-floor shop and turn it into the "Wan Chai Livelihood Place" (now known as the "Hong Kong House of Stories") providing a gathering place for residents and fostering a sense of belonging amongst them. I began my involvement with the project from the shop on the ground floor.'

Back then, the Blue House had not yet been included in the Revitalising Historic Buildings Through Partnership Scheme. However, soon after Tse completed the Wan Chai Livelihood Place, he heard news that the Urban Renewal Authority and the Hong Kong Housing Society had plans to acquire the place. Having spent some time in the area, Tse gradually became more acquainted with the neighbours, social workers and people who cared about the community. He had also gained a layer of affection for the place. So, together with the social workers from St. James' Settlement, he was running back and forth to the Town Planning Board, and drawing up several proposals. After some twists and turns, he finally managed to turn the acquisition initiative into a revitalisation programme. 'It was like being engaged in volunteering work, and it was when I took part in the Revitalising Historic Buildings Through Partnership Scheme with St. James' Settlement and won a bid that it finally became a legitimate project.'

The name 'Blue House' was passed down from an urban legend. According to Mr Lam Sair Ling, an expert on historic buildings, the government unit then responsible for maintenance happened to have unused blue paint and, for sake of convenience, the entire tenement building was thus painted blue; and this subsequently became an anecdote of the city. The Hua Tuo Hospital located on the ground floor of the Blue House was a pharmacy owned by Lam Cho, apprentice of the famous master Wong Fei Hung of Guangdong. This historic lineage later became a consideration for the government in preserving the Blue House Cluster.

The Viva Blue House (Blue House Cluster) won the 2017 UNESCO Asia-Pacific Award of Excellence for Cultural Heritage Conservation; it was the first time Hong Kong had won a heritage conservation project in this category. What made the Blue House a household name was probably not just because of its history and iconic blue façade; as Hong Kong's first revitalisation project under the concept of 'retaining both the house and the occupants', Blue House also represented the 'vitality' of revitalisation to its fullest meaning, and at the same time, it was one of the few bottom-up conservation projects in Hong Kong in which the neighbourhood could participate.

With a history of over a hundred years, the Blue House had been inhabited by four generations. 'When I first came into contact with the residents of the Blue House, there were about a dozen families living there, and while some wanted to leave, others wanted to stay.'

If a place carried certain emotions and stories, it ought to be closely related to the people. Walking into a unit of the Blue House, one could still see the partitions between these cubicle apartments. 'Just like the seventy-two tenants in those old Cantonese dramas, living in a space of 500 square feet with a dozen groups of people, you will get emotional.'

Tse's definition of good architecture is one that can carry some kind of emotion and memory. 'Nowadays many iconic buildings are just an expression of insolence; they actually do not have substance or meaning.' Although much has been disappearing in the torrents of time, Tse has been hard at work trying to retain something at least through his best effort. 'In the past ten years, I have often tried to allow for elements of the past to seep through into my designs. Sometimes they are just very small parts, like the handrails and the terrazzo of the Star Ferry; but if these details are ignored, these vignettes of the past will only become more and more vague.'

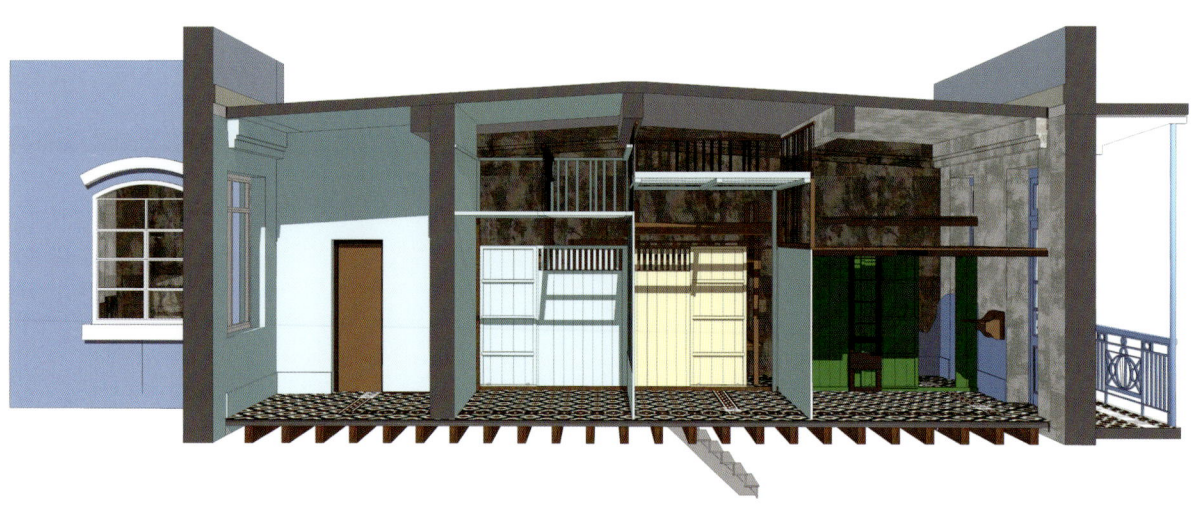

1. An illustration documents the layout of the former cubicle room. A 500-square-feet unit can be divided into more than a dozen bucket rooms, and dozens of people share a cooking space with only a stove and a tap.
2. Formerly deserted vacant land, it is now a gathering place for residents and their neighbours.
3. The adjacent yellow house is connected to the blue house and to the orange house to form a historic building complex.
4. View of the Orange House and public space entrance from King Sing Street.
5. The Blue House was formerly known as Hua Tuo Hospital, and was later changed into Hua Tuo Temple, where neighbours can pray to the divine for healing and receive free medical advice and medicine.

Island North

View of a partial façade of the Blue House on Stone Nullah Lane. The living-above-store concept is a functional feature of the tenement building, and the singled-out balcony decorated with chic flowers hanging onto the iron railing serves as a record of the daily life of residents.

Untold Stories   58

Hong Kong Waterfront Promenade
Central Market

Seventy-Three Kilometres

As night falls, the stars twinkle and are reflected on the surface of the rippling sea; accompanied by the gentle caress of the sea breeze, the sense of comfort is nonpareil. 'If you were to represent Hong Kong with just one photograph, it has to be of Victoria Harbour. Victoria Harbour is a natural asset of Hong Kong,' said Vincent Ng without the slightest hesitation. He has been engaged in waterfront promenade work for many years.

Growing up in Causeway Bay, Ng hung around the waterfront almost on a daily basis. 'The kindergarten I attended was near Paterson Street.' It was at a time when Paterson Street did not have light boxes and billboards. At most, there were a few neon signs, and most of the shops at ground level were also street markets and stalls. 'There were fishing boats selling seafood at the typhoon shelter, where I would often accompany my grandmother on her visits.' Recalling the past, Ng could not hide his excitement. 'But the waterfront seems to be getting further away from us.'

Some say Hong Kong is a city built on reclaimed land; and since land reclamation is inseparable from excavation, it seems that it is no exaggeration to use the phrase 'excavating mountains and reclaiming land' when describing Hong Kong. Through the torrents of development, the sea breeze that used to be salty, and fishy now seems only to be salty as the primitive and simple lifestyle of the small fishing village seems to have all but disappeared. In between the disputes arising from the question of whether or not to reclaim, Ng asked lightly, 'Why are we not thinking of returning the waterfront to the public?'

In 2004, the HKSAR Government established the Harbourfront Enhancement Committee, now known as the Harbourfront Commission, and Ng had joined on behalf of the Hong Kong Institute of Architects.

He had been engaged in waterfront-related work for over ten years. 'Everyone was so bold and said they had a vision of building the Victoria Harbour into an endless waterfront promenade and returning it to the people.'

The planned waterfront promenade totalled seventy-three kilometres. Work started in 2004, and, as of 2020, twenty-four kilometres had been completed. 'At first I was scratching my head over how we could achieve that, from Shau Kei Wan to Kennedy Town, Tsuen Wan to Lei Yue Mun…?' Yet it was through stroke-by-stroke, step-by-step, and two simple lines in his mind that constituted the driving force behind his consistent research, exploration and finding of ways to overcome the obstacles along the way. 'If you don't take the initiative to take a step forward, you will never know what difficulties you may encounter. Just like playing mah-jong, you ought to play the best hand you have and not wait for the best hand to come into play.'

'The typhoon shelter in Causeway Bay has the Tin Hau Temple on the water; the waterfront of Tsim Sha Tsui has the most prosperous Central night view by the sea; and the T-shaped pier in North Point, although a little untidy, is a favourite fishing spot for many in the evening. It is especially interesting to see the many stools placed around the area.' 'Which is your favourite promenade?' Ng did not have a definite answer. 'It depends on the mood!' 'Each has its own characteristics.' However, he did express that the Belcher Bay Promenade was his recent favourite.

In the past, the traditional management model was employed when dealing with waterfront projects, which generally required planning, consultation, design, collection of opinions and other procedures. These procedures were rather time-consuming and resistant to change. 'Now it's just start first, optimise later.'

Ng described the Belcher Bay Promenade as a testing ground.

The design of the Belcher Bay Promenade was unconventional, with occasional 'pop-up' installations found on the site. 'Whether they are beach benches or pallets, most of the installations are mobile.' And there are no special signs in the open space. 'You can skateboard, roller-skate, or even bring your pet along for a walk, if you like.'

Over the past decade, Ng has envisioned a waterfront that is intimately connected to people and their daily lives, reminiscent of childhood memories or the naturally unfolding moments of life. He remarked that his recent waterfront promenade work had been a different experience compared to his past work. 'In the past, I was working within the framework and never had the opportunity to experiment.'

In addition to new inspirations and discoveries, Ng expressed that once he had started designing his work outside of the framework, he could respond to everyone's needs much more quickly. 'It turns out that many people like parks with tables and benches, especially because the epidemic has led to the banning of "dine-in".' Hence, sporadic ideas such as 'Dining Table' and 'Work from Harbour' started gradually emerging, and spaces that had not been deliberately planned began to take on some form of consistency for everyone, which in turn created a feeling of interaction between people and space. 'I haven't heard this much laughter while strolling along the waterfront in a long while.'

Today, Ng still frequents Causeway Bay for a walk and view-finding to gain inspiration for his watercolour artwork. Aside from his work, painting has been his main source of happiness. During his school days, most of his peers read medicine, but he liked to paint. He started learning whilst at secondary school from the master of watercolour painting, Mr Maytin Kan; and his senior-in-training, Mr Stephen Yau, has now become a famous watercolour painter in Hong Kong. He lamented that reading architecture was a time-consuming affair. 'If I hadn't put down my brush then, I might just be like Stephen Yau now.' He couldn't help but laugh at his own remarks.

Starting one's own business was a path chosen by many architects, and Ng was no exception. However, for him it was an extremely dramatic undertaking. After graduation, Ng joined KNW Architects & Engineers, which was later restructured into K & N Architects Ltd, which then later became Kwan & Associates. The company had undergone rounds of reorganisations and yet he was still there. Back then, he was working as he should have been and had no desire to switch jobs, but the company eventually closed down. 'You can become your own boss just by working for the company until it goes out of business.' The humour and irony of this statement was not lost on either of us, and we had a chuckle about it.

Faced with the sudden closure of the firm, Ng said he didn't have time to give it much thought. 'I had no idea if it was fated, but it was like falling into the water from ashore. I had to get afloat immediately.'

The whole company was made redundant, and so it was either a matter of saying goodbye or coming together as a team. It was 1999 when Ng and three other colleagues decided, within the span of two to three days,

Untold Stories   62

In addition to the creatively designed lawn, there are also charming mushroom-shaped rain shelters.

1. If you want to take a break after a stroll, the chair is right in front of you.
2. Connecting the waterfront is no longer a dream; it now offers a variety of leisure spaces.
3. This large-scale installation built through an open competition is brightly coloured.

to found their own firm – AGC Design Limited. The ongoing construction projects suddenly became opportunities for the new firm to prove itself.

Going from more than one hundred staff to a team of fourteen, the volume of work suddenly reduced by a large margin. On top of that, the ever-watchful eyes of their competitors made the whole process as exciting as an eagle trying to prey on a chicken. Only a tenth of the projects remained, and some customers even told Ng directly, 'I can't trust young people like you' and then proceeded to engage other architects. The experience was undoubtedly a turning point in Ng's career and had a deep impact on him, but everything was so sudden and there was no time for him to thoroughly digest everything.

The firm has now been operating for more than twenty years and has covered a great number of different projects, many of which have been collaborations with other architects, for example, the Asia Society Hong Kong Centre with Tod Williams and Billie Tsien and the Jockey Club Innovation Tower for the Hong Kong Polytechnic University with Zaha Hadid. He also nearly had the opportunity to complete the revitalisation project of the Central Market with Arata Isozaki, 'but it didn't happen in the end, so I think it was at least some other form of experience'. He sounded a little disappointed.

In any case, the waterfront project that has helped secure the company's growth is now already well underway. 'We have completed twenty-four kilometres out of the seventy-three kilometres as of 2020 today. In 2021, I would like to complete twenty-five kilometres; in 2028, thirty-four kilometres…' More than a decade has passed, what has made him persist? 'Because it's not done,' Ng says without hesitation. So, is it necessary to complete the seventy-three kilometres in your lifetime? 'Actually, I haven't given much thought to this goal.' Ng said, very frankly. 'It has taken sixteen years to complete twenty-three kilometres. Perhaps you could just about complete this goal if you lived well and long – and got to a hundred years old.'

Ng has been nicknamed Kimura Takuya within the professional circle. With his fiery enthusiasm and mildly insolent temperament, he does actually look like the Japanese pop star himself, even though he speaks Cantonese. Although the entire waterfront project has been calculated in decades and might not be completed in a lifetime, seventy-three kilometres is a clear goal that carries with it the very bold idea conceived from the beginning.

'Some things just can't be forced, but the goal is to deliver as much as possible.' During the interview, Ng often found himself unable to contain his laughter, showcasing his abilty to approach challenging situations with a lighthearted attitude. Yet, at certain moments, those experiences were tempered into an indescribable calmness, inspiring confidence in those who crossed paths with him.

1. An outdoor space constructed from the atrium; this is an important venue for organising events.
2. Modernism was simple and functional, and for most people in Hong Kong who have been in and out of the Central market for decades, the wide staircase in the centre is the most comfortable aspect of the market, which has been preserved up until today.

Untold Stories

Hong Kong Museum of Coastal Defence
Fireboat Alexander Grantham Exhibition Gallery

Guarding the Memory of Hong Kong

The Hong Kong Museum of Coastal Defence, formerly known as the Lei Yue Mun Barracks, is now one of the branch museums of the Hong Kong Museum of History, and it serves a different role in guarding the harbour as well as memories of Hong Kong.

The Hong Kong Museum of Coastal Defence originated from the then Hong Kong government's proposal to find a storage space for the uniforms and firearms of the Royal Hong Kong Regiment (The Volunteers) before the Handover of Hong Kong in 1997. The Leisure and Cultural Services Department suggested that, with a little repair, the many abandoned barracks in the Lei Yue Mun area could be put to good use. Kenneth Tam, the architect in charge of the project, believed that if these museum objects were placed in a dilapidated stucture, they would not hold much appeal to visitors and the architecture itself would fail to fulfil its intended purposes as a suitable exhibition venue nor as a means of continuing a story.

When Tam visited the barracks, he accidentally found the Lei Yue Mun Pass Battery. The old battery was also very dilapidated. It had been leased to film companies producing movies on the Vietnam War. However, this bunker was special in that it had been built underground, and although the battery itself was in a state of severe disrepair, its design was very much ahead of its time. This aroused Tam's interest and prompted him to conduct site visits in different regions, and he found no similar design, neither in Hong Kong nor in the Mainland. This indeed spoke volumes of its historical value and attractiveness.

'I thought if you could put these museum objects in a bunker, it would be a complementary situation where people could better associate them with what happened during the Second World War.' said Tam. However, the government units responsible for this project held different views on the matter, especially as the bunker itself was not open to the public and was located within the flight path of the Kai Tak Airport; the civil aviation instruments that had been installed for calculating wind shear could not be simply be repositioned randomly, as their location and management were crucial for flight safety.

The first hurdle in resolving this impasse was the Urban Council. Tam held numerous meetings with members of the legislative council and even visited the site with them to better explain the idea of the project to them. Recalling the endless discussions amongst those who attended the meetings who generally held the belief that the problems involved were too difficult to be resolved – and that it was undoubtedly a controversial project – Tam said. 'If you don't try, you never know how it will turn out.' It was only when the eighty-year-old member of the legislative council Mr Brook Antony Bernacchi stood up and voiced his support for the great potential of the project that it began to gradually gain support from other members. Subsequently, other positive responses began to come in, too.

Hong Kong would certainly not be able to find another museum with an underground bunker, so when the design concept was submitted to the Urban Services Department, there was concern about the lack of suitable exhibition space. It was proposed that the sunken courtyard be covered with a canopy. Tam then formally proposed his design to the Urban Council, which opined that it could be a meaningful project after all and finally approved the design concept. Using 'the soldier's spirit' as a reference and inspiration, Tam began his formal design and included further elements of the tent that were originally proposed as well as the tabernacle in which soldiers had lived. Mr Jason Yuen, a member of the legislative council, even took the initiative and travelled to Canada to visit British military structure conservation projects being undertaken there. Tam visited the Mainland and Britain at his own expense to inspect similar architecture, and found that the Coastal Defence Museum indeed had a very advanced and distinctive military structure.

As an architect, Tam is often focused on the viability of a design concept. As the Handover in 1997 drew near, resources were being concentrated on related projects to welcome the special occasion. As a result, there wasn't enough manpower available to help out on the Museum of Coastal Defence. Fortunately, during the tender process he managed to bring together former colleagues from the Architectural Services Department. They first took time to organise the remaining civil aviation equipment, but while testing them, an accident involving a commercial airliner brought the project to a standstill for a while. In addition, as the positions of many of the testing instruments on site were already fixed, it was difficult to incorporate them in its design. Coupled with the shortage of manpower and resources, limited time and the complicated terrain, construction began without a complete plan and the team was literally building while finalising the plan at the same time.

Once the proposal was in place, it had to be approved by the Architectural Services Department and was subject to a detailed audit from the Urban Services Department. The Civil Aviation Department later relaxed the requirements for the positioning of the instruments and allowed them to be relocated, and when work finally commenced, they had to work out budgetary issues with Leighton Contractors. Time was critical during the design phase of the project, and Tam would receive countless enquiry emails from colleagues. According to him, in order to more effectively resolve the problems at hand, he visited the site every day, answered questions, rode his Jeep to different locations at short notice, made records and resolved issues, as well as presided over the overall design work.

The tensile structure of the Hong Kong Museum of Coastal Defence was the focal point of the project. It was designed by a German company, reviewed by a Hong Kong team and handmade in Sri Lanka using parts from the Mainland. A key element of the tensile structure was the aerospace material it employed, and Tam had to personally be in different places to follow up on its production. The support of the tensile structure also relied on the steel cable in the middle, and the height of the tensile structure was limited so as not to adversely affect the flight paths of the Kai Tak Airport. The design of the tensile structure had also undergone changes. The number of masts increased from one to four, and the base support points had to be adjusted to suit the position of the basement. After its completion, the tensile structure looked like a spider's web hanging in mid-air.

The work was eventually completed ahead of schedule, allowing the willing contractor to take time to improve on the details, meaning that everything was even closer to perfection than expected. From the architect and the design team to the contractors, the entire construction team had established deep friendship and trust working on this project.

On 25 July 2000, the Hong Kong Museum of Coastal Defence was officially opened to the public. What truly brought joy to Tam was that on its opening day, there was a large group of very excited children who visited, and for the first time, a school field trip to the site could consist of both indoor and outdoor museum experiences. In addition, the Museum of Coastal Defence had attracted customs officers from all over the world, including some veterans who were happy to recall, learn and share about military culture, connecting the many stories of the Second World War.

Today, the Hong Kong Museum of Coastal Defence continues to celebrate the history of Hong Kong's coastal defence through its museum collection and historical trails. Tam feels honoured to have been in charge of the project. Looking back, it was no easy feat for Hong Kong, especially when there were so many considerations to accommodate in the project's design. However, no effort was ever

The Hong Kong Museum of Coastal Defence celebrates the history of coastal defence in Hong Kong through the display of museum objects and historical trails.

wasted, and the museum has fulfilled its purpose by securing a home for valuable historical records and stories. In addition, it also provides a meaningful and educational experience for all its visitors – and that, indeed, is the most treasured part of a piece of architecture.

After completing his work on the museum, Tam became more confident in handling issues relating to historic building revitalisation and conservation. In 2007, he took on another such project: the Fireboat Alexander Grantham Exhibition Gallery.

The Fireboat Alexander Grantham Exhibition Gallery is housed in the firefighting vessel *Alexander Grantham*, a fireboat of Hong Kong, in active service from 1953 to 2002. The vessel was named after the twenty-second governor of Hong Kong, Alexander Grantham. It had fought numerous fires and participated in many marine rescues, and at the time of its decommissioning, it was still the largest fireboat in Asia. The exhibition gallery has an area of approximately 1,200 square-metres, is home to unique historical objects and provides informative and educational material about the various firefighting facilities and marine rescue work, as well as the firefighting history of Hong Kong.

At the beginning of the conservation work, the first issue to be researched by the team of architects was the potential placement of the vessel in the park. The Director of the Leisure and Cultural Services Department believed that although the damage caused by oyster shells on the boat's hull was serious, there was scope for remediation. While the repair was underway, the team was also focused on the next challenge: making the vessel more visible to the public. In addition, due to the size of the vessel, it was necessary to enlist the assistance of a search and rescue vessel from the Mainland for transportation. The vessel's firefighting equipment and rooms were later restored and the exhibition gallery was created and themed around the history of marine firefighting. The vessel itself bears witness to the history of firefighting in Hong Kong and reflects the achievements of Hong Kong's shipbuilding industry in the 1950s.

The interesting feature of this architecture project was the vessel itself, which was pre-existing rather than a piece of architecture that was built from scratch. Tam remarked that when approached to lead this project, he was actually in the midst of learning about conservation; how it involved preserving a historic architecture, to allow the public to learn about its people, their stories and the objects that remain. Tam even enrolled in a Master's program at HKU and has been involved in many conservation projects. He has since undertaken academic research to further his knowledge and expand his awareness in this important field.

1	3
2	4

1 The museum, formerly the barracks of the Lei Yue Mun Battery, now performs a different role: guarding the memory of Hong Kong Harbour.
2 Inspired by and referenced from 'the soldier's spirit', the museum's canopy looks like a spider's web from a distance.
3 Named after the 22nd governor of Hong Kong, the Fireboat Alexander Grantham Exhibition Gallery displays unique firefighting artefacts.
4 The *Alexander Grantham* sits on the promenade. Visitors can learn about various firefighting facilities, marine rescue work and firefighting history by boarding the boat.

Island North

Aldrich Bay Park

Further, Wider, Deeper

Around the corner of Shau Kei Wan in the eastern district of Hong Kong Island, there is a red wooden boat berthed at the base of several high-rise buildings. The water feature is a unique addition to the bustling city. This is the Aldrich Bay Park, designed by landscape architect Mr Ryan Lin.

From the large water feature to the design of the fishing boats, every detail is connected to the history and story of this place. The area around Aldrich Bay used to be a fishing village. When Lin took over the project, he immediately conducted a site visit – from overlooking the mountains from afar and spending time in the community to visiting the reclamation site and then the seaside. All in search of clues that would link the community with its historical and cultural context. The theme of the project was finally decided – 'Fishing Village of the Past.'

From the initial sketch to the completion of the entire park, Lin was very involved throughout the process. Aldrich Bay Park covered an area of approximately 22,000 square metres and was formerly a car park and golf course. The high intensity of light and noise used to cause a nuisance to the nearby residents; and due to restrictions brought about by the layout of public roads, it was difficult for residents to visit the sitting-out area nearby; thus, the whole environment felt rather unpleasant, and that became Lin's primary challenge.

Using the concept of the fishing village as a starting point, the fishing boats located at the Aldrich Bay Park were to be its focal point. The boats were genuine fishing boats, custom-made at a shipyard in Shanwei. They were towed to the site through the harbour, winched to shore and then pulled into the park by large trucks, attracting a lot of public attention on the way. There are many pavilions of different sizes in the park that serve to imitate the stilt huts of the old village; the streams and waterfalls of the area are replicated in the water features, which also provide a visual connection to the Shau Kei Wan typhoon shelter just outside the park. Standing in the park and looking out towards the sea, the ponds of the park will first come into view as it stretches towards the promenade beyond, which subsequently leads onto the view of the sea, forming a straight line that connects to nature.

There are also many details in the park worth discovering; the nearby Tam Kung Temple holds an annual festival with temporary theatres constructed out of bamboo branches. Lin took this as an inspiration and added bamboo elements to the design of the park to reflect the culture of the district. In addition, he deliberately pushed the facilities at the entrance of the park further backwards, thus leaving a larger entrance to allow the crowds easier access; and the large pavilion in the garden has been connected to a grassed area by a concrete pathway. As a result, if the pavilion is still not spacious enough to accommodate a large number of visitors, the grassed area is available.

As for the moderately sized children's playground, although during the day there are elderly people utilising the facilities for stretching exercises, the relatively static nature of their activities means that their voices would not affect the nearby primary school. However, once school has ended, children would flock to and gather at the playground, making the whole place lively and joyful. 'While designing the playground, I was thinking about the needs of the whole family.' Lin said.

For safety reasons, a glazed pavilion has been built around the entire playground to allow parents to watch over their children; there is also a designated place for strollers and for large personal belongings to be stored. Aldrich Bay Park has a lively ambience where everyone, from the young to the elderly, can rest and play. On the weekends, domestic helpers will also gather and some will bring along musical instruments

1 The water feature is matched with pavilions of different sizes, imitating the stilt huts of the old fishing village. The wooden deck brings visitors close to the water.
2 Through different water features, such as creeks and waterfalls, the park guides visitors from the main entrance of Tai On Street to the large water feature where the fishing boats are located; this visually connects the Shau Kei Wan typhoon shelter.

to liven the place up. All this is the result of the designer's meticulous attention to detail, careful observation, numerous experiments and subsequent implementation, 'I remember going to the park on the first weekend after its completion and the entire children's playground was full.'

However, since the design of the park involved the elements of water, it presented a major challenge to the architects due to potential safety risks associated with water features in public architecture. As a result, the park was subject to many revisions and compromises before its final completion. Lin recalled that, on one occasion, he and his supervisor, Ms Winnie Ho, attended a public consultation at the Quarry Bay Community Hall. They had parents expressing their concerns on the safety issues surrounding the reflecting pond. This subsequently led to the planting of flowerbeds and trees around the area, leaving only the fish shed as the access point. Fortunately, a colleague from LCSD at the time accepted the proposed change. 'There are things you just won't know until you try. The most crucial of all is to be unafraid; it is important to learn how to communicate with multiple stakeholders.'

The park finally opened in 2011 and Lin recalls seeing a group of children sitting by the barrier of the reflecting pond, gently touching its surface with their feet. The scene struck a chord with Lin; and he wondered if setting up so many safety signs was truly necessary?

Lin used to make woodwork furniture with his father when he was a child. Once he grew up, he pursued the study of environmental science and landscape architecture for which, back in the day, the department only had a quota of eleven students biannually. After graduation, he participated in the Hong Kong Wetland Park project as a landscape architect. Previously, he had worked for the Civil Engineering and Development Department where he had experimented extensively with different varieties of plants and tested their growth patterns (for instance, the depth required for aquatic plants to grow underwater); so when he was in charge of the wetland park project, he was able to apply the results of those experiments, and plants became an architectural language for him.

Within the Aldrich Bay Park, a close examination reveals many seemingly inconspicuous Boston Ivies. They reflect the change in season with the change of colour in their foliage: verdant green in spring and summer; withering and turning red in autumn and winter. Different to architecture, plants are always changing and the same holds true of people. As a landscaper, Lin is also changing. An architect needs to employ independent thinking and experimentation in order to overcome fear and obstacles. Public architecture has a long lifespan, often remaining for ten or twenty years, sometimes even longer. How architects connect these structures to communities and public spaces when designing them, as well as ensuring their upkeep, are topics worthy of contemplation. 'We must look further, wider and deeper.' This was the message imparted to Lin by his supervisor.

Island South

Reading Guidance

Island South includes The Peak, Pok Fu Lam, Aberdeen, Deep Water Bay, Repulse Bay, Stanley, Tai Tam, Shek O and other scenic areas.

Historically, the Peak was designated as an exclusive area for Westerners, and it was not until after the Second World War that those restrictions were lifted. Now, it has become a residential location for the affluent families. With the changing times, many beautiful, classical Western-styled buildings have been converted into luxury mansions. The Peak has its special elements, and we should respect historical facts including the story of the Peak Pavilion. Its earliest location was, in fact, not at the familiar Peak Tower or the Lions Pavilion next to it but an old pavilion not far away, at Mount Austin Playground. Nearby lies the site where the legendary late Zaha Hadid found her first success. In 1982, a Hong Kong businessman held an international design competition in a private club at the Peak, which Hadid won. Although her design, being too avant-garde, was never realised, it was the start of her subsequent, legendary achievements. I would like to take this opportunity to correct the claims made by certain foreign online news sources that the venue of the said competition was neither at the Kowloon Peak nor the Peak Tower.

Restoring the Classical Style of the Peak

The Peak Improvement Scheme was a unique project that stemmed from the Tourism Board's idea to improve facilities around the Peak for tourists. I undertook the project on my own initiative in collaboration with Mr K.C. King. The scope of the project was not limited to simply upgrading the facilities and adding a tourist information centre (converted from an old cable car). It also aimed to create a Western-style garden in its pure form, to restore the classical scenery of the Peak of the past. By replacing the more modern landscape facilities with more classical ones, a beautifully retro atmosphere was created.

Participating in this project yielded another interesting find that involved a brief episode of excavating some interesting artefacts. These discoveries were made beneath the foundation of the Peak Pavilion. Notable findings included fragments of the century-old tile flooring from the Mountain Lodge[1], along with vintage soda bottles of that time. Unfortunately, shortly after the excavation began, voices began to call for the protection of the pavilion which had been built mere decades ago in the 1970s. Subsequently, we received a formal notice from the Development Bureau requesting a halt to the excavation. It was truly regrettable, as we had no choice but to restore everything to its original state. Recalling the project's consultation phase, where we navigated opposing viewpoints and successfully transformed adversaries into allies, the experience of the Peak project remains a poignant and complex memory.

The University of Chicago at Mount Davis

Walking from the Peak to the Mount Davis Battery, one passes by a building on the hill that was originally a youth hostel and the award-winning work of two architects, Mr Wallace Cheng and Mr T.C. Yuet. The University of Chicago's Hong Kong campus is located in Pok Fu Lam's Battery area. The campus building was built on top of a white painted house where political prisoners were imprisoned during the British-governed period. It was designed by renowned Vancouver Chinese architect the late Mr Bing Thom and Mr Francis Yan. The streamlined glass curtain wall was designed to match with the terrain and slope to reduce the sense of volume and weight, so that people travelling in vehicles on the narrow roads would not feel constricted. As the glass curtain wall reflects the surrounding trees and mountains, the originally low building complex becomes more integrated with nature. In addition, Mr Bing Thom and Mr Francis Yan also successfully completed the revitalisation of the Haw Par Mansion as project architects, with Mr Roger Wu as project manager. Initially, the Haw Par Mansion was the property of Ms Sally Aw, which later became one of the projects under the Revitalising Historic Buildings Through Partnership Scheme[2] of the HKSAR Government. Under the design of Bing Thom and Francis Yan, the Haw Par Mansion was revitalized into the current Haw Par Music, mainly to promote art, culture and music. Born in Hong Kong, Thom had returned to his birthplace after making a name for himself in Canada and worked with his partner Yan to design several prominent projects for Hong Kong, including the Xiqu Centre in the West Kowloon Cultural District. Unfortunately, he died of a cerebral haemorrhage without seeing the completion of his work; that is perhaps an architect's lifelong regret.

The Béthanie in Pok Fu Lam was built in 1875 by the Paris Foreign Missions Society and was later taken over by the Hong Kong government. The intention was for it to be handed over to the University of Hong Kong and to be transformed into a beautiful second campus of the Hong Kong Academy for Performing Arts. The newly refurbished Béthanie is a testament to how the architectural language blends between old and new can be extraordinary. Mr Philip Liao was in charge of the renovation project. Adjacent to the Béthanie is a classical bungalow, once the property of the formerly known Dairy Farm International Holdings Limited, the restoration of which is a project under the Revitalising Historic Buildings Through Partnership Scheme named The Pokfulam Farm. Half a century ago, this area was originally a piece of dairy farm pasture land. I paid a visit there when I was young, and I recall that there used to be herds of cows with brass bells grazing on the slopes of the mountains. From afar, the sound of the bells and the mooing of cows vaguely conjured up the ambience of the Netherlands.

The University of Hong Kong (HKU) also has many campus buildings in the Pok Fu Lam area. Amongst them is the HKU Graduate House; the most beautiful modern building of them all. The huge difference in the height of the building within its site gave Rocco Yim the opportunity to showcase his strengths. Rocco's forte lies in creating accessibility through clever design and in connecting different spaces in a way that lightens up the often mundane experience of shuttling back and forth within the campus. Being an HKU alumnus himself, he is proud to leave behind a campus building for his alma mater. The HKU has a history of more than one hundred years and has had decades of settling in in the Pok Fu Lam area. Yet the replacement of the old buildings with the new ones has me reminiscing about the classical elegance of half a century ago which is certainly gradually disappearing. At today's HKU campus, even when walking into the Lok Yew Hall or Fung Ping Shan Museum (now the University Museum and Art Gallery of the University of Hong Kong), one would not be able to tell that the campus was once home to numerous great historical and literary figures.

A New Art District at Island South

Wong Chuk Hang has been transformed from an industrial zone into a new area that attracts the young. Due to lower rentals, it once attracted galleries that preferred the extra-large spaces available in these industrial buildings, and it gradually became the Hong Kong version of Chelsea[3] in New York. However, it cannot be denied that the biggest disadvantage of Wong Chuk Hang is the vehicle-oriented layout that makes walking inconvenient. To visit these galleries scattered in different industrial buildings, visitors must cross many footbridges and uninteresting streets. This inconvenience has hence driven the galleries back to Central. Nevertheless, a large number of new industrial and commercial buildings that cater to the preference for studios amongst the self-

employed young people have recently been completed.

The stylish Arca Hotel is the work of Mr Sam Ng and his partner Mr Peter Lampard. The exterior features a grey brick façade that looks like a woven sweater, while the interior decor is rough and lively to match the vision of the area's upgrade. Another architecture project of Lampard is the Hillwood House Hotel on Hillwood Road, Tsim Sha Tsui. It was no easy task for such a young architect to succeed with these large-scale projects. Drawing reference from many of the returning entrepreneurs whose stories are mentioned in this book, Hong Kong is no doubt a blessed place for young professionals to develop their talents.

On the way from Wong Chuk Hang to Stanley, the Hong Kong Ocean Park Marriott Hotel, with its vine-like façade and a slightly tropical design, comes into view. Moving on to Deep Water Bay, Repulse Bay and Chung Hom Kok, the mansions along the way are all unique in their own way, but the most prominent of them is The Repulse Bay designed by Mr Anthony Ng. Together with the shopping arcade of the former Repulse Bay Hotel, these are must-see places for tourists. Although The Repulse Bay has been around for many years, it is still very well maintained.

Southern European Vibe in Stanley

Stanley was originally the first place where the British army was stationed, but it was later moved to Central due to the soldiers' difficulty in acclimatising to the area. The

Stanley Military Cemetery had already been established by the early 1840s. The area has long been home to many foreigners, and the American Club is also located in Tai Tam. The American Club was designed by the late Mr William Turnbull Jr[4], who specialised in designing waterfront architecture. Making use of the chemistry between space and nature, he managed to skilfully grasp the relationship between seascape, landform and architecture, and he integrated them seamlessly. For those who have the opportunity to visit the clubhouse, they surely must agree that it is one of the most beautiful clubhouses in Hong Kong.

Stanley has been designated by the HKSAR Government as a key tourist area. Due to the waterfront scenery here, the historic Murray House in Admiralty was dismantled and rebuilt in Stanley, and there are many distinguished Western restaurants which appeal particularly to tourists, recreating the vibe of a Southern European town. The plan to renovate Stanley includes the construction of a Stanley Municipal Building designed by Mr Thomas Wan. Based on the narrow streets here, the curved corners are in line with the concept of the Chinese courtyard houses where facilities face inward and harmonise with each other. Here I would like to share a small side story: it turns out that in the early stage of the project, there were many complaints and harsh criticisms; some believed it was of an erroneous design while some feared the finished product would be unattractive, and it was only after the masterpiece was completed that the detractors finally had a change of opinion.

As for the renovation of the waterfront, it was jointly planned by Mr Thomas Wan, landscape architect Mr Tony Mui and myself. We first requested, rather boldly, the demolition of the large and clumsy temporary street market on the waterfront and for it to be replaced by a cluster of small shops shaped like surfboards that curved along the waterfront. This allowed room for the expansion of the boardwalk, making the extension to the entire new promenade to Murray House unobstructed. The design team went a step further by selecting a waterfront location adjacent to the Murray House for the construction of a 'Blake Pier at Stanley'. The original Blake Pier was built in Central in 1902 and was later moved to Wong Tai Sin Morse Park in 1967 and converted into a pavilion. It is as if the Blake Pier has returned to the sea again, as it was a century ago, but to a new location: today's Stanley waterfront.

St Stephen's College, located in Tung Tau Bay in Stanley, is the site of both old and new buildings. The new building refers to the school campus designed by the late Mr Tao Ho forty years ago. An A-shaped fair-faced concrete building was considered relatively avant-garde in those days, yet it is still attractive today. St Stephen's College Preparatory School is located at Wong Ma Kok Road in Stanley. Designed by Mr Philip Liao, it looks like a large square box piercing through the blue sky.

Stanley has a wealth of tourist attractions, from the new waterfront to the old bazaar, the cemetery to the old village house, and from the historic buildings to the eight houses[5] that had existed before the Japanese Invasion. Stanley is also a favourite spot for celebrities and a concentration of famous residences and public figures. Before joining the government, I had the chance to design the Stanley Crest, a project of six villas with panoramic sea views. They were originally boldly mud-red, but their colour has since been changed to a paler hue and they are almost unrecognisable to me now. Opposite

those villas are the Stanford Villa designed by Mr Steve Leung, Stanley Court by Mr Anthony Ng, and Mr Frank Yu's independent house on South Bay Road. The latter is a square box facing the sea, encapsulating a meticulously designed interior space with an elegant outdoor garden and a slender swimming pool, displaying another level of minimalist aesthetics.

The Exceptional Shek O

The reason why foreigners are particularly fond of Hong Kong is that it only takes a journey of twenty minutes to get from the colourful metropolis to the lush green mountains and azure seas, not to mention the big waves at the Big Wave Bay.

What makes Shek O extraordinary is that it is close to the city but also close to the countryside, which affords it a mixture of scenery and features. The most iconic of such features include the European-style Shek O Bus Terminal completed in 1955, which is the work of Mr Su Gin Djih, a modern Chinese architect master, as well as twenty-two unique Taipan houses. These are the properties of the renowned families who have come to Shek O since the nineteenth century, settling in this utopia which offers tranquillity and superb views. The grand mansions on view today were all designed by famous architects; each being unique in design and outstanding in its own right.

There is also no shortage of alternative architecture, for example, the Shek O Village House, which was transformed by Mr Kenneth Ko. Shanghai-born Ko made his first fortune by beginning with the transformation of his own cottage in Shek O. Demonstrating a unique blend of Eastern and Western styles, all of his neighbours subsequently appointed him as their designer, and it was this that helped his architectural style and reputation to flourish. The colourful cottages in Shek O have become an attraction for tourists. On Shek O Rocky Bay Beach, there are also peculiar Robinson-style rock houses, all of which bear testament to the fact that while Shek O may be small, it is exceptional.

Notes

1 Mountain Lodge: Former summer residence for governors of Hong Kong on the Victoria Peak. Its architectural design had evolved throughout history starting with its intial design in 1867. In 1899, Sir Henry Arthur Blake commissioned a second (design) of the Mountain Lodge which was built between 1900 and 1902.

2 Revitalising Historic Buildings Through Partnership Scheme: The HKSAR Government has been revitalising government-owned historic buildings since 2008. Grants are provided to non-profit organisations which successfully pass the application process. Nominal rents are collected, and it operates in the form of social enterprise.

3 Chelsea, New York: Manhattan's new gallery district.

4 William Turnbull Jr: American architect.

5 Pat Kan Uk, also named Pat Kan (the Eight Houses), is located at 2 Stanley Street. The Eight Houses are a historic complex of seven Grade II historic buildings and one Grade III historic building. The name derives from the fact that the houses are all adjoined.

University of Chicago Booth School of Business, Hong Kong

Born Here, Honoured Here

On 22 November 2011, during a lunch appointment I had with the late Mr Bing Thom, he gave me a copy of his complete architectural collection, *Bing Thom Works*. It is his story, and it captures perfectly the sentiments of many Overseas Chinese who want to give something back to their birthplace and Motherland.

Born in Hong Kong, Thom moved with his family in 1950 to Vancouver, Canada, where he was educated and began his career. Over the years, he developed into the outstanding architect that he is known as today. From my generation's perspective, he was also the role model of many in the city for having reached such heights in his profession within the overseas architectural circle. Many Overseas Chinese hope to do something for their hometown, and Thom was an architect with a vision and mission who shared this wish to leave behind the fruits of his labour and heartfelt sentiments to the city of his birth.

Thom later achieved his wish to return home triumphant when he collaborated with Mr Wong Kam-sing for the international design competition for Xiqu Centre organised by the West Kowloon Cultural District Authority. Wong, who was working at Ronald Lu & Partners at that time, was a mentee of Thom during his early years in Canada. Together, they secured the West Kowloon Opera Centre project by presenting their visionary concept of the Grand Theatre.

In order to realise the plan, Thom arranged for his partner Yan, who was also from Hong Kong, to return and set up a branch to further develop their business. In addition to the West Kowloon Xiqu Centre, during the same period, Thom had also won bids for the Haw Par Mansion Revitalisation Project and the University of Chicago Hong Kong Campus Project.

The Haw Par Mansion was originally the property of Ms Sally Aw. Having gone through some turn of events, it finally became one of the HKSAR government's historic building revitalisation projects which was open to public application. In view of Ms Aw's nostalgia for her former residence and her long acquaintance with Thom, she applied for co-application. Due to their special historical and artistic backgrounds, Aw and Thom won the unanimous praise and trust of the judging committee for elevating the revitalised Haw Par Mansion into the Haw Par Music.

At around the same time, the headquarters of the University of Chicago Booth School of Business relocated from Singapore to Hong Kong. The white painted house at Mount Davis was selected as the site of the new campus, tenders were requested for the design of the campus building. Of the twelve bids received, Thom's design was particularly favoured by the jury because his proposal respected the integrity of the original landscape and ecosystem, embracing nature while striking a harmonious balance between the old and the new.

His design was a transparent and lightweight glass building that appeared to float in mid-air; an effect which was ultimately achieved only through close discussions with engineers and contractors. It should be noted here that Thom had high standards for the level of architectural art and always believed in maintaining mutual cooperation with contractors.

Respectful cooperation is an essential factor for successful design; hence Thom took the interaction and mutual cooperation with contractors very seriously. It was also central to the 'design and build' model he had been practising in Canada, resulting in an architect-led product guarantee. This was very different from the so-called effective 'design and build' in Hong Kong, by which the contractor tended to control everything and made it difficult for the architect to take charge.

1   The glass curtain wall that emphasises the curve allows the building to be surrounded by the shadows of mountains and trees; blending into nature.

2   The architect used the glass curtain wall as the outer coat of the building to reflect the surrounding landscape, making the building appear lighter and more elegant.

3   The low-key and simple building, lined with ancient wood and broken artillery batteries, forms a contrast between solid and void.

The beauty of the University of Chicago Booth School of Business building lies in its design of wavy lines that create a ribbon-like smoothness, with clear glass being the primary material for the outer walls. This design provides students with a comfortable and open education environment, where they can sometimes interact with historic buildings or communicate with the surrounding foliage. The lightness of the architecture and glass reflections accentuate the elegance of the gardens, accompanied by the weightlessness in the spacial experience. This allows visitors to freely wander through different time and space, immersing themselves in the traces of the bygone years.

My acquaintance with Thom began at the West Kowloon Xiqu Center, where we had the opportunity for warm and meaningful exchanges. Amongst these interactions, what truly stood out was his unwavering affection and attachment to his birthplace, a sentiment that deeply resonated with me. His wish was later realised through his design of three remarkable pieces of architecture for Hong Kong. Regrettably, his sudden passing in 2016 prevented him from witnessing the completion of these masterpieces. However, he may rest in peace safe in the knowledge that the people of this city would not forget the beautiful architecture he has left behind, as his works continue to be a source of honour and pride today.

St Stephen's College Preparatory School
The Béthanie

Bringing History Into Life

'Is my dad my idol?' Philip Liao raised his eyebrows slightly and repeated the question. 'Definitely. When he was in charge of the Wah Fu Estate, he was much younger than I am, not even forty years old.' When it came to his father, Liao always unreservedly expressed his admiration for him. Talking to Liao about his fate with architecture, it was hard not to mention his father, Mr Donald Liao.

Donald Liao was an architect, the first Chinese Chief Secretary in Hong Kong, and was also known as the 'father of public housing in Hong Kong'. Since the 1960s, Donald Liao had started working on the fundamental problem of public housing construction, and the subsequent improvement of the poor living environment of these estates. Donald Liao used landscape design to bring greenery into the estates, designing a people-oriented environment with abundant supporting facilities. The most notable of all was the Wah Fu Estate, known as 'the civilian mansion'.

'He never asked me to be like him; he even told me not to study architecture.' Philip Liao recalled that when he first applied to the Department of Architecture, his father made time for a long conversation with him. 'He told me that pursuing a career in architecture required much endurance, and financial rewards may not necessarily be substantial; but most importantly, there is never the best, only better...'

After receiving this dose of ideological teaching, Liao said, still unwaveringly, 'Hopefully I won't starve to death!' And so he followed his calling and pursued a degree in architecture. 'Actually he's happy; but as a father, he ought to share his experience with me.'

Philip Liao graduated from Eton College and Cornell University. Thereafter, he worked in Toronto for three years before returning to Hong Kong in 1992 to join Wong Tung & Partners Ltd, where he stayed for ten years.

'I'm not a person who moves around; I don't even have a résumé for job applications.' Back then, Liao was already thirty-eight years old, and for an architect, it was a case of either switching jobs or staying there forever. 'At that time, I had just completed a West Kowloon project. Coincidentally, a relative had just returned from Shanghai and, after taking a look at my work, thought I was good enough to start out on my own. He later gave me my first assignment in Shanghai.'

In 2002, Liao founded Philip Liao International Co. Ltd. However, not long after its establishment came the outbreak of Severe Acute Respiratory Syndrome. 'Couldn't help it. The lease was signed for three years, and you couldn't just quit. So I travelled anyway, but with a mask. Fortunately, plane tickets were cheap.' Amidst the uncertainty, he remained steadfast and, despite the economic downturn and with no salary for himself for four months, he never missed payroll for his staff. Recalling the ups and downs of the old days, he had always taken it easy; speaking with a smile, he said, 'Aren't we all wearing masks now?'

Due to his father's influence, he never lacked opportunities to observe architecture from a young age. One of his weekend pastimes was to accompany his father on site visits, where early on he began to feel the resonance and emotions created by architecture and space. However, he was too young to understand where such a feeling was coming from. 'I used to show my homework to my dad, and I would watch for his facial

1. St Stephen's has had a long history and, under the mantle of merging the old and the new, new architecture added to the campus does not have a fancy exterior.
2. The old buildings suffered much destruction from the torrents of history. Their renovation gave them a new, modern look.

expression to get a hint of his opinion; but as I grew up, I seldom do that anymore. Once, when my parents were travelling, they happened to bump into the principal of St Stephen's, and during their conversation, the principal mentioned, "We really like the school your son designed for us." She also asked if my parents had seen it. As usual, we texted each other and arranged to visit if we had the chance.'

St Stephen's has a long and storied history that bears witness to the ebbs and flows of Hong Kong. In 1901, a letter was addressed to the governor of Hong Kong, penned by eight influential Chinese business leaders and esteemed members of society, expressing their wish to establish an English college dedicated to providing quality education for Chinese children. St Stephen's was officially founded in 1903 and underwent several relocations before settling in 1930 at Tung Tau Wan Road in Stanley, nestled along the shores of St Stephen's Bay. Notably, the primary school division continues to provide boarding facilities for students today.

During the Japanese invasion of Hong Kong in 1941, the college building was taken over by the British army and converted into an emergency military hospital. Just two weeks later, on Christmas Day, the Japanese army broke into the college building and murdered the patients, doctors and nurses. Later, this became known as the St Stephen's College massacre. St Stephen's was a Japanese internment camp until the Japanese surrendered in 1945.

St Stephen's still retains eight pre-war buildings, including the college building, Martin hostel, the old laboratory and five bungalows. Most of the campus was destroyed during the war. After refurbishment, although the old structures had been repaired using modern architectural materials, their original appearances have remained largely intact. In addition, as the number of students grew, new blocks were added to the campus, including the Ho Shung Yuk Building, which was completed in 2016 by Philip Liao.

The new building has no fancy exterior, with just simple lines and colour tones that work in harmony with the surrounding environment. Liao expressed that, given the size of the campus, space was an important element in both the old and new school buildings, as well as the interaction between people and space – which had also been the focus for the original design of St Stephen's. The top floor of the building includes a bridge which connects it to the main campus with its twelve classrooms, library and theatre. The exterior wall of the new wing has a rock climbing wall on it. The natural light and ventilation design features offer a seamless experience between the campus and the outdoor space; the core space at the centre provides an opportunity for learning and exchange, thus encouraging bonds to be fostered between teachers and students.

According to Liao, revitalising historic buildings, even for those that seek to combine both old and new elements, did not always require tearing them down and starting over. Some of these original structures carried historical values that were worth preserving. 'I recall one of my most memorable projects being the restoration of the Béthanie in Pok Fu Lam, which we were engaged shortly after we started our business.'

Built in 1875 by the Paris Foreign Missions Society, the Béthanie was once a missionary residence and sanatorium. On the granite lintel over

1. The Béthanie, founded in 1875 by the French Catholic church.
2. The only neo-Gothic style church in Hong Kong, with white façades and pointed arches, it is a popular wedding venue.
3. Stained glass windows are even more attractive at night.
4. Adding a glass roof to the original building instils a touch of modernity.

the entrance, an inscription reads 'Domine, ecce quemamas infirmatur. Jn III.', which means 'Lord! Please see that your loved one is sick!' The sanatorium has undergone closures and changes of function. In 2006, Liao completed the restoration work and converted the original cowshed into a theatre, adding a glass cover to the original building. The neo-Gothic style church makes it one of the most popular wedding venues in Hong Kong, 'There used to be more than 300 weddings held there annually.' To continue this legacy, it is now the new campus of the Hong Kong Academy for Performing Arts, the School of Film and Television.

In addition to his father's influence, he remembers going to Rome with a professor in his fourth year of university to see numerous examples of Italian architecture. 'The professor was an urban planner who saw not just what was in front of him. His perspective did not come from just one building, but from the city as a whole; and we took a similar approach when working on the West Kowloon project.' In 2002, Liao participated in the West Kowloon Cultural Arts District Design Competition, and he was ranked second only to Norman Foster.

Speaking to Philip Liao about architecture, the conversation was not confined to just the subject matter alone, but it also extended to the issue of global climate change. 'It's hard to restore once the ice melts. Look at Singapore, any new infrastructure needs to be built five metres above sea level, by law! What about Hong Kong? If we turn a blind eye and remain indifferent, in less than a century we will be in hot water...' In fact, it didn't take long before Liao brought up the issue of the system. He is a firm believer of architects having the ability to make changes for the city and the society, and these changes, or contributions, cannot be measured solely by financial standards.

Untold Stories

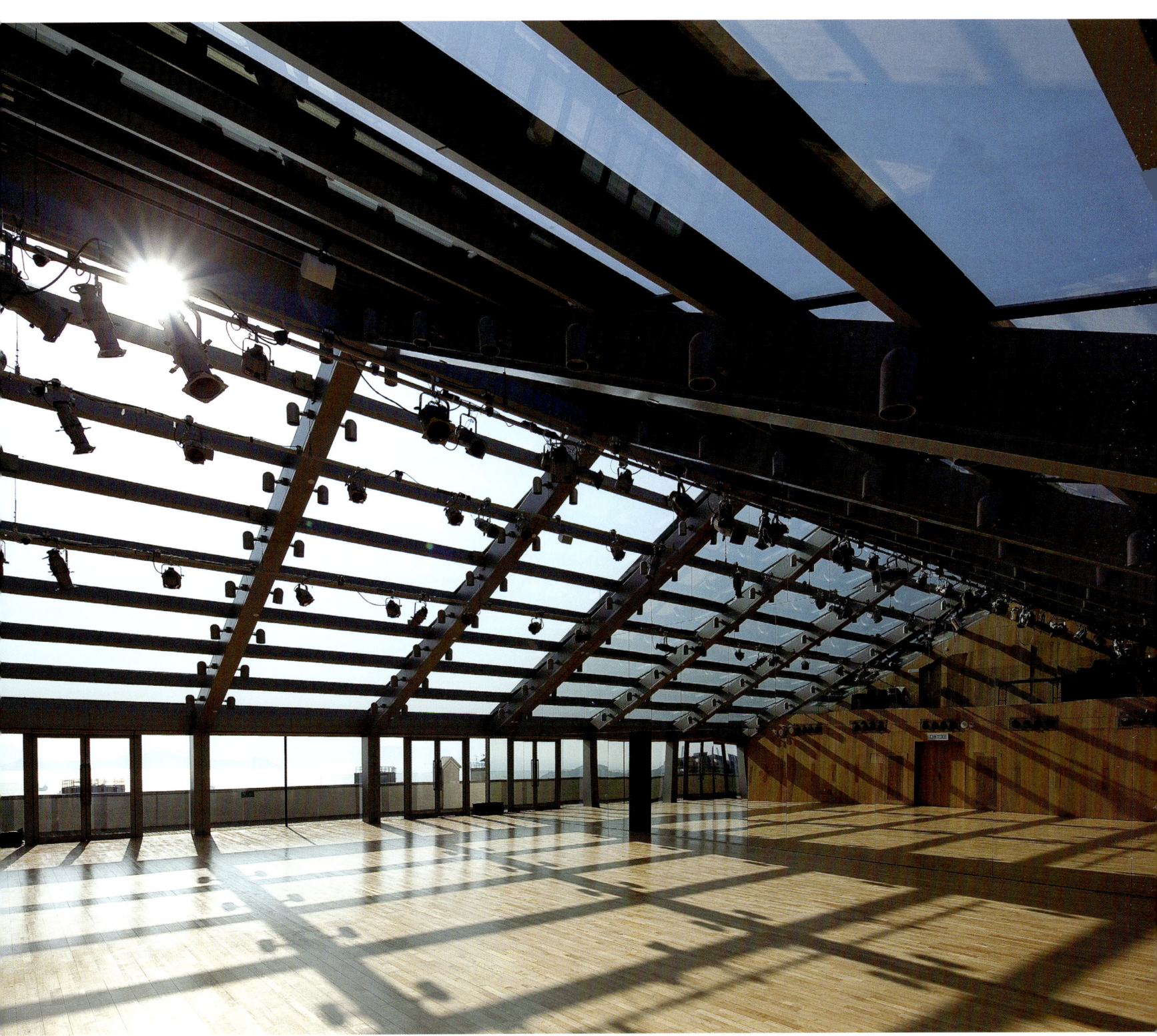

Victoria Peak Garden

Guardians

I first met Raymond Fung in an interview. I was very impressed by him, not only because of his kindness but also because the encounter was my first official face-to-face interview at my first job. That particular visit was very pleasant. He talked about his paintings, his life, yet not much about architecture; and that was pretty much how an entire afternoon had passed. It was only afterwards that I learnt he actually had this question on his mind: 'Why doesn't this reporter want to leave?'

When I was working on the interview piece, I recall it being both time-consuming and puzzling. I realised later that it was probably because of the emotional baggage I was carrying, as I was so nervous. Writing about him again today is still a challenge, as it is hard to write something new about him, considering the number of interviews he has done. With all these concerns in mind, I flipped through *The Untold Stories of Raymond Fung*, the book he gave me at our first meeting. Reading through his life from youth to adulthood, feeling his humour, his hardships, his fate with architecture, how he transformed tedious architecture into something playful, and how he gave life to architecture through his witty words – all these instantly brought me a warm sensation and a smile to my face.

At some point, Raymond has turned into a white-haired man who wears a pair of round-rimmed glasses. He explained that he was only slightly short-sighted (by 90 degrees), but it didn't hurt to wear a pair of glasses. Wearing them gave him a touch of the literati, and as long as he didn't speak, that look did give him a sense of distance. However, as soon as he spoke, he would quickly break the ice, and with only a few words he would easily make those around him laugh and the atmosphere more harmonious. It's quite a surprisingly stark contrast to his serious appearance.

In order to prepare for this book, we were given the opportunity to take three days to travel around Hong Kong. We were enthusiastic about participating in this 'City Hunt' which brought back memories of our time at university, carrying a list of tasks with us while running around Hong Kong, Kowloon and the New Territories from dawn till dusk. The process was joyful but, in all honesty, it was tiring, too. However, listening to Raymond's countless stories about architecture and history and his anecdotes of wherever he visited helped dissolve our fatigue, and also our impulse to utter the words 'I am tired.'

I still remember it was a cloudless Sunday, with the kind of clean blue sky that Raymond liked best. Arriving at the Victoria Peak Garden, far from the city, listening to the sound of the flowing stream with the occasional chirping sounds of birds; overlooking the green grassland in front of me with the sea and islands in the distance, all troubles were immediately washed away. The Peak Improvement Project was one of Raymond's pre-retirement projects, taking place at the same time as the Tsim Sha Tsui waterfront landscaping project and the Hong Kong Wetland Park. Accompanied by a cool gentle breeze, we walked along the Governor's Walk passing by the Peak Tower to arrive at the Mountain Lodge Guard House. 'The name in Chinese [literal translation – trail of common happiness] sounds very close to the people, right? But in English it is "The Governor's Walk", which is the backyard of the governor of Hong Kong.' Raymond switched to history class mode and went on with more stories.

Looking back at the history of the Peak, according to the Peak District Reservation Ordinance passed by the Hong Kong government in 1904, Chinese were not allowed to live in this area. The Peak therefore became

The antique-style pavilion shipped from England is not only cost-effective, but also exquisite and practical.

a special area for Westerners. The Peak was popular for a good reason: the weather in Hong Kong is normally hot and humid, but the temperature at the top of Victoria Peak is several degrees lower than that in the city. Therefore, the Victoria Peak became a place for Westerners to get away from the heat in the summer. Due to its cool temperature, the governor's summer house was built here, too.

This unjust Peak District Reservation Ordinance was not repealed until the Second World War. The summer house at the top of the hill was damaged during the war and eventually abandoned altogether following the construction of another Governor's Lodge in Fanling. Therefore, the once most-magnificent peak villa was finally demolished in 1946, leaving only the Guard House behind. In the 1970s, the Peak was converted into a park for public use, and a pavilion was constructed at the villa site in 1979, offering a panoramic view of Hong Kong.

Throughout the past century, the Peak has retained a multitude of Western-style architecture, resulting in its distinct character. In 2006, the Architectural Services Department embarked on the Peak Improvement Scheme, and in handling this project, Raymond did not add on new structures to the site excessively. He first demolished structures which he felt were out of place, including the gazebo and the public lavatories, followed by street lamps and the parterre; he then replaced them with English-style pavilions, street lamps and other facilities of a classical style, re-presenting the traces and faces of the past.

For Raymond, it was not difficult to let go of his own ego, but what was truly difficult was debating with the legislators. Some members of the Legislative Council questioned the objective of the Peak Improvement Project. 'Why do we need to go back in time and remember the architectural style of the past?' At the same time, there was concern that the replacement structures would be labelled as 'faux antiques', making another Song City out of Hong Kong. Raymond rebutted such a claim. 'The Legislative Council building where everyone works at is also an antique building, a copy of a Romanesque building, and the Chi Lin Nunnery in Diamond Hill is a copy of a Tang Dynasty building. Why do we not resist and instead have a liking for them?' To him, 'retro' at the Peak was not an imitation of an ancient town but a symbol of respect for history.

In fact, there had been a few small episodes during the Peak Improvement Project. When the Guard House of the Former Governor's Lodge was declared a monument in 1995, Raymond and his team had intended to transform it from a storage room into a 'history gallery at the Peak' to showcase a series of historical stories from Central to the Peak. However, because the proposed change could not take place within the project timeline and due to a lack of support, it never happened. Contrary to expectations, some of the major discoveries at the Peak never got to be showcased to the world.

One of the many improvements carried out at the Peak was the conversion of the Chinese-style pavilion completed in 1979 to a Victorian-style pavilion. During its construction, some objects were excavated, 'and we deliberately obtained a plan for the Lodge from the British Archives, having estimated that some of the objects of the villa would be hidden under the base of the gazebo. At that time, we

1 The public lavatory has been repurposed into a Western-style historic building and, together with the surrounding garden decor, including fountains, lighting, railings and furnishings, it brings a sense of nostalgia.
2 The design of the Victoria Peak Garden required the architect to abandon his own personal architectural style, opting instead for a blend of modern and classical, in order to restore the natural authentic look and feel of the Western-style garden of the past.
3 The pavilion and surrounding balcony left behind from the former Hong Kong Governor's Lodge have been rebuilt by the design team to better match the historical style of the pavilion. The withered trees beside the old white building also add a touch of gloominess with echoes of its former beauty.

also invited the Antiquities and Monuments Office to investigate and excavate the site together,' exclaimed Raymond with excitement.

'During the process, we discovered a large number of floor tiles produced by the British firm Minton Hollins. Eight boundary stones found were engraved with 'Governor's Residence' and two were from the military. There were supposed to be fifteen of these boundary stones from around 1910; so, along with the additional two found earlier in 1979 when the pavilion was built, a total of ten have been found. We had also arranged for TVB [a Hong Kong broadcasting company] to come witness the findings, yet...' Raymond patted his thigh and exclaimed with regret and anguish, 'some people mentioned that the existing pavilion was part of our collective memories and did not agree to dismantle it, so the plan was forcibly stopped.'

Although it was impossible to recreate this 'Peak Discovery', from the Victoria Peak Garden to the Austin playground, the Victorian design does bring the place a kind of continental beauty. Immersed in this, it is easy to find a quiet moment away from the hustle and bustle of the city. 'If you look at it from an architectural or design perspective, there is no personal characteristics, but I am satisfied because the stories and meanings have transcended architectural aesthetics.'

Ms Lung Ying-tai wrote in her *Notes of Hong Kong* that, 'Since Bilbao is an extremely ordinary and inconspicuous town, any distinctive building can easily stand out as a landmark. But Hong Kong is a magnificent place full of landmarks, which means you can hardly spot any landmark, bringing to the question of whether a landmark still has meaning.'

Raymond agreed wholeheartedly, 'Many assume that I have enjoyed the wetland park project the most, but, in fact, this project brought me even more joy.' The Peak Improvement Project was initiated by Raymond, and while it might not have been the largest in terms of scale, nor was the antique style his personal favourite, it was typical of him. He who would never put himself before any public architecture and local culture. Compared to personal preferences, he cared more about 'respect for history' and 'authenticity'. Perhaps, as Lung Ying-tai said, for a city as magnificent as Hong Kong, there is no need for another eye-catching landmark at the Victoria Peak Garden.

Looking at this cloudless blue sky and the towering tree next to it with its bare branches, there was a cold and poetic sensation hanging in the air, quietly waiting for the arrival of spring in order to flourish.

Stanley Promenade
Stanley Municipal Services Building

Coming to a Small Town by the Sea

Influenced by his father, Thomas Wan has been exposed to art since young. On the weekends, Wan's father used to take him to antique shops to hunt for treasures, which sparked his interest in art history. After completing high school in the UK, Wan secured a place at the University of Cambridge, where he studied architecture. He would often visit the university library to read architecture-related books in search for his own style. Since architecture is difficult to self-teach, he also looked for classes and workshops to learn about different approaches to design.

Wan believed that the study of architecture should be explored freely. At that time, there were few Chinese students studying architecture at the University of Cambridge. He had thought of studying at the Architectural Association but found that many famous teachers taught through mentorship, which meant that students had to design according to the teacher's wishes, whereas he preferred to study at a place where he had a high degree of autonomy to drive his own design.

Wan spent a great deal of time digesting academic theories and allowing them to settle. After graduation, he continued learning to refine his shortcomings. He read through many of the articles written by his professors and delved deep until he transitioned from the realm of pure theory to the field of modern architecture (Modernism). At which point, he began to feel a sense of ease and enjoyment, realising that for an architecture student to fully master the architectural language, this aspect cannot be lacking, as it would be hard to ascend to a higher level without it.

When he was in his third year at university, full of doubts, Wan visited the Notre Dame Cathedral. He sat down to rest in a dark corner, closed his eyes trying to feel the tranquillity of the space, and found tears in his eyes. 'At that moment, I realised what architecture was,' said Wan.

Although he had not been deliberately looking for such meaning, this particular experience at the Notre Dame Cathedral was more impactful and defining than his previous years in architecture.

Although he had plenty of doubts during his studies, he never did shy away from them; rather, he tried to discover and understand them one step at a time. 'Architecture is through building.' He believed that architecture was different from other forms of art such as painting and music, as the art of architecture was the only form which offered a uniquely complete immersive experience.

After graduation, Wan worked for an architecture firm in the UK and took up his licensing examinations. Later, in the wake of the economic crisis in the UK, he returned to Hong Kong and started working at a private architect firm, where he was expected to complete design drawings in just ten days. Eventually, through a fortuitous turn of events, he joined the Architectural Services Department, which, to his surprise, has given him a level of freedom in architectural design previously thought to be unattainable; thus, it seems that in life, a strong faith does lead to deserving opportunities for one to shine.

The Stanley Municipal Services Building was completed in 2005 and was a project referred to Wan by his supervisor, Mr P.L. Kwan. Wan wanted to create 'A town hall in a beachside town'. Referencing modern interpretations, he attempted to create something similar to the work of Finnish architect Alvar Aalto – the Säynätsalo.

The essence of the design of the Säynätsalo Town Hall is its fair-faced concrete façade that gives it a different look from the traditional Hong Kong municipal buildings. Wan designed an elevator in the atrium and added many windows to the building, hoping users would enjoy the view

1 The Blake Pier was used by governors of Hong Kong and other politicians, from 1902 to 1925, to travel to and from the Hong Kong Island. It was also used for welcome and farewell ceremonies, too, until it was replaced by the Queen's Pier in 1925.
2 As the sun sets, the pier stands quietly over the sparkling sea.

Untold Stories

from the inside. The central courtyard of the building is a copy of the Chinese courtyard house, with many open passageways and staircases that allow for natural ventilation, making it warm in the winter and cool in the summer. Lights have been added to the flooring of the roof garden to make the space look transparent from bottom to top. In addition, the glass platform of the central courtyard is also a skylight allowing sunlight to enter the community hall during the day and lighting it up at night. The design of the glass bottom was ahead of its time. Wan also personally chose to plant a large tree in the atrium to enhance the vitality of the environment. Meanwhile, the Stanley Municipal Services Building that is located on the slope echoes the surrounding environment, especially the curved wall at the bend which is predominantly made of glass, bringing a touch of lightness to the building; next to it, a flight of stairs leads to the roof garden and a completely different visual experience.

From the Stanley Municipal Services Building to the Stanley Promenade, through the narrow alleyways, there are kiosks with white canopies – like sails. Previously a temporary street market, it once blocked the view of the entire waterfront; but, immediately after its demolition, the view has been opened up much more to give the feeling of being connected to the sea. The architects have even widened the wooden pedestrian walkway on the outside.

The style of the Stanley area is quite diverse; arriving at the Stanley Main Street, there is an almost exotic feel, with a street of bars bringing a relaxing summer ambience all year round. There are many small shops in the narrow alleys that echo the sentiments and history of old Hong Kong. Next to the promenade, two revitalised monuments of historical significance have been relocated, namely Murray House and Blake Pier built in 1846 and 1902, respectively.

Blake Pier, formerly known as Pedder Pier, was originally located in Central at the current location of Exchange Square. The pier had undergone many demolitions and reconstructions until it was replaced by the Blake Pier, which was completed in 1902 as part of the reclamation project in Central. Blake Pier was used to receive then incoming governors when they first arrived in Hong Kong. In 1965, the pier was demolished again due to the reclamation of Victoria Harbour, and the second configuration of the pier was built in the same year. In 1993, this second iteration of Blake Pier was again demolished, this time due to the Central and Wan Chai Reclamation project, and the ferry service was subsequently moved to Central Pier.

The cast iron canopy of the Blake Pier was originally imported from the United Kingdom. After its dismantlement, it was relocated to the amphitheatre at Morse Park 4 in Wong Tai Sin, preserving its timeless design while utilising, for the first time in Hong Kong, a low-carbon steel supporting structure. In 2006, the Architectural Services Department restored this canopy to its original form at Stanley Public Pier, faithfully reconstructing it according to its original design. The result was the creation of the Stanley Blake Pier, which has now become a new landmark in Stanley.

Blake Pier at Stanley was the starting point for Wan's research into Chinese architecture. The design, combined with the concept of a fishing village, was influential in his future architectural designs, and paved the way for a more comprehensive and in-depth approach to his work as well as its presentation.

Following the design principles of the outdoor dining area on Stanley Street, the sea view at the rest space displays the unique aura of the Stanley Promenade.

	2	1	A glass platform in the central courtyard allows natural light to penetrate into the integrated auditorium on the next floor. The auditorium is illuminated at night through the glass platform.
1	3	2	The architecture is a modern interpretation of the city hall by the sea, using multiple vertical planes to reinforce the horizontal-facing balcony concept, creating multiple levels of architectural space.
		3	The Stanley Municipal Services Building is composed of small geometric space elements that meet the needs of different facilities while echoing with its surroundings in harmony.

Graduate House, The University of Hong Kong

Undaunted by the Highest of Mountains and the Deepest of Valleys

Mathias Woo once made a comment regarding Rocco Yim: 'Hong Kong is not without international-class architects, it just lacks owners with vision and culture and that is why it is so very painful to engage in architectural work in a serious manner. Whilst the Hong Kong government only thinks of architecture as a set of management tools, the property developers and the people of this city see architecture as some form of speculative tool for profit. Thus, most buildings in Hong Kong are "built for money", but not "built for the people" to serve to nurture human development. Rocco's works belong to the latter category. It might be a stretch to say that his talent has been underappreciated, but the people of Hong Kong have indeed wasted Rocco's talent for design.' Having read architecture in university, Rocco frequently publishes critical articles that spare no words in expressing his observations.

Born and raised locally, Rocco was not apprenticed by any internationally renowned master. Having worked for only two years after university, he founded Rocco Design Limited (now Rocco Design Architects Limited) with his friends. In 1983, at just thirty-one years of age, he entered the international architecture competition for the Bastille Opera House in Paris and won it. Although his proposal was never materialised, it gave him a good start for his career. One after another, his 'landmarks' began rising up in Hong Kong. However, perhaps the word 'landmark' is inappropriate here; after all, Rocco has always been resistant towards the so-called 'landmark building'.

In Hong Kong, from No. 1 Peking Road to the International Financial Centre; from the Graduate House of the University of Hong Kong to the Chu Hai College of Higher Education; from the Central Government Complex of HKSAR to the East Kowloon Cultural Centre and the Hong Kong Palace Museum, these are just some examples of his work which showcase his considerable talents. However, what constitutes sincerity to him in terms of architecture is his belief that the exterior must echo its interior. This is especially important in Hong Kong, a small, market-oriented city. So there is no point in asking him, 'What is your style?' Rather than superficial styles and exaggerated shapes, he pays more attention to the relationship between architecture and the environment, as well as the relationship between architecture and people.

Not only has Rocco left one mark after another on the Hong Kong architecture scene, the same goes for his work both in and out of China, as well. Turning to the University of Hong Kong, his alma mater, there is only one piece of architecture designed by him – the Graduate House of the University of Hong Kong. He remarked that he indeed treasured the opportunity to be able to leave behind his work there. The location of the Graduate House of the University of Hong Kong is an especially challenging terrain due to its varying degrees of elevation. Looking at this piece of land that was neither flat nor hilly, I could barely bring myself to ask if it had been particularly difficult to design. He recalled that at the beginning of the project, there were actually several questions on his mind. One of them was how to overcome the uneven height of the entrances so that when walking uphill, people would enjoy the journey instead of feeling exhausted by it? Another question related to the division of the building into the graduate dormitory, the graduate hall and conference centre; how could spatial connectivity be achieved amongst these seemingly separated parts?

'The height of the terrain can make an architectural complex feel independent, but how visual integration can then be achieved poses

  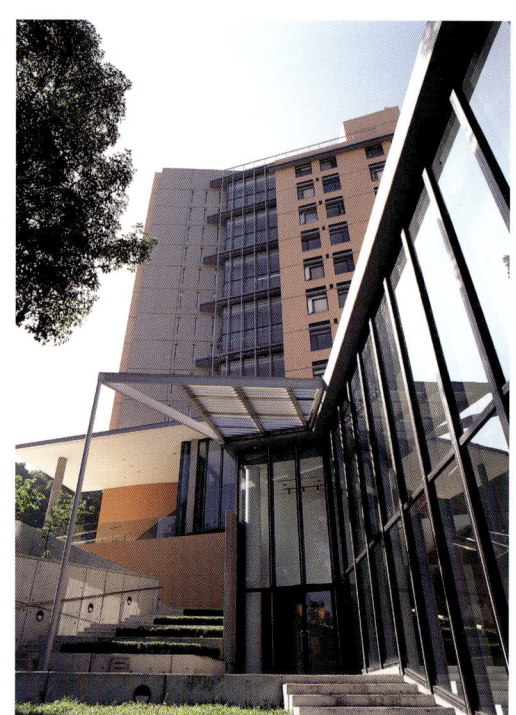

a challenge.' Rocco liked challenges, and where there were challenges, there were problems to be solved. 'Given the state of the terrain, attempts can be made to construct a "related" building, and use it to improve the relationship between the upper and lower levels of the campus to enhance the experience for the visitors.' This includes setting up green platforms within the building, so activities inside the building can be observed while coming down from the upper floors. One may choose to walk in, pass by or even stop by at the public space. This public space may hold exhibitions, classes and various activities to enhance the interaction between students and teachers. According to Rocco, Hong Kong's reality is apparent; but from the perspective of Rocco, restrictions are merely opportunities for breakthroughs. If talent were God-given, then enthusiasm and persistence are of one's own making. Rocco's road to architecture did not have the twists and turns and climaxes of a dramatic movie; he walks this journey one step at a time.

1 2 3 | 4

1 The atrium space of the conference centre can be used for exchanges and exhibitions.
2 The indoor and outdoor public spaces, together with their landscapes, have been integrated with one another.
3 The building conforms to the mountain and spirals downward. The outdoor and indoor public spaces depend on the terrain coming in from high to low altitude, connecting the campus from uphill to downhill, providing a place for teachers and students to communicate with one another on a daily basis.
4 From the conceptual sketch, it is evident that the architecture is harmoniously integrated with the surrounding landscape, seamlessly blending natural and man-made elements.

Untold Stories

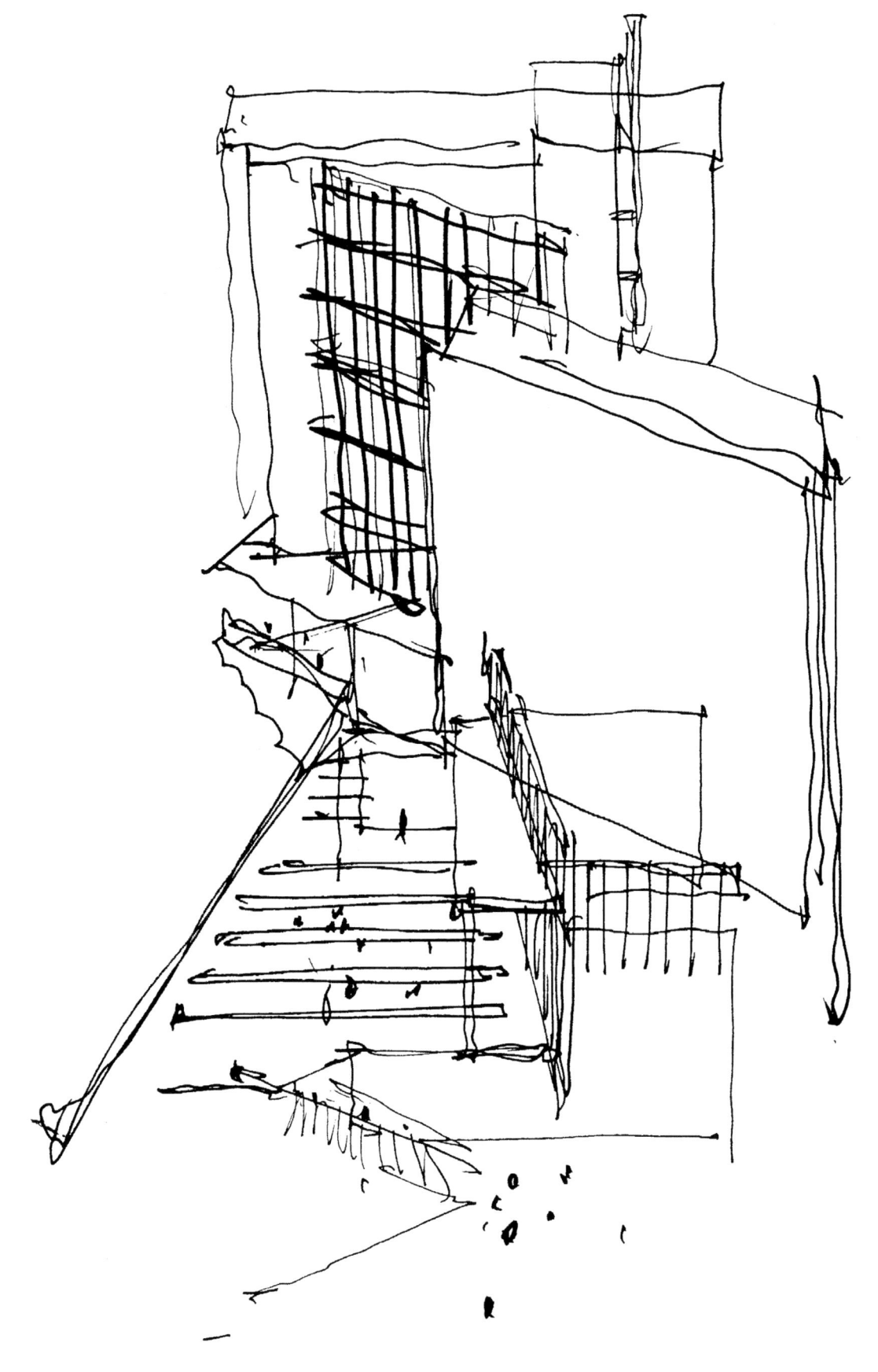

Kowloon East

Reading Guidance

How should the division between East and West work for Kowloon East? Using Nathan Road as the boundary, walking northward from the south: to the west of Tsim Sha Tsui, there is the Hong Kong Museum of Art, and to the east is the K11 MUSEA which brings together collective works designed by famous designers from all over the world. On the Avenue of Stars outside K11 MUSEA, there is a 'versatile' seaside food kiosk designed by Mr Otto Ng, Mr Yip Chun Hang, Ms Sherry Fung and the LAAB team. There is also a public lavatory nearby with a design focused on openness that has broken the stereotypes for this type of facility. It looks like a 'thatched hut', with various green elements thrown in. From the perspective of urban texture, the former, shorter incarnation of the Regent Hotel was better suited to the densely packed area of Tsim Sha Tsui, which served to set off the stunning views of the Victoria Harbour. It was designed in the 1970s by the American architecture firm SOM. Prior to that, the Tsim Sha Tsui Shui Hing Department Store (now Prestige Tower), designed by Italian architect Gio Ponti[1], was completed in 1962. Both buildings are examples of renowned architects leaving their marks on Hong Kong.

Untold Stories

In the past, the buildings of Tsim Sha Tsui were limited to the height of 61 metres due to their proximity to the flightpath of the airport. However, with the relocation of the airport from Kai Tak to Lantau Island, the height restriction has been lifted and it is believed that the skyline of Kowloon will undergo changes as development progresses. Currently, there is room for redevelopment for commercial buildings in Tsim Sha Tsui East. However, how this potential new redevelopment of the area will play out with its own distinctive character depends very much on the necessary investment from property developers and their will to improve the overall quality of the environment. The government of Singapore has formulated overall planning and regulatory development guidelines for each of its districts, while the Hong Kong Planning Department only has urban design guidelines, thus affording property developers a great deal of freedom and flexibility. Fortunately, the Town Planning Board and the Harbourfront Commission of Hong Kong have been acting as gatekeepers to ensure there will be no future arbitrary placement of skyscrapers along the waterfront of Hong Kong.

Along the waterfront from Tsim Sha Tsui to Hung Hom is the Hong Kong Polytechnic University (PolyU), a campus located at the most eye-catching location in the vicinity of the Kowloon side entrance (and exit) of the Hung Hom Cross-Harbour Tunnel. PolyU has evolved from the Hong Kong Technical College and offers a wide range of career-oriented courses. In order to facilitate accessibility for the public, the university is strategically located near an industrial area in Hung Hom. During its transition into the PolyU, the imminent and most challenging task lay in the need for expansion of its campus. The first design of the campus, carried out by P&T Architects, paved the campus with red bricks to deliberately create the atmosphere of traditional Western schools. When the initial campus designs of The Chinese University of Hong Kong, Lingnan University and Chu Hai College of Higher Education were being conceived, they similarly entrusted a single architect to oversee the campus design, resulting in a cohesive and unified architectural style for each one of them.

As the campus of PolyU continues to grow and develop, different architects have brought their unique styles into the mix. The Jockey Club Innovation Tower designed by Zaha Hadid broke away from the traditional red-brick style of the campus, with white aluminium plates packed into its streamlined shape, making it look like a lady's handbag – and giving it its nickname. Within the PolyU complex is another prominent building, the single-storey new wing of the Pao Yue-kong Library designed by P&T Group in partnership with Ms Angela Pang, whose masterpieces also include the new libraries of CUHK and Lingnan University.

Situated on the other side of Hung Hom is a building designed to look like a series of tightly packed boxes. The PolyU Hong Kong Community College was co-designed by Mr Wei Jen Wang and Mr Bernard Vincent Lim with the design philosophy of presenting the relationship between solid and void, as well as the interaction between yin and yang. Wei Jen Wang is one of the very few architects from Taiwan who had come to Hong Kong from the United States to teach at the University of Hong Kong. Over the years, he has become a local of Hong Kong and has contributed much to the city. He once described this piece of architecture as a demonstration of the concept of the Beijing Siheyuan while still maintaining the main colour tone of PolyU. It is unique architecture, worthy of a visit, and admiration, as it echoes and reinterprets the concept of traditional Chinese architecture combined with modern multistorey buildings.

To appreciate the local customs of Kowloon East, wander through the narrow alleys of the old districts that include the Ladies' Market in Mong Kok, Tung Choi Street, Flower Market Road and Kowloon City to get a sense of the community over its one-hundred-year history. The traditional streets and alleyways of the Mong Kok Dawn Market and the former Bird Market along the current Mong Kok East Station are expected to also disappear due to upcoming urban renewal plans and changes in the lifestyle preferences of the public.

Cultural spaces worthy of special attention in the To Kwa Wan area are the Cattle Depot Artist Village and the Cattle Depot Art Park. The former was transformed from a cow slaughterhouse into a cultural park, similar to the Redtory in Guangzhou or the Huashan 1914 Creative Park in Taiwan. Some may disagree about this comparison when judging it in terms of its popularity and visitor numbers, as the Cattle Depot Artist Village has not been all that lively for a long while. However, the common ground I wish to draw upon here are the predecessors of those two sites and the way in which they were converted. The Redtory was formerly a canning factory and the Huashan 1914 Creative Park was formerly a wine-making and camphor factory. Unlike the expensive projects of the Revitalising Historic Buildings Through Partnership Scheme, the conversions of both places were simple and sought to retain the rough and original flavours of the premises.

The Cattle Depot Artist Village is liked by many artists because it is simple and less restrictive; however, unlike many exhibition halls, it does not have air conditioning, which makes for an uncomfortable experience in the sultry summer of Hong Kong. The Cattle Depot Art Park, designed by Mr Jacen Lo, has been transformed from a cowshed. With many concepts relating to the combination of the humble cowshed with other cultural elements, the leisure space was created with much effort and attention to detail. Since these two places are located quite far away from the MTR station, not many young people are currently living in the vicinity of the Cattle Depot. It is expected that a youthful ambience will arrive in the area after the reconstruction of 7th Street in To Kwa Wan.

Mainland-Centric Hong Kong Architects

Amongst the many Hong Kong architects featured in this book who have left their imprints on the Mainland architecture scene, there are four professionals who have made career development in the Mainland their chief focus. They are: Mr Frank Yu, Mr Frankie Lui, Mr Au Fai and Mr Manfred Yuen. As for the reason why they have chosen to look far and forego what lies close at hand? While each of them has a different background story and reason, they all share this common opinion:

they say that the Mainland, with its vast land and far-reaching borders, has much to offer in terms of opportunities and possibilities; while opportunities for development in Hong Kong are comparatively more scarce.

There is a very plain, dark-grey building near Sung Wong Toi named the Oootopia Kai Tak. It is a serviced apartment block with a cool name, and without a doubt it must have been designed by very cool designers – and they are none other than Manfred Yuen and C.Y. Lau. Their masterpiece in Hong Kong is a hotel with a youthful style that is rarely seen here. This book has selected only a few hotels with distinct styles and personalities, namely the TUVE Hotel in North Point, The Arca in Wong Chuk Hang, the Hillwood House Hotel in Tsim Sha Tsui and Oootopia in Kai Tak. They share the common characteristics of simplicity on the outside and tastefulness within; they care not for the pursuit of the grandiose, but only for trendsetting creativity.

The Kowloon Walled City and Kowloon Walled City Park

Due to its proximity to the former Kai Tak Airport, building-height regulations restricted Kowloon City's buildings to low-rise only. Prior to its gentrification, it retained the old style of Hong Kong. It was nicknamed the

'Little Bangkok' due to the abundance of Thai restaurants in the area. The Kowloon Walled City Park was another outlyer, a special product left over from the history of Hong Kong. According to the agreement jointly mediated by China and the UK in early 1990, it was agreed to first demolish the unsafe and insanitary illegal buildings in the Kowloon Walled City and rebuild it into a Lingnan-style park. It was also expressly stated that there would be no profit-generating activities within the park so as to avoid any deferred benefits for either China or the UK.

My tuition fees were sponsored by a relative who had returned to Hong Kong from the Philippines after his retirement. Due to his limited savings, he was forced to live in a small dwelling within the Kowloon Walled City. Without a valid Use Permit[2], the installed lift would not service the floor on which he lived. Although the rent on the top floor was amongst the cheapest in the city, life was also at its toughest where he had to rely on other means for expensive water and electricity.

The surrounding environment was extremely cramped, cluttered and unhygienic, and seeing the sun from within the complex was something of a rarity. I knew well what it was like living in the Kowloon Walled City in those days, and it was certainly nowhere near as romantic as young people today might imagine. I do not agree with the preservation of many of such severely illegal and ugly structures and have no regrets for supporting their demolition. Many from the younger generation have lamented the passing of the Kowloon Walled City without having actually visited the Kowloon Walled City Park. I believe this has arisen from the publication of books on the Kowloon Walled City by foreign authors that were written from an outsider's perspective and with a novelty-seeking mindset. Such books sought to instil in their readers a misguided nostalgia for a past that was anything but rosy.

Kadoorie Hill is a small hill located next to the Mong Kok East Station in Kowloon. The Diocesan Boys' School occupies the largest area in Kadoorie Hill, and within its campus, there is a primary school building designed by Thomas Chow that is characterised by its emphasis on the interlaced relationship between horizontal lines and bumps. There is also a glass pavilion whose design combines transparent glass and structural steel I-beams

to express lightness and translucency in a very simple manner. The Kadoorie Hill is home to many celebrities, the outer walls of whose houses are often rendered with expensive materials. However, one of those houses has walls made of rough hollow blocks, which look unusually plain but curiously enticing. As it turns out, there are two modernist bungalows with tasteful exteriors within this complex, and they are the designer houses where three generations of the Chan family live. Norman Chan is both the homeowner and designer. Sitting comfortably in his cosy garden, we listened to his stories of rebellion and mischief in his youth.

Within the City University of Hong Kong in Kowloon Tong is the Run Run Shaw Creative Media Centre. Composed of several three-dimensional triangles, it is a particularly eye-catching piece of architecture in Hong Kong left behind by Daniel Libeskind[3]. Inside the Alliance Primary School in Kowloon Tong is yet another bold and creative work: the Wallflower Music Hall.

A breakthrough design by Manfred Yeun and C.Y. Lau, the concert hall's curved components create streamlined, organic spaces that have completely subverted the original, traditional architecture of the place.

Another piece of architecture that warrants a special mention is a white-coloured house named the Bridged House. Let's start with a little story: One fine day, the owner of this house called out of the blue asking for my opinion about designing a new house for him in Kowloon Tong. I immediately suggested two young architects – Ms Ida Sze and Mr Billy Chan – who were both working at Herzog & de Meuron Architekten[4] in Basel. Fortunately, the homeowner and his wife were willing to give these two young architects a chance. They flew to Paris for a meeting with Ida and Billy, and the four of them immediately hit it off. Because of this fortuitous introduction, both Ida and Billy returned to Hong Kong and started a new page in their lives.

Kowloon Tong is a high-end residential area with hundreds of detached houses. I am not ungenerous when it comes to introducing residential buildings in Hong Kong, but most of them are ordinary in appearance, and only a few of them can be appreciated from the perspective of architectural aesthetics. There are two high-end residences on La Salle Road in Kowloon Tong that have been designed by Mr Joey Ho. Joey was born in Taiwan, grew up in Singapore, and read architecture at the University of Hong Kong, after which he decided to settle in the city. His father had gone to all the effort of moving the family to Singapore, only to have Joey end up in Hong Kong.

He initially began his studies at the National University of Singapore, but after working in Hong Kong, he fell in love with the city and chose instead to continue his studies here. He gave up the career in Singapore planned for him by his father and did not inherit his business. His final decision to settle in Hong Kong is a true testament to the Lion Rock Spirit that reflects Hong Kong's success in attracting talents from all walks of life over the past century.

The Aura located on Waterloo Road is a high-end residence and the most prominent residential design in this area. The building gives the appearance of four pillars that have been buckled together to form a square box, leaving outdoor terraces at the four corners and thus forming a symmetrical architectural combination. I designed a two-tone (black and white) bungalow on Wiltshire Road that used the concept of sunlight projection to express the owner's sentiments of life. This design will be discussed in another chapter.

The Pure Land of Diamond Hill

Kowloon East and Diamond Hill are very much alike, with each area giving the general impression that it is filled with replicated public housing estates and non-distinctive factory buildings; most would not give the area a second look. Unexpectedly, though, there are pieces of work worth introducing. The Chi Lin Nunnery and Nan Lian Garden, a Tang-style building and garden that together are two of the city's finest examples of traditional Chinese architecture made with local contribution and participation. From the overall planning and the rigorous selection of materials all the way to its precise construction, ongoing maintenance and meticulous care, it is a marvellous place, not to be missed by visitors. To the surprise of many, an application was made for it to become a World Heritage Site despite the building itself only having a history of slightly more than ten years between its date of completion and the relevant application. The applicant's argument was: in view of the need to protect the architectural style of the Tang Dynasty, it is necessary to apply for the status of cultural heritage in order to inherit and carry forward the essence of Chinese culture.

Although the application was unsuccessful, it is a reflection that Hong Kong has spared no effort in conserving and maintaining traditional Chinese architecture.

Another surprise, not far from Chi Lin Nunnery, is the Diamond Hill Crematorium. Encircled by ring upon ring of housing estates, it is yet another pure land on earth. It is a design comparable to the masterpieces of Tadao Ando, yet it is almost hidden in a concrete forest, and nearby residents have no idea just how close they are to this elegant piece of architecture! The Diamond Hill Crematorium and the new columbarium were designed by a team led by Mr Stephen Tang that included the combined effort of Mr Patrick Luk, Mr Michael Li and Mr T.Y. Lau, all of whom had worked closely together to create a simple and refreshing environment with oriental wisdom. As to why Stephen had striven to change the image of funeral and burial buildings, an interview later in this chapter will provide an understanding of his genuine motivations. Every time a local of Hong Kong sees a minimalist design, they will immediately praise it as being 'very Japanese'! My particular appreciation for this project, however, comes from its representation of the Chinese culture – serene but not archaised, and derived from ancientry without being pretentious. If the style of Tadao Ando were to be used as a form of metaphoric comparison, it would be to praise the proper and balanced use of fair-faced concrete; one simply cannot equate minimalism with Japanese style, as the same can be said for Tang style.

Blake Pier in Wong Tai Sin

Not far from the Diamond Hill Crematorium is the Morse Park in Wong Tai Sin. Within the park is a large theatre facility with a little tale

the perspectives of women, and presents an optimistic attitude. The building is a lively sketch that can lift people's spirits and give them hope for recovery.

From Knowing 'Connie Chan' to Getting Acquainted with Kowloon East

When it first began to keep records, Hong Kong was just a trading post with a population of 6,000. This number increased to 600,000 during the Japanese occupation, and it increased to 2.2 million by 1950. The rapid increase in the immigrant population created pressing issues on all fronts that required Hong Kong's immediate response, and top of the list were land issues. From 1953 to 1954, the Hong Kong government launched a large-scale reclamation initiative, with Kwun Tong being the first satellite city to be developed. The coastal land was developed into an industrial area and, broadly speaking, this is still the blueprint of Kowloon East today.

I recall an unforgettable experience from 1969, when I was a clueless seventeen-year-old fourth-form student looking for my first summer internship. One day, without a clue, I took a bus to the Kwun Tong industrial area for an interview. As soon as I arrived in the area, pungent air entered my nostrils, and I knew exactly where I was! When the bus finally arrived at the Kwun Tong Ferry Bus Terminus, I got off and saw a thousand ladies coming towards me. I had never seen the female of the species in such a large crowd. As it turned out, my arrival had coincided with the clocking-off time, and the ladies were leaving work, en masse, to catch the bus home. Suddenly, I got to experience first-hand what it was like when 'Connie is Here!'

Back in those days, Hong Kong's average wage was low, and the main source of income for most families came from labour-intensive and menial roles. In that patriarchal society, women often worked in factories, and as such, the 'factory girls' were a large portion of society. Factory work comprised mostly general assembly operations that were tedious and uninteresting, and respite came in the form of watching movies for entertainment; and the character of the 'factory girl' featured in many films was immortalised by the actress Connie Chan. She became an idol of Hong Kong's blue-collar class, competing with Josephine Siao, who represented the white-collar class. Their popularity was equal but independent

behind it. When Morse Park was built in 1967, the cast iron canopy of Blake Pier in Central, completed in 1902, was relocated there. Why the relocation from Central to Wong Tai Sin? Though it is impossible to verify the story now, some said it was relocated there because when Central was undergoing land reclamation, Blake Pier had to be demolished and thus the cast iron canopy was to be discarded into the sea. Instead, the Morse Park project architect recovered it and had it reassembled as a pavilion in Morse Park. There were also speculations that the architects of the Public Works Department, who at that time were primarily British, could not bear the abandonment of traditional British architecture and so they had the canopy salvaged instead.

Many years ago, I discovered the cast iron canopy in Morse Park and proposed to have this historically meaningful structure relocated to the waterfront in front of Murray House in Stanley near the Stanley Waterfront. I wished we were able to bring together a number of such pieces and make a series of historic buildings so that a particular part of history could be restored. However, returning to the relocation (for the second time) of the cast iron canopy of the Blake Pier, the Wong Tai Sin District Councillors at that time were extremely surprised: although they had served in the district for so many years, they had been unaware of the existence of this 'accidental treasure'. However, giving up their treasure would surely entail certain conditions of exchange, and in the end it was a 'one for two' affair – replacement of the pavilion in Morse Park and the gift of a large-scale, covered theatre. And there is the tale behind Morse Park's large theatre. From Wong Tai Sin to Choi Hung, there are two other scenic spots: first, the improvement works of the original Kai Tak Nullah that has turned it into the Kai Tak River, with masterful project advice provided by Mr Wallace Chang. Although its scale was not comparable to the restoration of the Cheonggyecheon in Seoul, it was of great significance, as it enlightened the authorities on the subject of beautifying nullahs. Another small building of note, located near the Choi Hung MTR station, is the Hong Kong Breast Cancer Foundation Jockey Club Breast Health Centre designed by Tam & Philip So & Associates Ltd. What first attracted our team's attention was its rich and eye-catching colours, followed by the block casement windows of different sizes that are distributed across its exterior, slightly resembling the Dutch painter Piet Cornelies Mondrian's masterful handling of geometric lines. The design is aesthetically pleasing, with deliberate consideration for of each other, and their collective charm swept Hong Kong off its feet. Although I am no fan of Connie Chan, the surging energy that came from the thousand 'Connie Chans' on that fateful day was the deepest impression I have ever had of Kowloon East.

The Major Transformation of Kowloon East

Being an international city made up of immigrants, there is a natural state of flux in Hong Kong; an ebb and flow as people come and go, each for their own reasons. As immigrants form the collective mindset of 'eager for change', the people of Hong Kong, being composed of such DNA, are not only naturally eager to seek changes but are also equally good at adapting to them. Our self-proclaimed 'Street-Smart Kid' ideology compels us to always get ahead of the game; perhaps this is best illustrated by the saying: 'Losing out at the start is worse than losing everything'; such is the core value that has been deeply embedded in the hearts of the people. While this has indirectly driven the rapid development of Hong Kong, it has also inevitably led to changes of the human landscape in equal measure.

And so, half a century later, Kowloon East has been transformed yet again, this time covering Kai Tak, Kowloon Bay and Kwun Tong. This area is officially known as CBD2[5], which is Hong Kong's second central business district. After the relocation of the airport, the government planned to build a beautiful new urban area on this large piece of flat land.

For this purpose, it set up a dedicated office, canvassed opinions from across society, and held public planning concept competitions, instilling high expectations in everyone.

After more than ten years of development, Kai Tak is now close to completion. The cruise terminal was built first through the combined efforts of Norman Foster and Wong Tung & Partners Ltd. The relationship between Norman Foster and Hong Kong goes back a long way. He has undertaken work for some of the major transportation hubs in Hong Kong: Chek Lap Kok Hong Kong International Airport, Hung Hom Kowloon-Canton Railway Terminus, the new wing of the Tsim Sha Tsui Ocean Terminal and the Kai Tak Cruise Terminal. The cruise terminal located by the Kai Tak waterfront is 850 metres long; it is a large-scale structure with a sky garden on its top platform and an unrivalled location that allows visitors to enjoy views of both sides of Victoria Harbour.

The Long-Awaited New Town: Kai Tak

Kai Tak has now become a new treasure of Kowloon East, with the historic Lung Tsun Stone Bridge serving as a prominent attraction. Designed through an open competition, the Lung Tsun Stone Bridge Preservation Corridor, once completed, will become yet another iconic attraction within the district. It will serve as an integrated recreational space while offering the public an informative tour on the history of this bridge. The much-anticipated Kai Tak Sports Park is currently a work in progress, and there is no doubt that, when completed, it will be one of Hong Kong's

high-profile architectural venues. The HKSAR government has been planning and preparing for Hong Kong's infrastructure in anticipation of more diversified development in the future. It is looking forward to a diversified Hong Kong having not just the traditional finance and tourism industries but also the hardware to support industries such as culture, sports, entertainment and scientific research which will pave the way for future development opportunities for the younger generations.

The Kai Tak Sports Park covers an area of 28 hectares; the entire park has been designed by Populous, a subsidiary of HOK[6]. (HOK was also the architect for the Hong Kong Stadium, the appearance of which resembles a pair of shells with clean lines and a graceful shape.)

The upcoming Kai Tak Sports Park will have an industrial flavour with trendy tones added in, thus providing an architectural style more suited to a sports venue. I believe the public will not be disappointed with the finished product: a 50,000-seat facility capable of hosting large-scale sports events and concerts.

The Kai Tak Development project is another great place for admiring new architecture on the Kowloon Peninsula after the West Kowloon Cultural District. Noteworthy pieces of this project include the Kai Tak Sky Garden, the concept for which is derived from airport runways; there is also a newly established

school village, within which is the one-of-a-kind P.L.K. Stanley Ho Sau Nan Primary School, whose structure excels in its spatial variations with a masterful use of fair-faced concrete, giving it a very distinctive look that is instantly recognisable as the personal design style of Thomas Wan. The Refuse Collection Point on Shing Kai Road, a boutique project with geometrically shaped aluminium panels designed by William Tsang, is definitely worth a visit. Meanwhile, there is a green lawn in the nearby Kai Tak Station Square, as well as public facilities such as bowling greens and a pet garden, adding some breathing space into the concrete forest.

Review of the Second Central Business District

There are many industrial buildings in Kowloon Bay that are undergoing transformation as the district is being developed. Some have been rebuilt, while others are being revitalised. A successful example is the headquarters building of the Electrical and Mechanical Services Department, which was rebuilt from the former site of Air Freight Terminal 2 at Kai Tak Airport. It was designed by a team of three architects: Stephen Tang, T.Y. Lau and Michael Mak. The Zero Carbon Building, recently built in Kowloon Bay, is the result of a collaboration between the HKSAR government and the Construction Industry Council to promote the concept of zero carbon emissions and environmental awareness in the construction industry. The building is an information centre that integrates exhibition and education spaces over a floor area of 14,700 square metres. The design team included K.S. Wong, M.K. Leung and Tony Ip. Visitors can take guided tours that will enhance their environmental knowledge in a simple but informative manner. To further address the lack of civic development in Kowloon East, the government proposed the development

of the East Kowloon Cultural Centre in Kowloon Bay with Rocco Yim at the helm of its design. Rocco has already designed many cultural buildings in the Mainland, but this one will be his first such project in the city of his birth. However, due to numerous setbacks encountered during its development, his other cultural project, the Hong Kong Palace Museum, opened its doors first.

The former industrial areas of Kwun Tong are gradually being transformed into an integrated commercial space with recreational facilities. An example of this is the InPARK, near Tsun Yip Street. The first phase of the renovation for the park brought a modern design based on the Kwun Tong industrial theme, and in the second phase of its development, the Leisure and Cultural Services Department organised an outdoor sculpture competition with seven themes representing the former industrial specialities of the seven Kwun Tong districts, namely clothing and garments, textiles, toys, plastics, electronics, printing and timepieces. The prizewinners include many architects, including James Law, whose *Giant Robot* design in the toys category conjured up memories of the once-popular metal toys. His other works includes the transitional homes made with concrete water pipes on Hoi Hing Road, Tsuen Wan, which aim to partially resolve the housing problems faced by the young people of the city.

InPARK was a pioneering project for Kwun Tong's path to modernisation. Wei Jen Wang's team and Edward Wong introduced several cargo containers to quickly create an industrial-style outdoor space. It was also Edward's idea to create a new façade with aluminium panels to dress up the adjacent cooked-food market. Meanwhile, a new generation of property owners were eager to employ renowned overseas designers, including the American architecture firm ARQ[7], to turn this ordinary street into an extraordinary one. After the Dutch architecture firm MVRDV[8] renovated 133 Wai Yip Street, the existing tenants changed, and a 'trendy' group moved in.

Energizing Kowloon East

Kwun Tong was previously known as Kwun Tong Bay (derived from its ancient Chinese name, which translated to 'a rich salt pan') and was originally a place where urban refuse was processed. Later, the refuse pool was moved

to Gin Drinkers Bay as part of its development plan. As the Kwun Tong waterfront was a cargo loading bay in its early days, it was unsanitary, and the air was filled with unpleasant smells. The transformation of Kwun Tong Bay was a major operation, with its initial goals being the improvement of its water and air quality, and the reconstruction of the waterfront.

In order to carry out the first phase of this major operation, the HKSAR government set up a dedicated office – the 'Energising Kowloon East Office' by the waterfront of Kwun Tong with the aim to facilitate the transformation of Kowloon East into a smart city. It also serves as a testing ground of initiatives before their city-wide implementation. Under the premise of the CBD2 development, the government also intends to disperse the central business districts and diversify Kowloon East. However, the biggest problem has been the difficulties arising from each stakeholder putting their own interests first. Incidentally, the community had actually pushed for the development of an elevated monorail. However, after much analysis and review, the proposal was ultimately abandoned by the government. Elevated monorail systems were being phased out around the world which reflected the reality that such systems, whilst good for sightseeing, were not effective means of transportation. Instead, Hong Kong has fully developed its underground railway system, which is the ideal choice for a densely populated city with limited land area.

The pioneering team who volunteered to initiate the 'Energizing Kowloon East Office' was led by town planner Mr K.K. Ling, with Ms Winnie Ho heading a team of architects that included Mr Michael Li and, later, Mr Edward Wong. Mr Stephan Tang, then the Deputy Director of Architectural Services Department, suggested that the team should have its own independent office. However, before we proceed further on this, the following story must be told.

In the beginning, the Energizing Kowloon East initiative was modest in its management if not its outlook. No private commercial building was leased for the project team, as it did not want the public to suspect them of partiality. Rather, below the Kwun Tong Bypass flyover, in an area covered with weeds that had lain abandoned for many years, was where the team decided to practice what they preached. They started transforming this area for their own office by stacking together a series of cargo containers to form a building complex. By making full use of the space under the flyover, this example quickly drew attention from the public towards the architectural concepts of transitional housing and waste recycling centres. This endeavour not only highlighted the industrial flavour of Kwun Tong but also continued the memories and customs of this place. And it was totally worth it. I was invited to volunteer the design of the logo for Energizing Kowloon East; surprisingly, they are still using it. The office serves a full range of functions including design, contact, coordination and implementation. More importantly, the office also serves to allay the concerns of various parties and resolve the doubts of non-governmental organisations.

The project began with Phase I of the Kwun Tong waterfront. Mr Andrew Nam had outlined the design framework, and the team

that took it forward added further excitement to it. Together with the Hoi Bun Road Park co-designed by Mr Thomas Wan and Ms Selah Au, the originally lifeless space under the Kwun Tong Bypass flyover has been transformed, from being in a state of decay, into a magical place within the span of a few years. Today, the Kwun Tong waterfront has been transformed into a new, iconic location in Hong Kong, a leisure area full of colours and fragrances, and it boasts a romantic sunset view not to be missed by couples.

Notes

1. Gio Ponti: an Italian architect, designer and artist. Together with Lancia, Buzzi, Marelli, Venini and Chiesa, he founded Il Labirinto, specialising in high-quality, textured furniture.
2. Use Permit: refers to the permit for operating a lift issued by the Electrical and Mechanical Services Department. Since all of the residences within the Kowloon Walled City did not have the necessary Occupation Permit, the Electrical and Mechanical Services Department would not have issued any such permits for lifts. Thus, were a lift to break down, no required repair work would be carried out.
3. Daniel Liberskind: a Polish-American architect.
4. Herzog & de Meuron Architekten: an architecture firm founded by Jacques Herzog and Pierre de Meuron in Basel, Switzerland, in 1978.
5. CBD2: the proposed second Central Business District of Hong Kong, with smart city elements.
6. HOK: Hellmuth, Obata + Kassabaum, an architecture-engineering and interior design firm founded by George Hellmuth, Gyo Obata and George Kassabaum in St. Louis, Missouri, USA, in 1955.
7. ARQ: Arquitectonica International Corporation, an architecture firm founded by Bernardo Fort-Brescia, Laurinda Hope Spear, Andrés Duany, Elizabeth Plater-Zyberk and Hervin Romney in Miami, Florida, USA, in 1977.
8. MVRDV: An architecture firm founded in the Netherlands in 1993 by Winy Maas, Jacob van Rijs and Nathalie de Vries.

Bridged House

Rhythm in the Upstream

Forty minutes before my appointment time, I passed by the nearby H Queen's and Tai Kwun. Winter in Hong Kong is really short. It was January, the beginning of the year, and yet the cloudless sky had allowed the sun to be particularly intense at two o'clock in the afternoon. As I ascended the stone steps, I felt a sense of warmth emanating from within.

Ida & Billy Architects, founded by Ida Sze and Billy Chan, had moved from Sai Wan to an office in Central located just across Wyndham Street from Tai Kwun. Although it lacked the quietness of the Sai Wan alleyways – sitting by the window, one could hear the horns of the nearby traffic – it wasn't too noisy. Adjacent to the century-old Stone Slabs Street and facing the rare public space of Tai Kwun that had been transformed from a cluster of historic buildings, this area had a strong historical and cultural ambience.

As I looked out the window towards Tai Kwun, Billy told me a story from Switzerland from over a decade ago. In 2009, Billy left his job at Rocco Design and moved to Switzerland alone to begin a new chapter at Herzog & de Meuron. This would be his fifth change of jobs. In his slow and gentle tone, Billy said, 'Each change was not for promotion or salary increase, but for the pursuit of betterment.' It was not initially clear what he meant by 'betterment'; however, the story of the many vicissitudes of the career path that followed his salad days at university revealed the answers. Two years later, Ida also flew to Switzerland, and she and Billy became colleagues.

Billy and Ida had been classmates at university, and more than twenty years later their acquaintance turned into love. Ida joined the Architectural Services Department shortly after graduation and during her tenure of six years, she was trained in the ways of the 'unbeatable spirit'. Prior to leaving for Switzerland, she had worked for Steven Holl Architects in Beijing and Rocco Design for a period of time. *Why did you leave Hong Kong?* Not long after the interview began, they answered with this statement: 'Because we were lost.'

Billy and Ida spoke elegantly. They were dressed very simply, one in black the other in white, and both looking as if they had come out of Muji. However, in their bones, they both carried traces of unwillingness – the unwillingness to stand still, to follow trends, and to deny themselves – because what they think differs from others.

Hong Kong is a varicoloured city filled with sensual pleasures. Along with prosperity, the free economy also brought with it the inevitable dominance of a market-centric economy. 'Sometimes when you operate within the framework of a business model, the space for creativity will be limited.' Billy was calm and relatively reticent. He spoke only occasionally, and when he did, it was in a measured manner. Ida, on the other hand, was more talkative; she recounted her inner struggle and confusion of the past. 'I often felt that our beliefs were in conflict with Hong Kong's norms, and sometimes we even wondered if we were too weird. But after going abroad, I found out that our thoughts were actually normal.'

During his time in Switzerland, Billy felt enlightened, 'I was really doing architecture.' Ida added that, 'In fact, it was just like how we were taught back in university. Before starting to draw and design, the team would first engage in research work on the local history and the surrounding environment and its needs before taking the next step.'

Untold Stories

1   A new steel bridge connects the two houses. The wall of the original swimming pool was demolished, and water from the swimming pool spills over to form a waterfeature, which becomes the landscape of the indoor dining room.
2   The stair space is a gallery of shape and light. Tailor-made handrails have been designed with an emphasis on feel and touch.

The experience of living in Basel came with other perks. Not only does it have the first public art museum in Europe – the Basel Art Museum – but it is also the city with the highest density of museums in Switzerland. Basel had an ambience that oozed art, yet it was the simple life that Billy and Ida both loved. 'At lunchtime, I could take my sandwich and find a place by the river to sit cross-legged: that was daily life.' The subtle yet undeniable joy and the abundant feeling of good fortune were enough to embellish life. There was softness and yearning in Ida's eyes. 'There was nothing fancy on that large lawn; everyone could do whatever they wanted and were very close to nature and felt very comfortable.'

In 2013, a project brought them back from Basel to where they had left off, and they started their own firm. It was the renovation project for the mansion of Mr Henry Tang. In 2008, Ida and Billy had participated and taken the top spot for the concept design competition for the Hong Kong pavilion at World Expo. During that occasion, they were acquainted briefly with Mr Henry Tang, the then Chief Secretary for Administration, who was the judge that awarded them at the ceremony.

'We like to take things apart.' Ida said with a smile. When considering design concepts, the first thing to do was to take things apart. 'Many things are overdone in this era, but what we truly need is simply space.' Since her days at the Architectural Services Department, the idea of 'separating the wheat from the chaff' had been imprinted in Ida's mind. 'Just adding on a little is enough after taking it apart.'

The previous design of this mansion in Kowloon Tong consisted of two separate houses, that, at first glance, appeared independent and characterised by distinct styles. Upon their arrival, Ida and Billy first emptied the platform of the atrium and transformed it into an open and spacious garden. The previously modest swimming pool shed one of its walls, allowing water to cascade down, forming a two-meter-high water curtain that gracefully landed on the pebbles below. The marble cladding on the inner walls were completely removed and replaced with a touch of minimalist white to adjust the sense of modernism. As for the exterior walls of the house, they were modestly finished with fair-faced concrete. 'We didn't dare to propose it back then. When you spoke of concrete walls, the immediate reaction would often be associated with the place having no renovation, design nor decoration.' Fortunately, there were still those who appreciated it.

'With the five colours combined, the human eye will blind; with five notes in one sound and the human ear confounds.' Ida explained her attitude and views on architecture with the three philosophies from Lao Tzu's *Tao Te Ching*. There were two separate houses, one for the parents and the other for the children. 'The only request they had then was linkage.'

In between the two minimalist and pristine houses, Ida and Billy connected them with a glass bridge, instantly establishing a linkage between two once separate entities. 'Making them look like they belong to the same house, yet with a certain amount of private space.'

The house was named 'The Bridged House'. The bridge not only separated space but also connected it; this feeling of being neither friendly nor aloof immediately added a layer of fun and depth to the space.

1. The unpainted fair-faced concrete wall with fine wood grain finish presents the first impression of the house.
2. The two houses face each other across the garden on the second floor, like neighbours in a small town, connected by a bridge.
3. The staircase has been remodelled and is shaped like a sculpture. Tailor-made furniture echoes the shape of the house. Natural light floods the corridor from above, leaving behind a new spatial dimension for the interior space.

The interior space, from the primeval stone floor to the warm wooden staircases; the linear design extending from the terrace to the skyline; and even looking up at the skylight – all of these features echo with nature and the landscape outside. The roof containing the skylight is constructed out of fair-faced concrete, echoing the exterior wall at the entrance. 'Not many are accepting of the idea of having a concrete ceiling; but, in fact, the surface of concrete can also be very natural.' Billy said quietly, 'Sitting on the stairs at night and looking up, you could be forgiven for thinking that you are sitting outdoors.'

Ida and Billy paid close attention not only to the space but also to the building itself and its interior design. Under closer observation, visitors will note that not even the handrails on individual stairs have escaped Ida's and Billy's attention. For example, the handrail near the balcony is wider than the handrail going up the stairs. 'If you hold a small event at home, you can put your wine glasses there.' Billy continued, in his quiet voice, 'Some people thought the place was built entirely from scratch; in fact, we tried to keep it intact as much as possible. Not everything had to be completely removed. As long as we removed the excess and opened up the space, we could make the place *feel* brand new.'

Ida added, 'We are not following extreme simplicity; instead, we are using a simple method to solve a seemingly complicated problem to improve the quality of life.' Just like the contemporary artist Donald Judd said, 'If you like simple forms in art you will not make complicated ones in architecture.' Donald Judd and Henry Moore were two of Ida's favourite artists.

Because they were 'lost', the two set out to find the answers. 'Aesthetics, Nature and Humanities', the few simple elements and basics were the architectural beliefs they were looking for during their days of leading a wandering life. In the midst of our chat, they added, 'If you didn't go abroad, you wouldn't have been able to absorb and experience the alternatives, nor have the affirmation of your own architectural beliefs, and so, naturally, you wouldn't have dared to take on this project.'

In this world, it has always been easy to go with the flow, yet difficult staying true to one's original beliefs. Living a life full of contradictions, and having hovered around the edges of established principles and bottom lines many times, when ideals run counter to reality, can one not help but question whether we are truly the masters of our own lives, or even our own saviours? Perhaps it is just as Rousseau had mentioned in *The Social Contract*: 'Man is born free; and everywhere he is in chains.' However, despite this reality, there are always those who are willing to exert the extra effort to find their rhythm against the current.

I dare not say for certain how exhaustively Billy and Ida have tried to consciously break all the norms, but, at least on 'architectural belief', they can respond to their own convictions with absolute clarity.

Diamond Hill Crematorium

Ponder Deeply, Move on Gently

When his father passed away in 1989, Stephen Tang, who was in his thirties at the time, was inconsolable. The mood at his father's funeral was dark and the atmosphere oppressive. It dawned on Stephen that, for such a solemn occasion, no real consideration had been given to either the deceased or the living. Faced with such an uncomfortable and difficult situation, most would just brush it off and say, 'This is Hong Kong, just accept your fate!' However, as an architect, Stephen began to wonder: Do we really have to accept this, and is there a way to turn this around?

This idea found a lasting place in his heart. In 2006, Stephen was given the opportunity to work on the Diamond Hill Crematorium project. Initially, he was only responsible for about 10 per cent of the entire design, but knowing how rare such an opportunity was, he spared no effort in acquiring the project despite his busy schedule. At that time, few were willing to engage in a project dealing with the issue of death. Even his superiors had their doubts and urged him to think twice. However, Stephen persisted, hoping to design a facility that could take care of the soul, show respect for the deceased and give comfort to the living.

Stephen, along with Patrick Luk, Michael Li and T.Y. Lau embarked on designing the crematorium with a new form. He meticulously crafted a space that was both spiritually enriching and comfortable, allowing the deceased to depart this world with dignity, while those bidding farewell to their loved ones could embrace hope. When Stephen conceived the design of the crematorium, he began by addressing functional processes and facility requirements. For instance, they designed routes for farewell and paths for memorial ceremonies, with an aim of creating a serene environment for contemplation. As the hearse carries the deceased into the service hall through the rear of the parking lot, the bereaved family members enter the service hall through a separate staircase, ensuring that different groups do not cross paths.

The design of the hall is modest, simple and spacious, featuring skylights that create an open and unconfined atmosphere. Users are able to gaze upon the pristine sky outside, and as the sunlight seeps through the skylights, it creates a stark contrast to the traditionally dim environment of a crematorium. Adjacent to the hall, there is a restroom also equipped with skylights. Bathed in natural light, people can not only change their clothes but also wash their tear-stained faces, evoking a sense of harmony, tranquillity and warmth throughout the space. As for the stones placed in the centre of the hall, they were excavated during construction. The architect team believed that these stones have been polished and baptised by nature and if they could be utilised, it would bring meaning and create resonance with those who visit.

Furthermore, the four service halls are positioned at the cardinal points along the north-south and east-west axes. There are no religious distinctions, ensuring that farewell ceremonies for individuals of any faith can be held here. Death is not only the end, but it also carries a glimmer of light. The water in the pool is flowing quietly, implying the endless circle of the human life.

Diamond Hill Crematorium embraces a strong connection with nature throughout its premises. In addition to the interior design, the architect has also adorned the roadside gardens along the path leading away from the crematorium with fragrant flowers. These flowers serve as a gentle reminder to individuals, after bidding farewell to their loved

1. The architect insisted on a simple fair-faced concrete design, and also reserved a place for plants to climb up the stone wall, using them to represent the ever-continuous vitality of life.
2. The small garden in the round courtyard of the Diamond Hill Crematorium, with the light seeping through the skylights, creates a stark contrast to the traditionally dim environment of a crematorium.
3. Asymmetrical platform garden and lotus pond. The flowing water in the pond implies the endless circle of life.

1. The green roof of the Diamond Hill Crematorium breaks the long-held impressions of crematoria with a large number of green elements.
2. The cremation chimney adopts the highest environmental protection standard in the world so that the smell will not affect the surrounding environment.

ones, to accept the gift they have received and continue living their lives to the fullest upon returning to the earthly realm. At the exit, there is an archway with intricate patterns, revealing the enigmatic code that represents two hexagrams from the *Book of Changes*: 'Ending' and 'Beginning', symbolising the endless circle of life.

Just a few months after its completion, members of the public complained that rainwater absorbed by the fair-faced concrete walls of the crematorium made it look tear-stained, thus creating a sense of sadness. There was even a suggestion from another department that the wall material be changed. However, the architect in charge insisted on keeping the fair-faced concrete, as walls with such a finish would allow the climbing plants to cling to them, and those plants were intended to represent continuity of life. Fortunately, this concept proved successful six months later, and the crematorium was even chosen as a filming location for a movie, thus averting the misfortune of having its walls replaced. Additionally, the crematorium's chimney for the cremation process adheres to the highest global environmental standards, effectively mitigating any impact on the surrounding environment and addressing sanitation and environmental concerns. The Diamond Hill Crematorium, serving as a pioneering example of a garden crematorium, has set a new design direction for future crematoriums in Hong Kong.

Stephen's career path as an architect began with small-scale engineering projects after joining the Architectural Services Department. During this time, there was a significant event that greatly influenced him – the design of a small park in Repulse Bay. Initially, he was advised by his colleagues to employ the most conventional method and just simply place a few chairs in the park. However, upon visiting the site, he found that there were numerous coconut trees in the park and decided that the design should incorporate them. He made the extra effort, believing that architecture should also be responsible towards the environment. This small park later won him his very first design competition, serving as a tremendous source of encouragement to him. As a senior architect, Stephen believes that even experimental projects could and should be implemented, especially while working for the Architectural Services Department where there are resources available for such endeavours. Lessons can be learnt through both the successes and failures of these experimental projects, and this is also what separates public sector architecture from commercial architecture.

Kwun Tong Promenade • Energising Kowloon East
InPARK • Hoi Bun Road Park

The Secret That Lies in Patience and Perseverance

The Kwun Tong Promenade, with a total length of about one kilometre, runs along the waterfront parallel to the Kwun Tong Bypass. This promenade was formerly known as the Kwun Tong Public Cargo Working Area and is now part of the Kai Tak Development project. The concept of the waterfront development is to revitalise both sides of Victoria Harbour by allowing nature into the city, and it is therefore focused on the construction of green spaces. An abundance of trees planted beside the promenade provide shade for visitors while they rest on the lawn.

In 2008, the HKSAR Government initiated preparation work for the transformation of the Kwun Tong waterfront. Beautifying the underbridge and the first phase of the Kwun Tong Promenade was the responsibility of Mr Andrew Nam. The initial brief for the project was to create an interesting and unique look that had never been seen before in Hong Kong. With respect to the specific design, the architect was free to showcase his talents.

Andrew recalled that during his first visit to the Kwun Tong waterfront, he was completely overwhelmed by it. What created the most lasting memory, however, was not the view of sunset or nightfall over the waterfront, nor was it the clean and tidy space, but the foul stench of the place! There were piles of waste everywhere with several two-metre-tall fences built around them. Upon further investigation, it turned out that due to this accumulation of waste, no one had actually seen the real Kwun Tong waterfront for more than forty years. 'A sense of mission came to me at that moment, and I wanted to regenerate this polluted environment and turn it into the most beautiful waterfront!' When he first started working on the project, Andrew thought of the water mist, LED lights and music elements of the Millennium Park in Chicago and the Cheonggyecheon in South Korea. He believed that if a place could be interpreted through art performances, it would be a fascinating and refreshing experience. He also recalled that when he was visiting his relatives in the United States back in 1992, he and I had arranged a meeting and had taken a walk along the waterfront in Brooklyn, New York. He saw the simple timber decking and expressed surprise that such methods could be employed to help visitors get closer to nature.

'A good design should be simple and proximal.' Andrew's professor at university used the word 'proximity' when lecturing on seventeenth-century English gardens, emphasising the need for a close connection between man and nature. This principle is evident in the Kwun Tong waterfront, where the design focuses on our connection with greenery, as well as the sea. The entire design carefully takes into account the resonance of existing materials, such as the shades from corrugated paper and iron gates.

Andrew also mentioned the term 'folly'. Under its architectural definition, the term 'Folly' emphasises the architectural function of enhancing a given space. Some forms of Folly also use this to explore the possibility of changing the relationship between people and space, adding an interesting element into the mix. For example, during the second phase of the project, there was a rather decorative metal-box sculpture on the observation deck which was endowed with the concept of 'past, present and future'. Visitors could move about freely, allowing them the possibility of intervening in the 'relationship between people and space.' The Kwun Tong Promenade (Phase I) was completed in 2009 and Andrew was also involved in planning the 800-metre-long second phase which was completed in 2014. His contribution has helped define the initial appearance, as well as the distinctive character of the Kwun Tong waterfront.

The Energizing Kowloon East Office (EKEO) was established in 2012. The principal lead hired a consultant team comprising professionals from different fields including scholars, historians, architects, planners and overseas experts to jointly carry out the 'The Spirit of Creation – Study on Industrial Culture of Kowloon East'. Planners, architects and designers implemented various public spaces, facilities and architecture projects in Kowloon East to realise the strategic vision of the initiative with its four main themes of Connectivity, Branding, Design and Diversity.

Architects are widely recognised for their robust professional training and a well-defined thought process. When they receive a brief from a client, they set out to do their best within that framework, and it is a customer-oriented process throughout. During her time working on the EKEO led by planner Mr K.K. Ling, Ms Winnie Ho realised that the role of a planner was more multi-dimensional than that of an architect, as the range of issues to be tackled by a planner was much greater. She also realised that her understanding of urban planning was not of sufficient depth and so, under the leadership of KK Ling, Winnie's role was to resolve specific issues and execute solutions accordingly. From the Kwun Tong Promenade to the establishment of EKEO all the way to the end of the development plan, a total of more than ten projects have been completed, including reconstruction, demolition, connecting roads and communities, management and innovation.

At the time of their first visit to the Kwun Tong waterfront, there was severe pollution. The top layer of the water was literally black. While Winnie Ho and Michael Li were considering a solution to this problem, they thought the emphasis should first be placed on promoting the overall development of the entire road section. Along the way, there were many stories and obstacles. For instance, at the Kowloon Flour Mill site, the gate leading to the ferry terminal was tightly shut, and it took the team four full years to lobby the many relevant government departments to reopen the ferry terminal. As Winnie was sharing the bits and pieces of those stories, she lamented that it was indeed no easy feat. However, the experience has made her realise that solving those problems would require coordination and engagement with many communities within the city.

According to EKEO, 'the "Fly the Flyover Operation" is a critical place-making strategy in the Energizing Kowloon East initiative. The Operation aims to utilise unused spaces beneath Kwun Tong Bypass for creative, arts and cultural uses.' Fly the Flyover 01 was opened to the public in January 2013, allowing different performing groups to hold various activities in this informal performance venue. In the early days of the initiative, many artists believed that the project destroyed their original creative ecology. Michael then designed a simple stage on the site, adopting an open design, to provide the public with a freely accessible space for use; through this, the community could decide what would happen in that given space, much like planting a tree that can grow in unexpected ways. After the stage was built, we saw children coming here with their segways, while others chose to play music or held dancing competitions and community activities.

In the beginning, there was no specific government department responsible for the management of the area. The EKEO was charged with the overall arrangements but was given limited resources. As resources were scarce during the construction of the Fly the Flyover 01, the result was clearly inadequate. Subsequently, the Flyover 02 and Flyover 03 were opened for tender with a budget of HKD 20 million to allow a social

1   1   Located in the heart of a former industrial area, InPARK is like a secret garden for the local community.
2   2   The metal grille and frosted glass louvers of the façade allow natural light into the washroom while maintaining privacy.

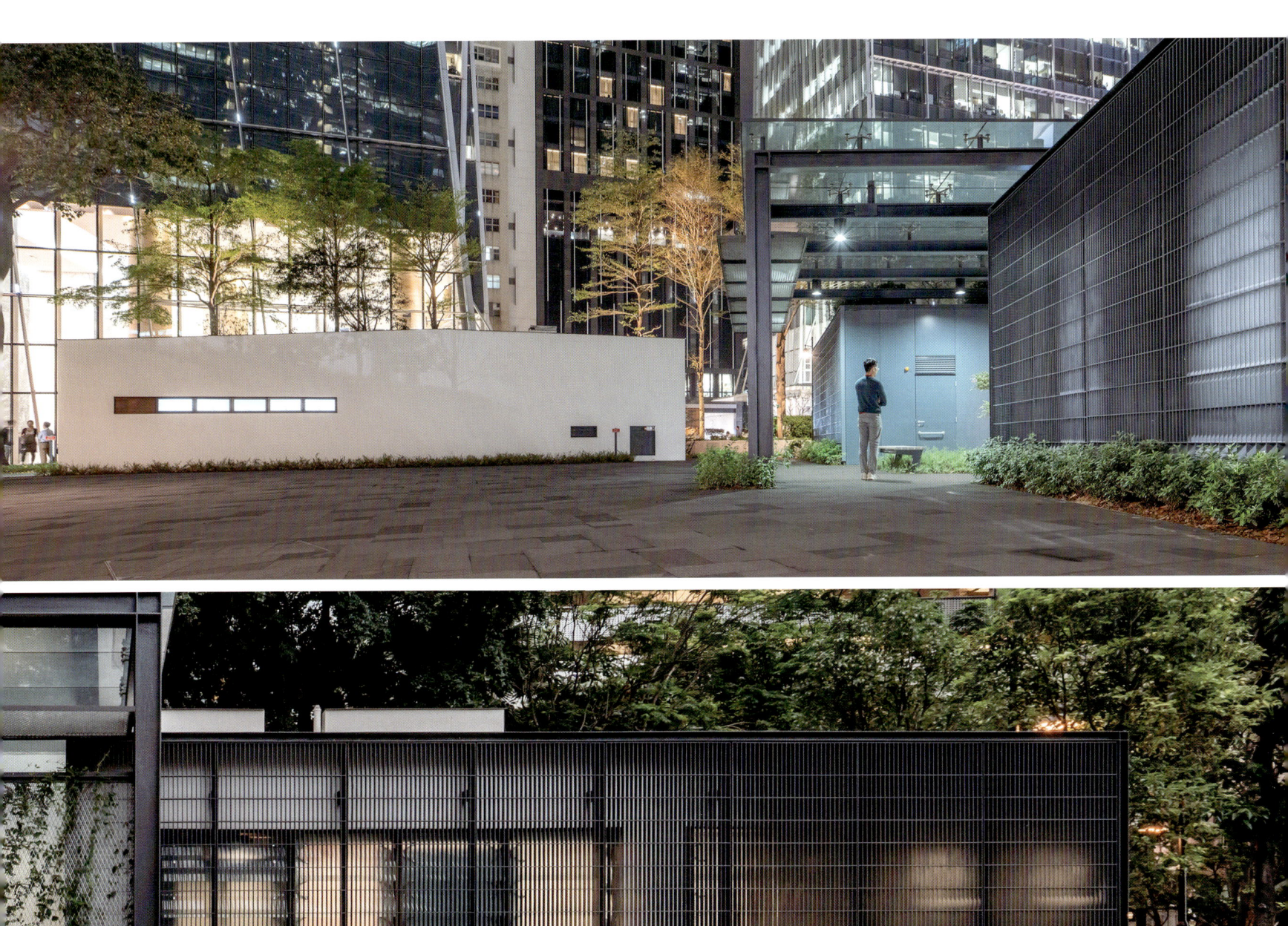

1, 2 The EKEO is the first low-carbon temporary office in Hong Kong.
3 InPARK combines industrial cultural elements with architectural design. Seven groups of artists created artworks inspired by the main industries of the past, such as clothing, textiles and plastics; people are able to find memories of the past while enjoying the park facilities.

enterprise to join and promote the initiative. After soliciting proposals through an open invitation, the EKEO awarded the tender to the non-profit organisation HKALPS to manage and operate the three venues under the 'Fly the Flyover' initiative. Edward Wong was responsible for communicating with contractors and implementing the plan.

From the seaside and grassy areas of the Kwun Tong Waterfront to the adjacent small community, underpasses nearby as well as the surrounding roads, there are multiple layers of design. In order to create another central business district in Hong Kong, K.K. Ling personally surveyed the area prior to the commencement of the project and identified ten areas that needed improvement. Michael and Winnie were the architects in charge of this project, with landscape architect Ryan Lin responsible for the greening master plan.

In her youth, Winnie didn't have many hobbies. However, on one fateful occasion, she accompanied her senior to visit an architectural firm and was captivated by the numerous architectural models on display. This experience sparkled her interest in the field, and she saw the industry as being professional yet lively. Her first year at university was an emotional roller coaster due to unexpected changes to the academic system that caused her to to have doubts about her abilities. She even had thoughts about giving up on the subject. Fortunately, with the encouragement of her teachers, she persevered and successfully completed her studies.

Winnie worked for the Architectural Services Department well into her thirties. She once casually mentioned that she had hoped to retire at forty-eight and enjoy life. A friend said to her: 'You will change your mind!' And that piece of comment has stayed in her mind ever since. At the age of forty-eight, a friend reminded her of that conversation, and it made her think seriously about what she would want to do if she were to leave the profession. Her answer from within was, 'Serve society, engage in meaningful activities, and help others.'

When you can truly do something you want while being an architect, why would you want to leave? Confronted with all sorts of feelings, Winnie found herself at a major turning point in her life. She began to feel more at ease, and, coupled with her own sheer enthusiasm, she hoped to devote more of herself to her profession. She felt that working at EKEO was a good fit for her personality, as it allowed her to do what she truly wanted while still embracing different challenges. She needed to be more patient in her work and engage in empathetic and meaningful communication with the local communities, while also engaging in intelligent and logical communication with professional

1 2
3

1   Translucent glass brick walls bring in soft sunlight to the public lavatories at the Hoi Bun Road Park.
2   The park can be enjoyed throughout the day by the public. During the day, it is common for families to gather on the grassland; as dusk falls, many will come to capture the beauty of the sunset.
3   The service facilities curve around the circular lawn at Hoi Bun Road Park, which can be used as a multi-functional outdoor space.

departments. 'The experience from the Energizing Kowloon East Office had changed me from being an architect to being a person,' Winnie said with a sign of relief in her tone. It all echoed with what was central to her belief in terms of the meaningfulness of her work and the boundaries that needed to be broken. Winnie is now the Secretary for Housing of the HKSAR.

Michael Li, who was also part of Winnie's team, has been passionate about drawing since childhood. He later studied architecture at the University of London and returned home upon graduation, where he worked in an architecture firm to lay a solid foundation for his career. Looking back on this journey, Michael has gradually formed his own views on architecture. He joined the Group 18 of the Architectural Services Department – which, at the time, was led by me – to participate in the Wetland Park project. This period also coincided with a time when Michael was composing a number of church hymns. From the introduction of the melody to a song, he found that music and architecture shared many similarities. Recalling the flexibility entrusted to him by the EKEO project, and having had the experience of working in other departments, he found that sometimes it was not wise to delve too deeply into a profession, as it would serve only to stifle creativity. When he retires, Michael aspires to achieve success in the realm of musical creations, and continue to indulge in his enduring passion for composing and arranging music.

Regarding the InPARK project of the Energizing Kowloon East initiative, the formerly known Tsun Yip Street Playground was originally built in 1973 and primarily served the families of the workers in the Kwun Tong Industrial Area. As the area began to transform into a business district, the Tsun Yip Street Playground underwent improvement works to better suit the needs of the community. Upon its completion, the Tsun Yip Street Playground was renamed InPARK in reference to the industrial culture elements of the area through the park's facilities and installations and was officially opened in 2019.

Designed by Wei Jen Wang, the park is made up of a rain shelter and an exhibition space formed from four modified cargo containers. It showcases the possibilities of revitalisation of small public spaces and the reuse of existing features. This space combines exhibition and leisure, community and culture, and public art in the daily life of the city. There is also the Kowloon East Discovery Map made of screw caps and rusted iron. Industrial materials have been integrated with the relevant background stories, and large-scale neon lights are installed on vertical containers to represent the diverse industries of Kowloon East with lights, colours and culture.

During the second phase of the Tsun Yip Street Playground initiative, the original facilities were improved upon and the public lavatories and the central lawn were rebuilt. The Art Promotion Office of the Leisure and Cultural Services Department and the EKEO jointly organised the Public Art Scheme at Tsun Yip Street Playground and extended open invitations to local artists, architects, designers and art teams to propose artworks for InPARK. Seven groups of selected works were installed on the central lawn to represent the major industries that used to operate in Kowloon East, including printing, clothing and garments, textiles, toys, plastics, electronics and timepieces. These works not only highlighted the characteristics of Kowloon East's industrial culture; they also demonstrated the vision of combining future business development with creative designs.

When walking from the promenade to the intersection of Wai Yip Street, one passes by the Hoi Bun Road Park, which was opened to the public in August 2021. The renovated park has lawns, gazebos, lavatories, changing rooms, resting facilities and rain shelters. Looking down at the park from the overpass, one can see that Thomas Wan and Edward Wong employed a circular layout to keep the facilities closely connected, including a group of covered multi-purpose spaces and the central lawn. At night, both moonlight and artificial light permeate under the covered multi-purpose space, allowing the starry sky above and the shadows of the trees below to echo with one another.

Edward Wong had worked with Thomas Wan in the Architectural Services Department. He was posted to the EKEO and put in charge of the second phase of the Tsun Yip Street Playground. He has always had a strong sense of space. When he was in his sixth grade, his parents took him along to a festive light display. He was intrigued by the round window grilles of Jardine House. He asked his father how those round windows were built. 'Architects will know'. And that was a clue for Edward's future.

Now that he has become one, Edward believes that, consistent with everyone else's description, the EKEO is a magical place. With many colleagues of different departments coming together, Edward has been able to learn the art of communication. That was quite unlike his previous experience, where he was stuck in a rut and could only ponder things on his own. However, post-EKEO, Edward has learnt to think outside the box, and has become what Winnie has preached: achieving 'coordination of all four limbs'. With a smile on his face, Edward said that architecture was always in his blood and has become a part of his daily life. On every trip with his wife, he always reserves three days out of seven to admire architecture, train his eyes and, most importantly, to recognise and understand beauty.

The park introduces green elements into the Kwun Tong Industrial Zone. Through the integration of concepts of both Oriental and Western gardens, the trees preserved on the original site are interwoven with new architecture, providing the area with an urban oasis.

Untold Stories

With the transformation of Kwun Tong into a business district, the Tsun Yip Street Playground underwent improvement works and was renamed InPARK.

Concert Hall of the Alliance Primary School,
Kowloon Tong · Oootopia

Pyrophoric

Watching Manfred Yuen's TED Talk on screen, you can almost feel his contagious charm. This charm walks a fine line between strength and gentleness, effortlessly intoxicating his audience with his swirls of words. Suddenly, he asked a sharp rhetorical question that went straight to the root of a problem. Many were not only caught off-guard, but were also, perhaps, enlightened. More importantly, he is the most good-looking architect in Hong Kong. At least that is how he has described himself in his other interviews. So I wasn't about to let go of this chance to tease him further. However, jokes aside, we began our interview.

Manfred first graduated from the Faculty of Architecture at the University of Hong Kong, followed by the Department of Architecture at the University of Cambridge. After graduation, he and some other young architects formed a band called Groundwork, and he played music and was also engaged in curatorial work. 'The things I used to draw were both radical and strange. I was looking for challenges everywhere.' At the age of twenty-eight, he was already a lecturer at Kingston University, and before turning thirty, he was appointed the China representative at the Austrian firm Coop Himmelb(l)au. Referring to that appointment, he humbly joked that he was more like a senior translator. Manfred's early career was certainly plain sailing, and he was considered, by many, to be 'the chosen one'.

There is a saying: the higher you climb, the harder you fall. After resigning from Coop Himmelb(l)au, he founded Groundwork Architecture + Urbanism. Unfortunately, the path of entrepreneurship was not as smooth as he had expected, and he recognises this period as the lowest point in his life. Due to ongoing financial difficulties, the firm shrank until he was the last one remaining. ' I wondered why this was happening to me. But we human beings tend to prevaricate when we can't achieve something. We will blame anything else rather than admit the problem lies within ourselves.'

'This world is interesting; it won't shut you off from all paths, but you have to put in the extra effort.' After the initial slew of extraordinary achievements came to an end and were replaced with challenging times, Manfred backtracked onto a path he knew well. He began teaching at Hong Kong Polytechnic University. 'At least I had a job.' Through a chance encounter, he met with Mr Suen Kwai Ping, who, at that time, was engaged in building rehabilitation projects. Thus, Manfred came into contact with and became more aware of social issues, which became the focus of his later projects. One of them was the Hawker Reload, a project that commenced after the devastating Fa Yuen Street fire. 'I realised that the theory we had learnt was severely out of touch with reality in Hong Kong.' Since then, he has been determined to position his firm as one that will bear social responsibilities and has started engaging in projects with that focus in mind. 'Life is a never-ending process of self-refinement. Slowly but surely, you will find your focal point.'

After experiencing the many ups and downs of life, Manfred exudes a sense of confidence and courage to face up to challenges, and these qualities have even extended to his designs. Located in a corner of Kowloon Tong, there is a spaceship-like object that has been suspended in mid-air within the campus of the Alliance Primary School. As it turns out, it is the concert hall of the primary school. Their concert hall was unlike any that were built for schools in the 1990s. Johann Wolfgang von Goethe once said, 'Architecture is frozen music.'

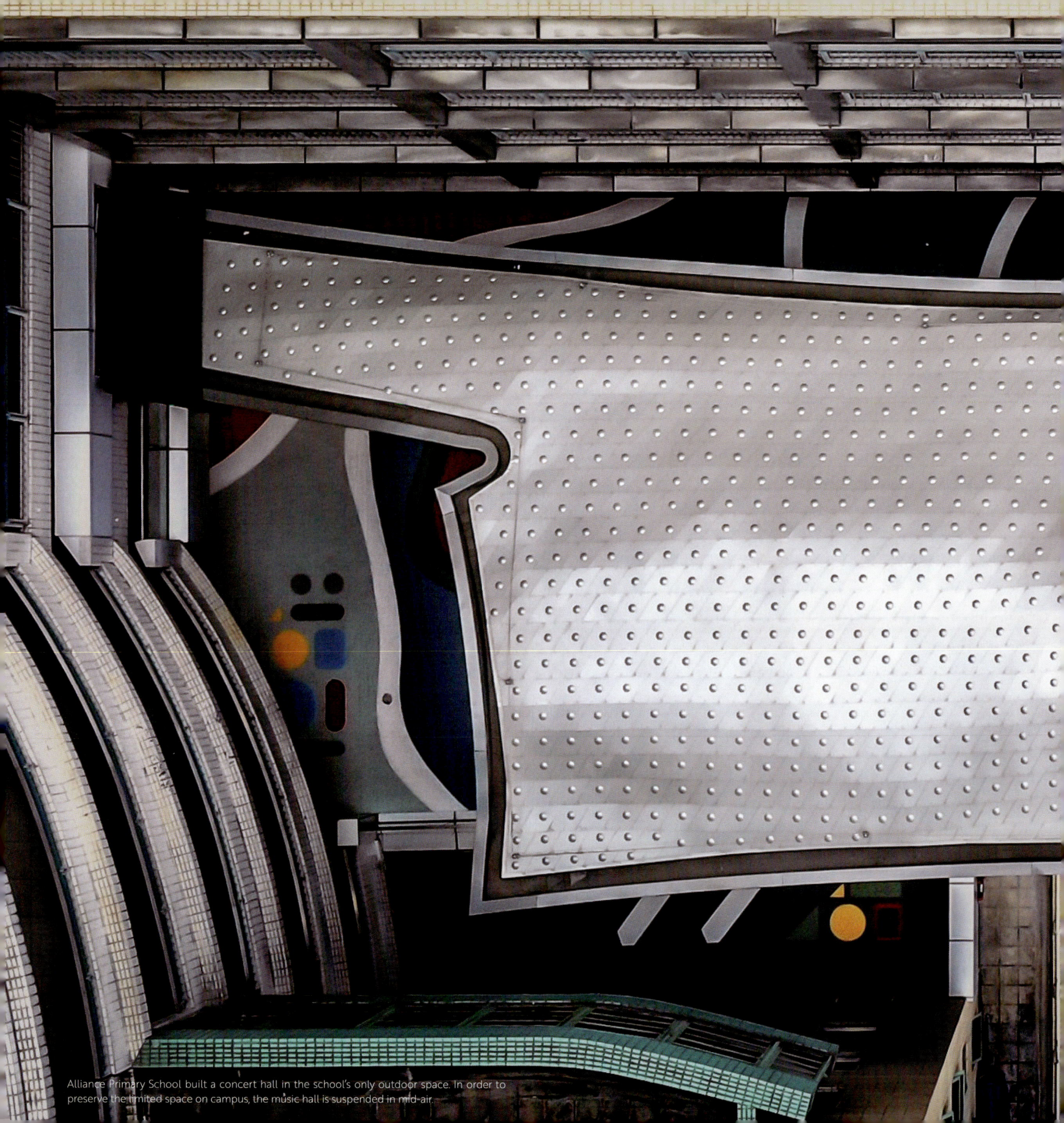
Alliance Primary School built a concert hall in the school's only outdoor space. In order to preserve the limited space on campus, the music hall is suspended in mid-air.

Manfred employed flowing lines as his design elements and wandered within the realm of delights. The top section is covered with metallic textures and the outer wall is made of black, circular copper plates which have been arranged neatly next to one another, projecting a high-tech and futuristic feel. The semi-open space is bounded by wooden acoustic panels decorated with translucent chiffon. Looking up to the ceiling, it is as if one is underground looking up at rolling hills. Much like *Alice in Wonderland*, it exudes a sense of the surreal.

Aside from his refreshing works, one can also observe Manfred's subtle and consistent effort in community projects through another design of his. The Oootopia is a co-living space that sits quietly in the corner of a bustling city. On stepping into the space, however, one is immediately greeted by a sense of cosiness leaving the noise and the stress of the city behind. Upon being awarded the project, Manfred was in no hurry to begin its design. Instead, he chose to begin researching and understanding the needs of the intended users of this co-living space. This included their lifestyles and habits, so that he could shape a design that would fit the way of life of the youth of today. Further, the concept of co-living is a form of social life that requires connection with others. Thus, in the layout of its space, a lot of communal areas have been reserved for tatami tea rooms and casual cafés decorated with warm wooden elements, so that people can have the space to breathe in this fast-paced city.

Whether he is standing on high ground or has fallen into the cracks, Manfred will always strive to find a way out. Like him, his works have also shown signs of struggle, contradiction, contrast and shock. 'So, are these elements your symbols?' I asked him. 'What virtues or abilities have I to bestow symbols on myself? It sounds very arrogant, and I wouldn't dare to say such things.' Nevertheless, he seemed inspired in that moment and said, 'Living, for me, is full of contradictions, just like the symbols of my works. These contradictions sometimes erode me, and seeing that others can concentrate on one single endeavour and excel in it, I wonder why can't I do the same? However, it is precisely these contradictions that have allowed me to experience the meaning of life. I like Chinese culture and also Western art; I like helping people, but I also like making money…' With his ever-eloquent silver tongue, he said that in one breath. 'I wonder how I should go about incorporating these extreme elements in my work.' In the end, he asked himself a rhetorical question, the answer to which perhaps already lies within his works.

1		
	2	3
	4	5

1. The Concert Hall was built because of Alliance Primary School's focus on developing its students' musical expertise.
2. The interior of the concert hall is covered with wooden acoustic panels with translucent chiffon to achieve the ideal acoustic effect and visual aesthetic.
3. The design of the concert hall uses the superposition and interconnection of spaces, aiming to create a space where students can explore freely and have fun.
4. Oootopia in Tai Kok Tsui is a serviced residence that promotes the concept of co-living.
5. Floor-to-ceiling glazing in the 2,000-square-foot communal area makes it a very bright place.

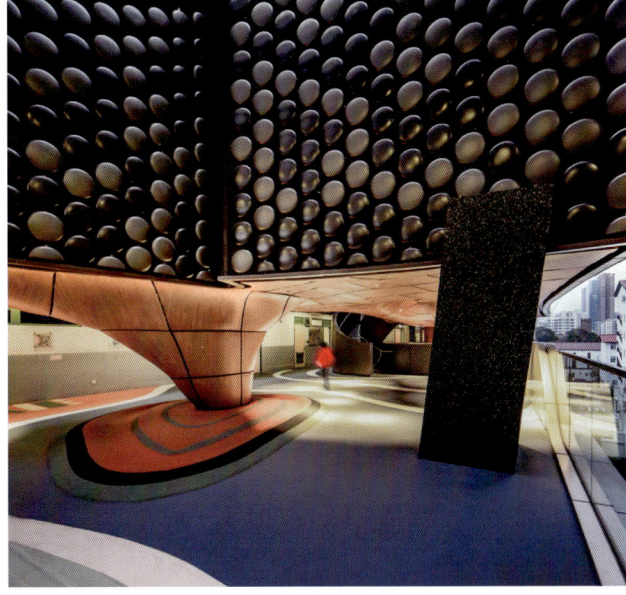

Morse Park
P.L.K. Stanley Ho Sau Nan Primary School

Miniature Community

Morse Park is the second largest park of the Kowloon district after the Lai Chi Kok Park. It was named after the late Sir Arthur Morse, the chairman and chief manager of the Hong Kong and Shanghai Banking Corporation, to honour him for his lifelong contributions to Hong Kong. The park, built in 1967, sits in the Wong Tai Sin District and is divided into four areas identified by numbers. Facilities within the park include a jogging track, a Tai Chi garden, an open plaza, a palm garden, a century-old well, a swimming pool, a children's playground, indoor and outdoor sports facilities, and Hong Kong's first amphitheatre.

According to Thomas Wan, the park was inspired by the Midway Gardens, a European-style concert garden designed by Frank Lloyd Wright. Built in 1913 with yellow bricks and patterned concrete blocks, the entire complex was adorned with intricate geometric ornaments. It was a place where the public could dine, drink, rest, and enjoy performances.

The Morse Park had been heavily criticised prior to its renovation. Funding was finally approved in 2015 by the Finance Committee. Renovation work began in 2016, and the project was completed in December 2018. One of the renovation projects was the amphitheatre in Park No. 4, which had an open design that increased natural lighting and ventilation. According to the project architect, Mr Donald Leung, 'The project's challenge came from the fact that it was very much a heritage conservation project.' Important elements of the past had to be preserved, while their functions had also to be improved, including the expansion of the canopy over the spectator stands and stage area and replacement of the stone benches with new seating. All with the aim of attracting more locals and tourists alike to visit and watch large-scale performances by Cantonese opera and local theatrical troupes, who were frequent performers at the park. A lawn was installed to both add beauty and improve public amenity by allowing more room for community activities.

Aside from parks, Thomas was also in charge of school projects. A school is a miniature community and its campus is a miniature city. People often believe that a school is not just a garden of learning for children but it also serves to imperceptibly but positively influence them through education. The design of the campus is a form of education in and of itself; thus, it follows that the designer of the campus will also be the architect of the children's souls.

The P.L.K. Stanley Ho Sau Nan Primary School is situated in the Kowloon Tong district. Within its campus there is a traditional Chinese garden that has been reinterpreted using modern methods; its design seeks to reinterpret the Chinese traditional culture by creating an oasis within the city. The front, centre and rear courtyards, with their gardens and bridges – each with their own functions – are linked by a long corridor, thus creating a sense of community by bringing everyone closer together.

Thomas had noticed that the students carried heavy schoolbags on their daily trips to and from school. In response to this, he relocated the sports ground to the first floor (previously located on the ground floor) to reduce the distance students had to travel between their classrooms and the outdoor activity spaces. Other initiatives of his included the relocation of the assembly hall to a lower level, resulting in a campus built over four levels instead of eight. High fences were replaced with lower ones, allowing the campus to integrate more naturally with the surrounding community, thus setting itself apart from a typical school campus.

Following a visit to the walled villages in Tin Shui Wai, Thomas was inspired to incorporate traditional building structures into his design with the concept of 'a city within a city'. 'In the process of planning and design, the language of space was my foremost consideration. Materials such as raw concrete, wood and metal were supplementary, and so were the colours.' Thomas pointed out that when designing the school, his

first step was to have basic materials such as plain, unpainted concrete on the exterior. Some function rooms had sunroofs to let natural light into the campus.

Ms Tuesday Li, who was also involved in the project, lamented the severe lack of space in the city. Throughout her career, she has always been concerned about quality of life. 'Architecture is meant to create spaces for people to live in.' In front of the school library lies a spacious green lawn, providing students with an inviting and comfortable setting to come together and bask in a warm and relaxing atmosphere. The architect's meticulous design showcases his thoughtfulness by extending campus activities to the outdoors and creating a natural, green and comforting environment. This will undoubtedly enhance social interactions between students, foster a love for reading and allow them to fully enjoy campus life.

1. The amphitheatre can also host concerts, bazaars and recreational activities, becoming a focal point for the community. The amphitheatre has been preserved and optimised to promote traditional culture according to the traditions of Cantonese opera.
2. The design of the rest area of the Morse Park Amphitheatre uses a modern approach to interpret the design of pavilions and screens of traditional Chinese gardens.
3. The P.L.K. Stanley Ho Sau Nan Primary School adopts a low-rise building design, breaking the tradition of the eight-storey school building. With only four storeys, the distance between the various school spaces has been reduced.

The campus is screened with woven steel mesh panels, which are combined with greenery and basic building materials such as plain concrete and timber to create a variety of spatial experiences.

Cattle Depot Art Park

First Step to an Interesting Path

The complex popularly known as the Cattle Depot is located at the junction of To Kwa Wan and the Kai Tak Development site. It sits on the formal site of the Ma Tau Kok Livestock Quarantine Station, which was closed in 1999. From the very early stage, the Kowloon City District Council had wanted to develop the area around the Cattle Depot. In 2009, a group of artists entered the area known for its cluster of red-brick buildings, and, together with a group of opera enthusiasts, set up the Cattle Depot Artist Village. Jacen Lo would often visit and watch their performances, but like everyone else in the community, the only thing he knew about the area south of the Cattle Depot was that a lot of it had fallen into disrepair.

It was not until 2013 that the Leisure and Cultural Services Department appointed the Architectural Services Department to design the Cattle Depot Art Park. Jacen Lo, the architect leading the project, was very excited, but, due to the limited budget, he chose to modify the park rather than to rebuild it. From a site visit undertaken at the beginning of the project, the neglect of the previous twenty years quickly became obvious, with moss growing in the water tanks and the brick walls in a dilapidated state. Jacen had grown up in To Kwa Wan and would often pass the 13 Streets and Sung Wong Toi where the Cattle Depot was located (in between the tenement buildings and new developments). Jacen believed that, through alterations, he could transform this place into a 'connector' between the old and the new: 'Helping others to see things from different angles' was his ultimate goal.

In his secondary school years, Jacen used to enjoy walking to and from school along Gascoigne Road, passing the United Services Recreation Club and barracks along the way. He loved the atmosphere of the area. He would stroll along the road and wonder if people would still be attracted to this quiet and comfortable space if buildings were erected on the meadow next to the main road. That was how the idea of architecture came to him. Reading medicine had been his first choice, but, due to unsatisfactory interview results, he chose instead to pursue the subject that interested him: architecture. As Jacen was reading an introduction to architecture, he realised that he was also learning about philosophy at the same time. It was precisely this overlap with other disciplines and scientific fields that architecture offered that truly captivated him.

He felt that learning was merely a process of absorbing knowledge, and what truly drove him to become fully invested in architecture arose from his experience attending a concert after his graduation. While waiting in line for the concert, a public exhibition of gold jewellery at the Hong Kong Cultural Centre caught his eye. He realised that although there was no apparent connection between jewellery and architecture, the art pieces in front of him had, nevertheless, been made using the same processes and materials. 'I thought if I could utilise such techniques in a knowledgeable and comprehensive manner, I could then materialise everything I had learnt at school.' And that was the calling that inspired the flexibility in his work.

While working for commercial firms, Jacen realised that even the top decision-makers in the firms did not enjoy much freedom. This was simply because of the urgency that came with commercial projects and also the unexpected changes demanded by clients. He later decided to work for the government in the hope of enjoying greater design freedom.

Every project comes with the possibility of taking up different forms, and Jacen has always been at the forefront of exploration and experimentation. The Cattle Depot Art Park, a complex covering an area of 6,000 square metres and themed around the history of the Cattle Depot, was officially opened in September 2019.

Many of the original structures of the Cattle Depot have been preserved, such as the barn, number plates, the remains of the well, the pavilion and even the iron frames in the park have been recycled. Trees, a gift of nature, had naturally taken root here. Jacen wanted to respect and preserve the trees that had grown and become twisted together over the years. His design allowed people to walk freely across the roots if they chose to, while those with limited mobility could use a boardwalk. He chose to preserve some collapsed red-brick pillars in the state they were found, thus 'allowing for an organic combination of the man-made and natural.' In order to respect the site as much as possible and give its users a different perspective, Jacen deliberately left those fallen trees and dilapidated brick walls in place, as they represented something that had taken place within a time and space on the site; and he was unwilling to interfere with its history or replace anything. As revealed through the design of the Cattle Depot Art Park, Jacen Lo's view is that things that have been lost do not need to be recreated purely for the sake of nostalgia.

In recent years, Jacen has gained a better grasp of algorithm design. He has ultilised software to aid in his design of the fluid, multi-dimensional red-brick walls in the Cattle Depot Art Park; as well as to visualise and design cattle-inspired forms and silhouettes using metallic materials. These additions further contributed to the authenticity and liveliness of the space. In addition to its connection with the nearby Cattle Depot Artist Village, the Cattle Depot Art Park is also involved with the forthcoming redevelopment of the industrial area. Looking towards the paper mill on the opposite side of the road, one can anticipate the complete transformation of the entire Cattle Depot area.

Recalling that path along Gascoigne Road, Jacen Lo eloquently shared, 'Actually, the path will only become interesting once you set out to take the first step and explore its intricacies.'

1	3
2	4

1. Park designers employed digital techniques to create the Tree Shade Arbour.
2. Art installations of cattle silhouettes on the outer wall of the Cattle Depot Art Park.
3. The pavilion and its chairs are a fusion.
4. The red-brick columns are historical architectural remains in the Cattle Depot Art Park.

Kowloon East

Zero Carbon Building

Beauty out of Thrifty

Before starting our interview, Mr K.S. Wong, the former Secretary for the Environment, asked if we knew about the Zero Carbon Park. The park is located on the way to Megabox (a place we frequent), and it is hard to miss. Mr M.K. Leung, who was in charge of the project, jokingly asked, 'Do you feel that even after ten years, the site hasn't really presented itself properly?'

CIC–Zero Carbon Park is located in Kowloon Bay and is surrounded by industrial buildings. Unlike the other public parks in the city, its doors aren't opened wide. Looking at its walls covered with climbing plants, it might be hard to imagine what it is all about just by walking pass it.

Speaking about the Zero Carbon Park, K.S. Wong traced the story back to more than a decade ago when Ms Carrie Lam, the then Secretary for Development, first introduced the concept of 'Green Building'. Having looked at the zero-carbon buildings that were beginning to take shape around the world, she wondered if Hong Kong could also create a demonstration model of zero-carbon building. At the time, K.S. Wong was working at Ronald Lu and Partners, and green buildings were his forte.

Very early on in his life, K.S. Wong had already crossed paths with environmental protection issues. His graduation thesis had been on how to create a space for environmental education in a country park. 'Back then, there was not a single book on green building in the library,' he lamented, 'Sometimes being too ahead of your time may not give you the best result, because there is no reference.'

In the early 1990s, green buildings were starting to attract the attention of the masses and after graduation, K.S. Wong joined Anthony Ng Architects and started working on architecture projects related to environmental protection. Thereafter he furthered his studies at the postgraduate school of The University of British Columbia on sustainable building and environment. 'I was very fortunate to have met the father of green building – Mr Raymond Cole.' Like reeling silks from a cocoon, K.S. Wong started elaborating on his story of acquaintance with green buildings.

After completing his studies, he returned to Hong Kong and founded the Environment & Sustainable Development Committee of the Hong Kong Institute of Architects. 'It is difficult to drive the entire industry and society forward solely by oneself. No matter how well one performs individually, the impact remains limited.' Therefore, soon after establishing the committee, K.S. Wong organised various continuing education programmes, including a series of green tourism initiatives, aimed at exploring environmentally friendly architectural practices in different parts of the world.

Climate change is a critical concern of the twenty-first century. It is not just the concept of a green lifestyle that has become a trend, but saving energy and reducing the carbon emissions in the buildings of the future have also become global responsibilities. As Hong Kong's first and only zero carbon building at the time, designers of the Zero Carbon Park faced the enomous challenge of not having any precedents while having a timeline of just fifteen short months to materialise it out of thin air.

The moment one enters Zero Carbon Park, the surrounding hustle and bustle disappear, and a spacious, open lawn comes into view, providing a breathing space away from the dense urban life. Of course, what makes Zero Carbon Park exceptional isn't just this expansive lawn; it's also the innovative design and techniques applied within it. In addition to being a public space to be enjoyed, it also serves the purposes of demonstration and education by showcasing the possibilities of the concept of zero carbon.

'Zero carbon' was the soul of the project. K.S. Wong, as the project director, undertook to achieve this goal within a short period of time. To accomplish this, he had two tricks up his sleeve. 'And do you know what they were?' he asked rhetorically. M.K. Leung and the project architect, Mr Tony Ip, who were both present at this interview, made no sound at all, though the corners of their mouths rose slightly, involuntarily. Out of curiosity, I stopped writing and waited for him to reveal his secret tricks. K.S. Wong pursed his lips and then continued, with a smile. 'The first trick is to be thrifty and not extravagant. The second trick is localisation and the creation of renewable energy.'

His tone was flat, yet we hung on his every word. 'So, what's the trick in being thrifty?' He continued to ask questions and answer them himself. 'Air conditioning actually amounts for a large part of a building's electrical consumption. The weather in Hong Kong is hot and humid, and turning on the air conditioner is unavoidable. Yet it is not necessary to do so in every season. In autumn and winter, the temperature is actually very comfortable, and saving up a few months still counts for something.' What about exhibition halls, cramped offices, and in dense cities, how can we feel warmth in winter and coolness in the summer and save months of air conditioning consumption? K.S. Wong enunciated the words: 'Natural ventilation.'

The prevailing winds of Hong Kong's summer usually come from the southeast and southwest, and they somehow manage to slip through the gaps in the adjacent Megabox. Zero Carbon Park has a long ventilation corridor, not a grand lobby. It not only directs the wind to the space but it also benefits the adjacent roads. 'It's the most comfortable place to have a nice cup of coffee.' In between his words, he made sure we knew how much he liked the coffee shop.

In addition to ensuring that the building itself would save electricity, the surrounding microclimate was also very important. 'Imagine this: a concrete sports ground absorbs heat from the sun and then bounces it back. Naturally, you would feel the heat just by standing next to it.' While K.S. Wong was introducing his ways of being thrifty, he also mentioned the plants in Zero Carbon Park. The Urban Native Woodland, half of the area of the park, has been planted with over two hundred native trees and over forty varieties of shrubs, and different types of climbing plants grow on each of the four walls. In response to different microclimates, they provide heat insulation and cooling to alleviate the city's heat-island effect. 'So even if the weather is obviously hot, it doesn't feel that way here.'

Zero Carbon Park is the first zero-carbon building in Hong Kong and is also one of the few zero-carbon buildings in the world whose design has fully considered the carbon used in the structural materials of the building, the energy consumed during its construction and the carbon emissions in the building's ongoing operational energy consumption.

The greening ratio of Zero Carbon Park is as high as fifty per cent. It contains Hong Kong's first urban native woodland, the planting of which prioritised local species including 220 native species and more than forty native shrubs to creat a diverse and natural ecological environment in the concrete forest.

After sharing his trick of saving electricity, he then discussed the utilisation of renewable energy. Zero Carbon Park has two main methods of generating electricity. The most visible is the curved rooftop with its 606 solar panels that produce up to a third of the Park's electricity requirements. According to Tony, 'It is necessary to consider not just the precise latitude and longitude of sunlight reception, but also the reflection of the solar panels and whether it will affect the surrounding environment. Therefore, the angle and position of each solar panel is different.' Solar panels are usually rectangular shapes: isn't it difficult to make curved ones? Tony shook his head and continued, 'No, it's not easy. It's a give-and-take situation to ensure that the overall aesthetics of the building will appear lighter, and also that it will not block the sunlight for the buildings behind.'

The fated acquaintance between Tony and green buildings started with his course on environmental engineering back at university. After three years of edification, he gradually came to understand the goals of environmental protection and developed a sense of duty towards it. Later, he visited Brazil and Peru while participating in the 'Green Holidays' organised by the Hong Kong Institute of Architects. 'It was mainly to visit one of the most environmentally friendly cities in the world back then: Curitiba.' After having visited this small Brazilian city that had done such a great job of promoting environmental protection, he couldn't help but ask himself why Hong Kong couldn't do better. However, the biggest benefit of the trip was the chance to meet with a group of individuals who shared the same vision and with whom he could collaborate in creating more green buildings.

From the first design plan for Zero Carbon Park to what it is today, Tony explained, 'Countless modifications and improvements were made, and different shapes were tried. However, the general direction is still facing towards the sun and towards the centre of the park. The angle of slope echoes the path of the sun and the surrounding landscape.'

From the positioning of the panels to the consideration of wind direction and the path of the sun, and even the desire to balance function and aesthetics, the design team spared no effort.

In addition to electricity produced by the solar panels, the remaining two-thirds of the electricity demand is generated by biodiesel refined from used cooking oil. Not only is waste material being turned into energy but the problems of waste treatment and energy production have also been solved; and this is just the icing on the cake.

Zero Carbon Park is undoubtedly low-key in appearance. It doesn't even have a grand lobby. Regarding the question of balancing function and aesthetics, M.K. Leung said, tongue in cheek, 'If you were to take this project to a beauty pageant, you would definitely lose.' He continued, 'But if you were to consider the concept behind it, you would stand a better chance of winning.' The starting point for Zero Carbon Park was not simply about beauty or otherwise. Its beauty did not lie in the appearance of the building itself; rather, it was reflected from within.

Compared to Tony's 'against all odds' path to architecture, M.K. Leung's path was more about inner struggle. 'I muddled along without an aim and became an architect.' He recalled the words of a senior who was sharing his memories of studying architecture: 'You don't need to study for architecture'. Whether it was intended as a joke, that statement had stuck in M.K. Leung's head. He said, bluntly, 'I was lied to by my senior.'

However, since it was the path he had chosen for himself, he had to keep walking it in earnest. After completing three years of his study, M.K. Leung chose to take a year out to decide whether or not he should join the architecture profession. He asked himself questions such as, 'Is meeting client's demands my life mission?' and 'Why strive for awards and good grades?' With these doubts in his mind, he kept switching between studying and working until he finally returned to school at the University of Cambridge to further his studies in environmental architecture and sustainable design.

'Back then, it wasn't called "green building"; it was "passive design".' During this experience, he realised that, intentionally or otherwise, architecture had an impact on the environment. 'I felt like I was beginning to find a meaning to it all, at last.' On his return from the UK, M.K. Leung chose to teach and also founded his own firm. 'Did you think that was it?' After a few years, having completed some projects of different scales; including some that he liked and some that he didn't, and taking part in some 'Green Holidays', he got to know K.S. Wong and Tony. 'K.S. Wong made me feel envious of him, as he was doing everything I had always wanted to do.' And so M.K. Leung handed over his firm to his partner and went on to Ronald Lu & Partners. While it was common for architects to start out on their own, going back into the job market after having your own firm was unusual. 'I still think that it was the right decision. I often pondered how I should go about being an architect. And now I can finally see a direction.' Undoubtedly, there were many dramas within M.K. Leung's heart. 'Sometimes overthinking is a torture to yourself. However, knowing when to take a step forward, and do so at the right pace, and, at the same time, to do it with the participation of others with similar pace – that is the wisdom I am seeking.'

La Villa De La Salle

Frozen Zeal

Joey was in no hurry to return to Singapore after graduation and instead heeded the advice of a mentor and worked at Rocco Design (now Rocco Design Architects). 'Leslie Lu told me to be more mature and practical. He advised me against engaging in my imaginative and unconstrained designs, and that I should learn real and grounded architecture.' And so he spent the next three years following up on the Hollywood Terrace project. 'It was only then that I felt like I had truly graduated and could become an architect.'

However, soon afterwards, he chose not to continue working in architecture, and left the firm to open a secondhand bookstore with his friends. He had always been unexpected in his ways and prone to do whatever came into his mind. A flash of inspiration had prompted him to open the bookstore. During a seasonal sale at Page One, Joey and his friends saw so many queuing up at the counters to buy books that he thought to himself, 'Do the people of Hong Kong like reading that much?' Soon after, together with three architects and a friend, he started a secondhand book café called Architude (Architecture + Attitude).

After the opening of Architude, his parents asked him to return home to Singapore. His father owned a timber manufacturing business there, with its own factories and manufacturing lines, and Joey, the eldest son, was the natural heir to the business. However, given his passion for design, he felt conflicted; nevertheless, he took on the challenge, splitting his time between two roles. He ran his own sudio, iipod, as well as working in the family business. This took a toll on him, both physically and mentally.

Then came the unfortunate event of the September 11 terrorist attack in the United States. As he watched the World Trade Center towers collapse, he felt it was not only a disaster for the whole world but also a rude awakening for him. He was struck with the realisation that life really was short and fleeting, and he felt compelled to let go of all his doubts, risking falling out with his family to pursue his dream for design on his own in Hong Kong. Although he didn't have many resources upon leaving his family, he had to give it a try. 'Looking back at everything, if I hadn't made the decisions I made back then, I wouldn't be who I am today.' Perhaps everyone needs to arrive at the lowest point in their lives to find the answers they need.

Between the years of 2002 and 2016, Joey ran the Basheer Design Books HK bookstore. 'It was initially meant to be a simple realisation of my childhood dream of owning a bookstore.' The name of the bookstore – the literal translation of which is 'I can afford to lose' (Cantonese pronunciation of the word for 'book' is the same as for the word 'lose') – was in no way a statement of heroism from Joey; he was merely preparing himself mentally for the worst-case scenario. This actually had the reverse effect and made him more optimistic in the face of challenges. He also became bolder in overcoming them. Some say the value of life comes from conscientious hard work. What is important is not the result of the hard work, but the satisfaction of the work itself and the enjoyment derived from it. Hence, those who understand this can truly enjoy life and make the most of it.

From Point Architecture to Joey Ho Design and all the way to PAL Design Group, from his initial goal of pursuing architecture to switching to interior design, Joey seems to have it figured out. 'Whether it is architecture, cartoons or interior design, or even opening a bookstore, it is all a process of creation,' he claimed. However, despite his various ventures, he could not shake off his love for Hong Kong and his passion for architecture. 'Deep down, I still wanted to prove myself as an architect.' An opportunity later presented itself when a client came forward with a request to build a private residence. 'I poured all my

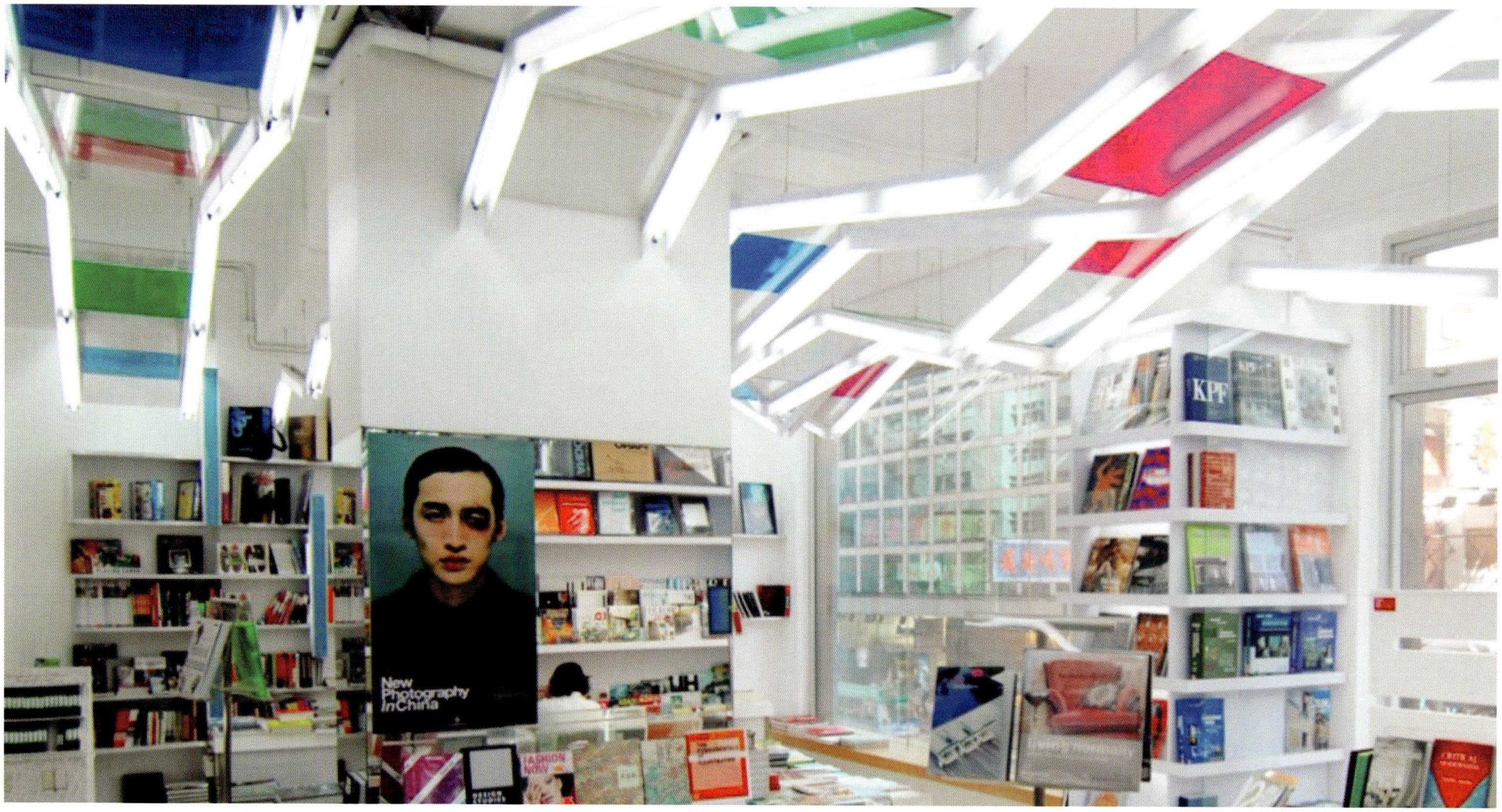
KPF
New Photography In China
FASHION NOW

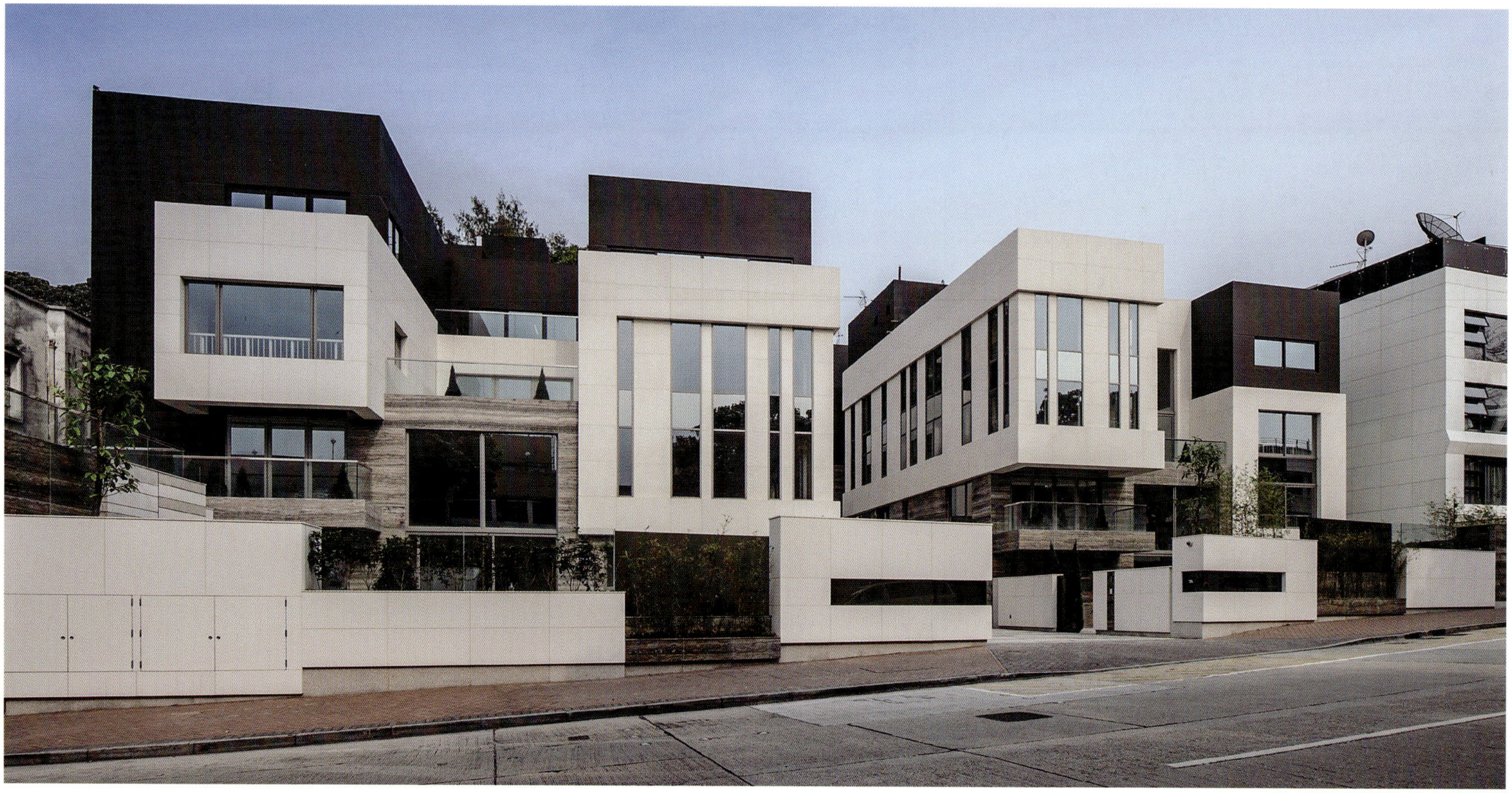

1. Basheer Design Books HK was opened to satisfy the owner's desire of owning a bookstore. The store offers a diverse range of books on design, art, fashion, painting and photography.
2. The design includes many 'empty spaces' that allow homeowners to enjoy and appreciate their living space to the fullest.

love and frustration into this project, giving it my all during the initial design phase.' His perseverance led him to two years of negotiation with the government of Singapore to acquire a larger land area. It was akin to a test from above, and, unfortunately, his design did not turn out as he had envisioned. 'My enthusiasm was dampened two years later,' he recounted. Upon reflection, Joey stated calmly, 'Sometimes all you need is a bucket of cold water to wake you up.' However, in the end, he did complete his first architecture project with the mindset of contentment.

With the first steps taken, the next ones naturally followed. Soon after came an architecture project in Hong Kong: La Villa De La Salle – four blocks of detached houses located in Kowloon Tong. This time around, Joey wasn't coming at it from the perspective of an architect but from that of a 'lifestyle connoisseur'. I have always been fond of the analogy put forth by British architect David Chipperfield, who likened a designer to a writer. 'A good writer doesn't flaunt his interest in his rhetoric. Instead, he uses it to tell a story, and the readers will also appreciate the beautiful words hidden within, but mainly be moved by the story.' As suggested by its name, the owners of 'La Villa' had wanted a home built of luxuries. 'I told them the first principle was the luxury of space. Given that in Hong Kong "one foot of land is worth an inch of gold", great luxury comes from being able to waste space.' Hence, Joey employed 'empty spaces' in his design that allowed the owner to freely enjoy space. More interestingly, though, Joey said his inspiration for stealing space came from the 'free-for-all unauthorised building works' of the ungovernable Kowloon Walled City.

Le Corbusier once said, 'Architecture only exists where there is a poetic emotion.' For Joey, the focus of design lies in the senses of people. Thus, design only exists when the door to these senses are opened. 'We must first understand how practicality is defined in modern society. The design of space has already surpassed the requirement for its basic function and has extended into the realm of taste and an attitude towards life.' Design has already become a part of Joey's life, and he is a firm believer in 'design to inspire' – improving the quality of life through design and blending it with the seeds of romance, so that the user may explore and experience the beauty of life and ultimately create their own unique attitude towards it.

West Kowloon

Reading Guidance

Moving on to West Kowloon, there are two landmarks that immediately come to mind. The first is the Hong Kong Cultural Centre in Tsim Sha Tsui, and the other is the West Kowloon Cultural District.

Any mention of the Hong Kong Cultural Centre brings back fond memories of the Old Tsim Sha Tsui Terminal. Replacing the old terminal with the windowless Hong Kong Cultural Centre was one of the biggest regrets of the architecture community. If they could go back in time, perhaps the designers and experts for the Cultural Centre would consider integrating parts of the exterior of the old terminal, or, even better, utilising the original, intricate classical colonnades as a design feature for the new building. They certainly should not have allowed the consulting company to relocate the six Doric columns to the Chatham Garden. At the time, conservationists had strongly demanded that the Tsim Sha Tsui Terminal should be preserved. However, their demands were met with an indirect refusal by the Urban Council, which was of the opinion that the layout of the terminal did not align with the design layout of the two theatres in the Cultural Centre. In the end, only one famous landmark of the past – the Kowloon-Canton Railway Clock Tower – was preserved, and it has since become lonely and silent, its former glory slowly diminishing.

In 2006, Mr K.C. King and I had just completed our work with the Tsim Sha Tsui Promenade Beautification Project, a project which encompassed the area from the Clock Tower to the square right in front of the Hong Kong Cultural Centre. During the same period, the HKSAR government was working on plans to relocate the Star Ferry Bus Terminus to facilitate the expansion of the area around the square into the Star House, by providing space for sidewalk cafés. To promote the initiative, the government had organised an open competition for its design and had built a bus terminal in Tsim Sha Tsui East for the sake of alignment. Ms Au King-chi, who was the then Commissioner for Tourism, once said that the new square should match the beauty of London's Trafalgar Square. Unfortunately, this once-in-a-lifetime opportunity never came to fruition due to resistance from various stakeholder organisations.

I had been brooding over this matter ever since and so I turned my attention towards making the bell of the clock tower, which had lost its voice for the previous seventy years, ring once again. With the combined efforts of Mr Xinbao Ding, Mr Shun Chi Ming, Mr Lau Chi-pang and Mr Cheng Cho-Ming, the clock finally rang again at 6pm on 9 December, 2021. While lost historic buildings cannot be retrieved, we can still trace the footprints of our past by regaining a familiar voice. Silence was not golden in this instance, but sound most certainly was.

West Kowloon – Not Just a Cultural District

The most important infrastructure in West Kowloon is the West Kowloon Cultural District. As for the ins and outs of West Kowloon, readers may refer to Chapter 3.12 ('The Love and Hate Relationship with West Kowloon Cultural District') of my book *The Untold Stories of Raymong Fung*. While everyone was joyfully shuttling back and forth

once ridiculed as a cultural desert, into the cultural hub of Asia. Now it appears that this decision showed great foresight. In less than two decades, Hong Kong has evolved from a city that was once described as a 'borrowed place' into the metropolis of today where people have a strong sense of belonging. The West Kowloon Cultural District initiative has garnered much attention from cultural communities worldwide through its global architecture competition. After two failed attempts at organising art exhibitions many years ago, another event, the Hong Kong International Art Fair[2], has made a comeback, and its subsequent success has even attracted the internationally renowned Art Basel to come looking for a slice of the action. Since then, Hong Kong really has established itself in the Asia art scene.

The overall design of the West Kowloon Cultural District has undergone two rounds of international competition. In the first round, Norman Foster won with his design for the world's largest glass canopy, which would cover more than ten giant cultural facilities. People were very proud that their city would be able to boast such a masterpiece, but they were not aware that the canopy would need to exceed thirty storeys in height to cover the entire complex. It was only after experts had carried out rounds of technical analysis did they understand the technical problems involved, which included the following: the spatial obstructions posed by the huge supporting structures; the greenhouse effect caused by the huge canopy; safety issues likely to arise during adverse weather conditions and the overall long term maintenance costs, which would no doubt entail an endless stream of repair costs. Once the reality had dawned on everyone, it was decided that this extravagant white elephant of a design was to be abandoned.

The West Kowloon Cultural District of today is selected from the second master plan, and although it once again adopts the design of Foster, this time it is a very practical proposal; seventeen building complexes neatly lined up along the work-in-progress Art Avenue, with the Artist Square being the focal point. Readers should note that only the Xiqu Centre, the M+ Museum of Contemporary Visual Culture, and

through the West Kowloon Art Park, I recalled the art exhibitions held in Hong Kong many years ago. The first one was held at the China Resources Building in Wan Chai, but as visitors were few and far between, it died a death after just two rounds of exhibitions. I was worried the West Kowloon Cultural District would turn out to be another white elephant.

Looking back over the past twenty years, the people of Hong Kong had yet to develop much interest in cultural endeavours. When the announcement was made that a piece of land by the waterfront with a market value of hundreds of billions of dollars was to be used for the construction of cultural facilities, it was met with much criticism, as it was perceived to be an empty gesture designed solely to improve the image of the government. There were reasons to believe that the decision-makers at that time were inspired by the Bilbao revitalisation project in Spain[1], London's Southbank Centre and Millennium Park in Chicago. The government was determined to realise the vision of turning Hong Kong, a city

the M+ Pavilion and Competition Pavilions, which were added later, were the result of architecture competitions. The rest, including West Kowloon Art Park and the Blackbox Theatre, respectively designed by West 8[3] and DLN Architects Limited; the Lyric Theatre Complex designed by UNStudio[4], AD+RG Architecture Design and Research Group Limited; the WKCDA Tower and Conservation and Storage Facility designed by Herzog & de Meuron Architekten; and the Hong Kong Palace Museum, Artist Square Tower, Artist Square, and the hotels and exhibition halls of West Kowloon, amongst others, all came into being through different means and approaches. Most of the West Kowloon projects were designed by internationally renowned architects with local companies mainly in charge of engineering management. The core purpose of this book is to introduce the masterpieces designed by Hong Kong architects and designers; hence, under this premise, only the Hong Kong Palace Museum designed by Ricco Yim, the Xiqu Centre co-designed by Bing Thom Architects and Ronald Lu and Partners, the M+ Pavilion designed by Mr Vincent Pang and the four locally designed pieces at the Competition Pavilion by Mr Paul Tse and Ms Evelyn Ting will be introduced in later chapters.

The West Kowloon Cultural District is not the only public leisure space in Hong Kong. Nearby, in Tsim Sha Tsui, is the Hong Kong Cultural Centre and surrounding cultural centres and museums, each facility playing its own individual role. The cultural facilities managed by the Leisure and Cultural Services Department aim to promote the art and cultural scene of Hong Kong, and the core objective of the West Kowloon Cultural District is to attract the best artistic talent into Hong Kong, so that, in turn, more visitors are attracted to the city, thereby transforming Hong Kong into the art centre of Asia.

From the perspective of an architect, the most pronounced achievement of the West Kowloon Cultural District is the provision of its spacious green lawn – something that, prior to its creation, people in Hong Kong could only dream of. Indeed, there are forty hectares of green space in which people can wander freely and enjoy themselves. The construction of underground car parks and roads, despite the cost, demonstrated a desire to follow Norman Foster's original proposal to create Hong Kong's first garden district – a precinct in which pedestrians and vehicles would be kept separate. Such people-oriented urban design leaves a deep impression on visitors of the West Kowloon Cultural District. As the unfenced promenade begins to take shape, it has added a sense of lightness and relaxation brought about by walking through the green lawn. This is the refinement this city deserves, and it is a source of pride that has been long overdue. In comparison with the Sydney Darling Harbour, London's Southbank Centre and the Chicago's Millennium Park, the fact that land-scarce Hong Kong has created such a vast green space makes it all the more precious.

Causes and Effects of the Renovation of the Hong Kong Museum of Art

There are other large structures in the West Kowloon area, such as the Kowloon Station and the tunnel ventilation shaft designed by Farrells and the high-speed rail terminus designed by Aedas, all of which are landmarks showcasing the talents of internationally renowned architects.

In the direction of Tsim Sha Tsui, the new wing added to the front of the Ocean Terminal is also the work of Norman Foster. This wing is in harmony with the original architecture style of over half a century ago; its design is not one that highlights Foster's personal flair. In the same district is the Hong Kong Museum of Art, whose renovation plan was first proposed by me twenty years ago. Together with the then chief curator, Mr Gerard Tsang, we planned and submitted the draft proposal for the transformation of the museum, but to no avail. A few years later, when Mr Tang Hoi-chiu took over as the chief curator, I made yet another suggestion to build a new Hong Kong Ink Painting Gallery next to the museum. Again, the proposal received no feedback whatsoever. Two more years passed, and Ms Eve Tam took over as the museum director and implemented a major renovation plan, entrusting the Architectural Services Department to coordinate the initiative. Ms Vivien Fung was put in charge of the design and related consultation. As expected, it was riddled with many challenges which were eventually overcome and success was reaped.

The successful transformation of the Hong Kong Museum of Art led to the subsequent large scale renovations for the Hong Kong Museum of History and the Hong Kong Science Museum, both of which went through open competition processes to determine their designs. Each participant was required to design a façade for the existing building. At first glance, there was nothing special about these 'new clothes', but the judges appreciated the fact that the designs could be modified according to changing times. With a project that takes eight years to complete, the more flexible and adaptable the plan, the more relevant it will be. The development of such flexible plans also showed what might be possible for the future transformation of other cultural venues managed by the Leisure and Cultural Services Department.

Aside from the sparkling new masterpieces of the West Kowloon district, many visitors have made a beeline for the stunning beauty of 1881, the former Marine Police Headquarters Compound. However, many friends in the profession see 1881 as an example of how not to revitalise a historic building. Because Hong Kong's historic structures are as rare as hen's teeth, the people of this city are keenly sensitive to how those structures are treated. Even ordinary-looking buildings such as old military barracks are regarded with special interest, for example, the three barracks in Kowloon Park that have been preserved, graded and even rebuilt. I designed one of them and rebuilt it into the Health Education Exhibition and Resource Centre, and this was followed by the remaining two barracks which were repurposed by the Leisure and Cultural Services Department into the Hong Kong Heritage Discovery Centre. It has been reported that Barrack No. 58 will be rebuilt from the current collection repositories of the Hong Kong Museum of History into a restoration centre for Chinese antiques.

Pondering on the Mismatch of Historic Buildings

Although there are very few of them in Hong Kong and some are still left empty or are unpopular with their users, the question of how we can better utilise historic buildings is an interesting one. Upon further examination, there seems to be a contradiction caused by resource mismatch. The people of Hong Kong may have double standards when it comes to historic buildings; they appreciate their classical beauty, yet are stingy when it comes to paying for their maintenance. The inconveniences common to unmaintained historic buildings – lack of electricity, leaking windows, termite infestations and outdated facilities – are gradually becoming valid reasons for their unpopularity with users. However, if these buildings were handed over to those who appreciate history, art and culture, they would probably apply to the Revitalising Historic Buildings Through Partnership Scheme for use of such buildings, and they might receive the desired feedbacks and support. Since the Scheme is voluntary in nature, most applicants are more than willing to deal with the potential problems that arise from the use of historic buildings. The historic buildings left in Hong Kong today are mainly the old police stations and the Court of Final Appeal Building. Look at the

original appearance of Tai Kwun; it underwent chaotic modification and addition, which was unfortunate, to say the least. However, once it was revitalised under the Scheme and taken on by those who loved art and culture, it has received positive feedback from all walks of life.

I shall use the North Kowloon Magistracy and the Kowloon Magistracy as examples to illustrate the problem of resource mismatch. The former was left desolated for years, and it was later transformed into the Savannah College of Arts and Design through the above mentioned scheme. Although it was put to a suitable use at first, the school was unfortunately later closed down due to insufficient student intake. The Kowloon Magistracy is an elegant piece of pseudo-classical Greek architecture. The building has a colonnade of Ionic columns, which is very rare in Hong Kong. During the Japanese occupation, it was used as a military office and the building was decommissioned in 2000. It was subsequently converted into a court storage facility, then later repurposed into the Lands Tribunal.

It is utterly inconceivable that, on the one hand, society realises the rarity of historic buildings, yet, on the other hand, continues to abuse them. It suddenly occurred to me that if the two magistracies had been repurposed into museums, their elegant aspects and the content within would have been perfect complements. The Chinese YMCA of Hong Kong Centre located on Bridges Street is another example. During the early days of Hong Kong, it was a community hall used for public events. The founder of modern Chinese literature, Mr Lu Xun, gave two speeches there on 18th and 19th February, 1927 – 'Silent China' and 'The Old Tune Has Been Sung', respectively. The building contained Hong Kong's first indoor swimming pool and a

suspended indoor running track shaped like a circular pan. Part of the building is currently being used as a residential care home for persons with disabilities.

As Hong Kong transforms into Asia's cultural hub, I firmly believe that this city has the necessary conditions to revitalise the aforementioned buildings. Considering the cultural characteristics of Hong Kong, their potential tenants could include: the Hong Kong Literature Museum; the Hong Kong Film and Television Museum; the Hong Kong Ink Museum; the Hong Kong Comics Museum; and the Hong Kong Intangible Cultural Heritage Archives.

Conservation Issues Concerning Old Buildings and Districts

I encourage readers to visit the old districts regularly before they disappear, including areas that are filled with local flavours such as Yau Ma Tei, Mong Kok and Sham Shui Po. The leather shops along Tai Nan Street in Sham Shui Po have experienced a rejuvenation, with new cafés springing up in the area, earning it the nickname New Brooklyn. The Cheung Sha Wan Catholic Primary School is the newest and hippest school building, with a refreshing layout based on a circular corridor.

The Yau Ma Tei Fruit Market, Temple Street Night Market and the Apliu Street Wet Market are now rare examples of local customs in modern Hong Kong. The frequent requests to the government or the Urban Renewal Authority to preserve these local characteristics are very often just wishful thinking on our part. Even if the appearance of these buildings could be preserved, declining industries therein will eventually become unsustainable and disappear naturally. The Broadway Cinematheque, hidden in Prosperous Garden, is one of the very few commercial theatres in Hong Kong that screens non-mainstream movies. The cinema has been given an alternative style, designed by Gary Chang. It has been twenty-five years since it first opened, and the original design has long since faded. In 2012, Kenneth Tse took charge of the renovation work for both the cinema and the Kubrick bookstore next to it. It is an alternative bookstore themed around movies, and it has witnessed the persistent love for movies shown by the people of Hong Kong.

The West Kowloon Mediation Centre located in Cheung Sha Wan was designed by Mr William Tsang. The eye-catching design comprises a row of red boxes connected in a series, making it especially eye-catching. Tsang specialises in using metal materials and he likes hard geometric shapes, as well. This approach has also been reflected through his other masterpiece, a new waterfront facility located on the Long Mei artificial beach at Tolo Harbour. The facilities there are a set of smooth, wavy metal structures that very much reflect his usual style.

There are three hidden architectural works worth visiting in the area. The first one is the Correctional Services Department Staff Club designed by Mr Kevin Li. Composed of several square boxes, it is a modern building made delightful by its accentuation of colours. A lot of effort must have been put into the design for it to have been approved by the Disciplined Services back in those days. The second building, hidden on a hill, is the Jao Tsung-I Academy co-designed by Humphrey Wong and P&T Group.

The design has cleverly integrated the old premises into the new building, thus combining Eastern and Western elements while not appearing too old-fashioned. Both the garden and the space within create a peaceful effect. In addition, the 'collision' between the white walls of the upper area and the red bricks of the lower area lightens up the place with an understated beauty. There is also the Jockey Club Creative Arts Centre located in Shek Kip Mei, another masterpiece co-designed by P&T Group, Humphrey Wong, Steven Chu, Anson Tsang and Kenneth Tse. It was rebuilt from an old industrial building which serves to provide artists with an affordable working space, adding an artistic ambience to this old district.

The third piece of architecture is located near the Mei Ho House, which was the earliest resettlement building in Hong Kong and became the model for many public housing estates. Mei Ho House is located within the Shek Kip Mei Estate, which was developed after the unfortunate Shek Kip Mei fire[5]. During the redevelopment phase of the Shek Kip Mei Estate, the government preserved one of the buildings and, through the Revitalising Historic Buildings Through Partnership Scheme, with AD+RG Architecture Design and Research Group Limited leading its design, the Mei Ho House was transformed into an affordable youth hostel. Inside the hostel, exhibitions detailing the development history of the resettlement areas including the public housing initiatives were put on show so that their history could be preserved. That part of history is also a collective memory for the people of Hong Kong who were seeking to settle down at that time.

Walking up from Shek Kip Mei along Nam Cheong Street, there is a building named the Public Health Laboratory Centre, which was built in response to the 2003 outbreak of the Severe Acute Respiratory Syndrome. The building is sympathetic to the features of the surrounding terrain and incorporates carefully

crafted contours of proper proportions, all of which have been masterfully designed by Winnie Ho.

Tai Kok Tsui gives the public the impression that it is a depot for metal equipment. It is hard to imagine that there is a creative miniature workshop therein called Solo, designed by RAD. On this otherwise nondescript street, I am attracted by the dynamic yellow boxes hanging on the outer wall of the workshop to cover the radiators of the air conditioning system – a clever functional addition that also enriches the overall appearance.

Notes

1 The Strategic Plan for the Revitalisation of Metropolitan Bilbao: Located in northern Spain, Bilbao was once the leading industrial city in Europe. As a result of the low prices in Eastern Europe and Asia, it later experienced a severe economic recession. In the 1990s, the Bilbao Municipal Government decided to abandon its industrial role and rebuild itself as a capital of culture and art, especially the Guggenheim Museum, which has become a world-renowned piece of architecture.

2 Hong Kong International Art Fair: Hong Kong International Art Fair, also known as Art HK, was founded in 2007. It was later acquired by Art Basel in 2013 and renamed Art Basel Hong Kong.

3 West 8: An urban planning and landscape architecture firm established in 1987 in Rotterdam, Netherlands, by Adriaan Geuze.

4 UNStudio: United Network Studio is a Dutch architecture firm founded in 1988 by Ben Van Berkel and Caroline Bos.

5 Shek Kip Mei fire: On Christmas night, 1953, a fire broke out in squatter huts in Shek Kip Mei, Kowloon, leaving some 50,000 people homeless. The incident led to the birth of public housing in Hong Kong.

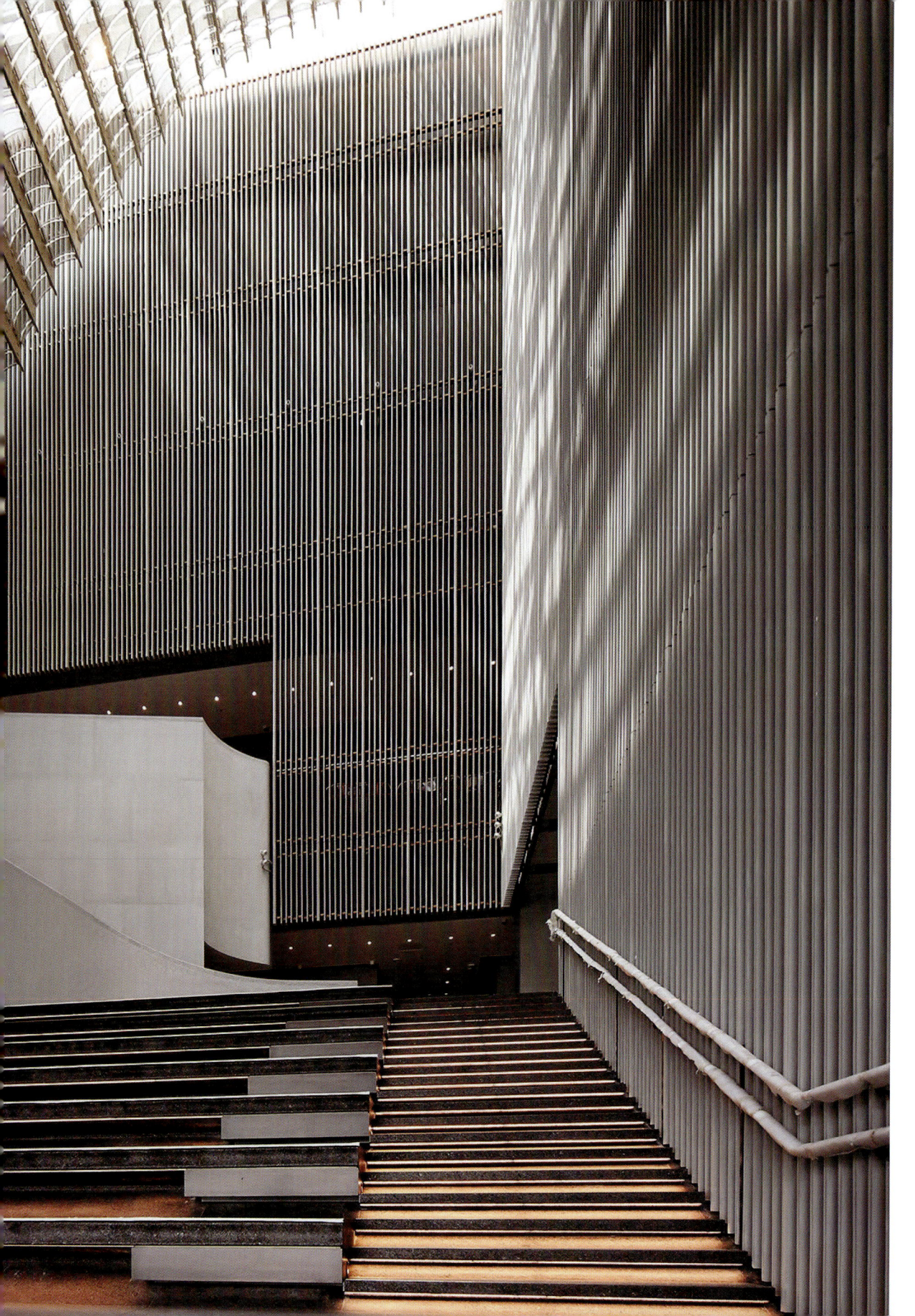

The Hong Kong Palace Museum

Every Cloud Has a Silver Lining

Every time I visit the West Kowloon Cultural District, I am enveloped in a comforting feeling that permeates my whole being. As I stroll along the waterfront with my bare feet stepping on the soft, feather-like grass and the warm sun shining down on me, I am able to feel a gentle, soothing heat on my cheeks. The sea breeze carries with it the mingled scent of fresh, fragrant grass. In the distance, a building in beige-gold hues stands proudly on the grassy ridge, emanating shimmering traces of gold in the sunshine.

On the occasion of this visit, the construction work for the Hong Kong Palace Museum was in full swing. Rocco Yim spoke eloquently in his office, telling stories about the Hong Kong Palace Museum in a chronological order. This was not the first time Rocco had designed a museum, but it was his first in Hong Kong.

The Hong Kong Palace Museum was inspired by The Palace Museum in Beijing, but Rocco did not intend that it would merely be a copy. 'The impression that The Palace Museum in Beijing gave me wasn't about the structures; it was the sense of cohesion manifested by the enormous square.' The Chinese culture is one of the few in the world that has never experienced a cultural discontinuation. There is a strong sense of continuity. Graceful tolerance with the cohesion and continuity of space are the essences of Rocco's design of the Hong Kong Palace Museum.

The Hong Kong Palace Museum sits on a grassy slope, creating a continuity with the space of the park in front of it. The predominant shade of beige-gold exudes the elegance of the Chinese dynasty and the temperament of ancient Chinese cultural artefacts and relics. The interior interprets Chinese culture through imagery. The museum encompasses five floors, featuring nine exhibition halls. 'Due to its topography, the upward development model has become a feature of Hong Kong, but few museums need to be built so tall; usually, three floors are enough.' There are three atriums in the museum, each one facing a different direction and taking in different vistas of Hong Kong. 'You can see Hong Kong Island to the south, Lantau Island to the west, and the entire West Kowloon Cultural District to the east. This is the urban landscape of Hong Kong.'

Inspired by traditional tiled roofs, Rocco opened up three atriums with a unique outline. Although divided into five floors, the connection and fluidity between the atriums creates a strong sense of continuity in the overall space. The curved mesh at the ceiling of the hall ensures it is bathed in patterend natural light. With the interlacing of curves and straight lines, it pulls the viewer in and takes them upwards. 'Just like the spaces in Chinese architecture, you will not see everything at first glance. New vistas open up as you journey through the space; a bit like the concept of the silver lining, compelling one to explore slowly and discover more.' The design of this imagery is likened to the substance and characteristics of Chinese culture, which is deeply meaningful and intriguing.

Unlike the streamlined tiled roof, the exhibition hall, theatre and backstage areas are designed mainly with straight lines. 'This relates to the exhibits we display. For example, in Frank Gehry's Guggenheim Museum in Bilbao, you can see the modern and contemporary works of art the museum displays working with the exhibition hall, so even if curved elements are added, it will still be feasible. However, if you want to display calligraphy and painting, wouldn't a square space be exactly

1   2

1   The stacked heights and visual axial transitions of the three atrium spaces are shown.
2   The Hong Kong Palace Museum is located at the west end of the West Kowloon Cultural District, an end point of the main east-west axis of the district, and it is in dialogue with the M+ Museum in the middle of the axis.

Untold Stories

 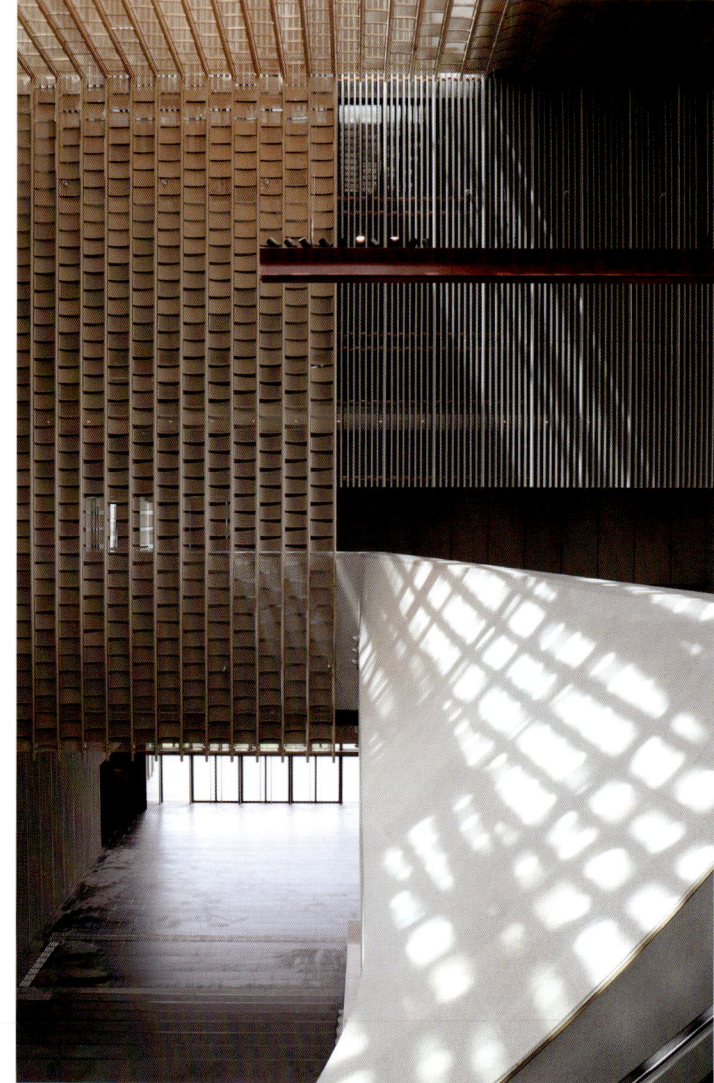

| 1 2 | 3 4 |

1   Natural light passes through the transparent ceiling like a veil, illuminating the large steps of the atrium on the second floor.
2   Looking down at the atrium on the second floor from the fourth floor, one appreciates how light and shadow can highlight the changes in time and space.
3   Within the atrium there are cloud-shaped wooden chairs designed by Andre Fu so that visitors can stop and rest after their visit.
4   The 400-seat lecture hall is the central element of the Palace Academy, located on the lower ground floor.

Untold Stories

what you need? Therefore, design must also respect its content and function.'

While formulating the concept plan for the West Kowloon Cultural District in the early years, Rocco took inspiration from the famous handscroll painting *Along the River During the Qingming Festival*. He had hoped to explain that the attractiveness of a place did not necessarily come from its various landmarks but, rather, from the cohesion and energy generated by the various activities in which the local community participated. Although this concept plan was never adopted, the design of the Hong Kong Palace Museum was still inseparable from his architectural language. 'I have always insisted that the shape of the building should reflect the character and needs of the inner space. The streamlined design of the East Kowloon Cultural Centre is born in response to the flow of people, and the Hong Kong Palace Museum symbolises a certain meaning and has a statement.'

Looking at the enlarged manuscript diagram of the East Kowloon Cultural Centre behind Rocco, I am suddenly reminded that also progressing in parallel with the Hong Kong Palace Museum was the East Kowloon Cultural Centre. Rocco's first cultural project in Hong Kong should have been the East Kowloon Cultural Centre. However, due to disruptions that stretched over many years, the Hong Kong Palace Museum took over and was completed before it.

Unlike the location of the Hong Kong Palace Museum which is within the West Kowloon Cultural District, the East Kowloon Cultural Centre is located in the downtown area and is surrounded by lively communities. Thus, it is not just a place for commuters to pass by, but also a recreational venue, for example, for tai chi and games of chess – activities that contribute to the very character of the community. 'This area is very mature and rich in urban fabric, so from an environmental point of view, the objectives of the two cultural projects are quite different.' Rocco has always refused to design buildings that are out of tune with their surrounding environment. The East Kowloon Cultural Centre is integrated seamlessly into the existing urban fabric.

Regular theatres are usually only crowded when there is is a performance; when nothing is playing, visitors are few and far between. Rocco has a different understanding of cultural venues. 'With or without performances or shows, I hope that the East Kowloon Cultural Centre will be crowded every day and that passers-by will be exposed to different cultural information.' This idea has been squarely reflected in the design of the architecture.

The design of the East Kowloon Cultural Centre focuses on circulation, and yet at the same time it also incorporates a streamlined design that allows visitors to naturally 'go with the flow'. The lobby of the cultural centre is also the antechamber of the theatre, conveniently connecting all parts of the community. In addition to being a formal performance venue, there are also small-scale dance studios, rehearsal rooms and other venues used daily by the community, 'It is like a community hall, not only an elite performance venue, but also designed to influence the community and the people around it with culture.' In fact, this also reflects another design technique of Rocco's: blurring the boundaries of different functions. 'Be it boundaries or what-not, I don't like to distinguish them clearly. Of course, after blurring these boundaries, unnecessary interference on the users cannot possibly be avoided.' Although Rocco's voice was not loud, it was sonorous, 'I don't want the East Kowloon Cultural Centre to be a big white elephant.'

Following the Guangdong and Yunnan Provincial Museums, Rocco finally brought his first museum design to Hong Kong. Was there still any other architecture on his wish list that he wanted to design? Rocco paused, then continued in his soft voice, 'Actually, I don't care much about the type of architecture, but I want to continue challenging myself in terms

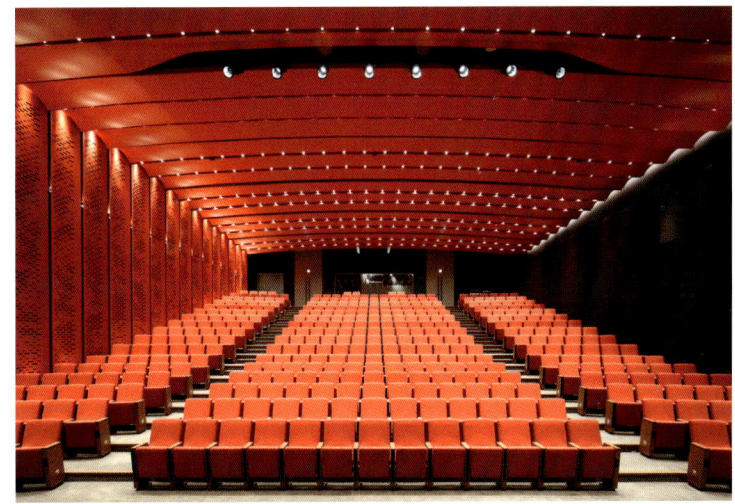

1	2 3	1 The East Kowloon Cultural Centre not only provides a performing arts venue that was lacking in the district, it also uses the architecture to integrate with the existing urban fabric. It optimises the public space system and improves the three-dimensional pedestrian network.

2 The lobby of the Cultural Centre is also the lobby of the theatre, and it serves as a commuter thoroughfare connecting all parts of the community.
3 The indoor public spaces of the Cultural Centre are integrated with cultural facilities to establish a dialogue with the outdoor square.

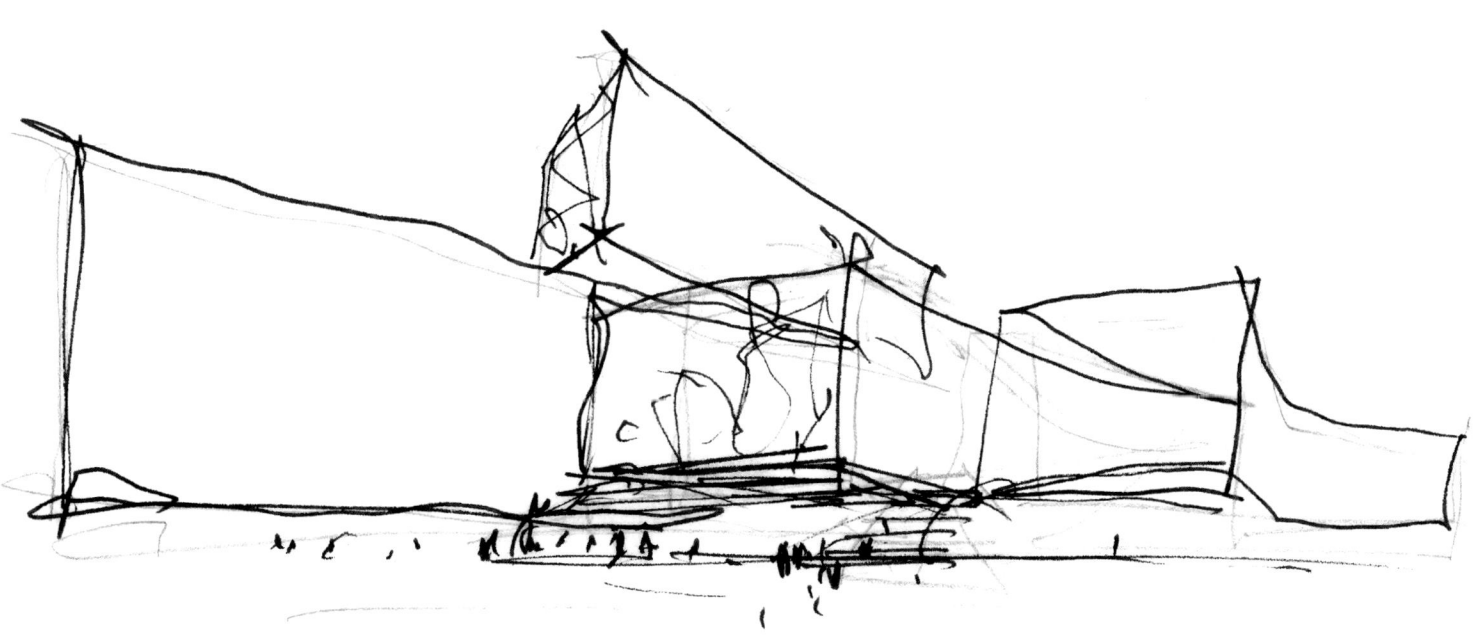

of design style.' The style he mentioned is not about changing to an exaggerated architectural language but adhering to his consistent belief and attitude towards architecture. With sincerity and authenticity, to establish a design that complements the environment, space and form, 'It is very rare to be able to bring to people a refreshing feeling under this circumstance.' Uncharacteristically, he raised his voice to describe the new generation's insatiable appetite for novelty. As opposed to the architects of the previous generation, such as I.M. Pei and Paul Rudolph, who were satisfied doing the same thing all their life, 'Is it a must for an architect to create something new instead of doing one thing consistently?' Rocco pondered this, but he did not give an answer.

Over more than four decades in the field of architecture, Rocco has had his share of encounters with naysayers and disappointing outcomes, yet he has nevertheless managed to roll with the punches while keeping his calm. Perhaps this attitude is better summed up by a passage written by the Chinese writer Yu Qiuyu in *Notes from My Mountain Abode*:

Maturity is a bright lustre but not a dazzling brilliance; a mellow sound but not annoying to the ears; an unhurried steadiness that cares not the reactions of others; a grace and ease of taking things as they are without undue complaint; a smile indifferent to noise and excitement; a kind of apathy that washes away the extremes; a profundity that needs no publicity; and a height that is not precipitous but commands a fairly distant view.

Hong Kong Museum of Art

A New Cubic Look

The renovation of the Hong Kong Museum of Art initiated by the Architectural Services Department, began in 2012. Instead of building a new museum from scratch, the HKSAR government completely renovated the old architecture, preserving its original cubic shape and connecting it to its surroundings with the addition of glass curtain walls.

Initially, the project was intended to be an interior renovation of only the restaurant and bookstore on the ground floor, but during the design process, the architect found that, even if those two spaces were to be redesigned, apart from adding a sense of fashion to the interior, the relationship between the Hong Kong Museum of Art and the surrounding architectures would not improve, and it would remain merely an interior renovation. Therefore, the architect in charge of the project, Ms Vivien Fung, proposed a major transformation to make the museum more connected to its surrounding environment and facilities: as well as introducing striking elements in its expansion to create a brand-new look.

Vivien enjoys reflecting on the relationship between community and individuals. However, during her time in school, she frequently stated her desire to become a dentist. Her family even once suggested that she pursue a career in medicine. Vivien's decision to become an architect has a back story. One day, her father, an engineer, returned home and expressed his frustration at being bossed around by an architect at work. Vivien realised that, despite being head of the household, her father faced opposition in his professional life from an architect. This incident, coupled with the passion she had had for drawing since young, piqued Vivien's interest in architecture, and she eventually pursued the study of architecture in the UK. After graduation, she obtained her professional qualification and subsequently worked in London.

Due to the economic situation in the UK, she returned to Hong Kong in 1993 and worked for Tao Ho Design International Limited and Foster + Partners, where she worked on interior design projects for the Hong Kong International Airport and Hung Hom Station. Having worked with international teams while abroad, she found the direction and style of local teams to be very different. She had learned to discuss the implementation plan with the contracting team at the very beginning of a project rather than producing a design first and then simply passing the plans on to be implemented. Due to the increasing number of commercial projects, she decided to join the Architectural Services Department, because she did not want to be too constrained, and working there would better suit her personal preferences regarding the pace of work, space and project selection.

During the preparatory phase of the project, Vivien visited the Hong Kong Museum of Art to view the collections there. She marvelled at how rich and valuable they were. The old museum had an inconspicuous appearance. Vivien first took down the large archway in the public area and transplanted the old banyan trees to locations that gave them space to continue growing. She designed an art square to be used as an exhibition venue and also set up signage along the route from Nathan Road to the Museum to improve its connection with the community. The original architectural design was inward-facing, but now with the early additions and modifications made to the museum removed, a striking, multi-level framed floor-to-ceiling glass wall facing Victoria Harbour has been erected, linking the stunning views of the harbour to the public space and creating a more open layout. The renovation project was completed in 2019 and, in 2021, Vivien had a meeting with Mr Kenneth Cho Yau Kan, the original designer of the museum. During their exchange, Mr Yau shared insights into the design origins of the museum, giving the architecture a newfound meaning.

Another individual who was part of the renovation project for the Hong Kong Museum of Art was Mr Tony Lau. He graduated in Australia in 2003 and is a film fanatic who enjoyed making short films when he was a student. His decision to study architecture stemmed from his belief that it was a combination of reality and fantasy, akin to using construction materials to build stage scenery. He was also influenced by Mathias Woo, a writer who specialised in architecture and liked to dabble in architecture, art and film to explore the close relationships between the three. In 2013, Tony Lau joined the Architectural Services Department and became part of the redevelopment project for the Hong Kong Museum of Art. He reflected that, back then, he was still in a learning stage, and when he learnt of the West Kowloon Cultural District, Lau began to wonder, why wasn't it enough to simply improve upon the existing cultural facilities in the area, especially since the Hong Kong Museum of Art and the Hong Kong Cultural Centre were already in existence.

As a young architect, he has seen first hand from the renovation project of the Hong Kong Museum of Art that many public places in Hong Kong can be given a refreshed look. He aspires to actively participate in the renovation work of controversial buildings in the future, while also hoping that he might have more opportunities to showcase his talents while working at the Department.

Untold Stories

1. The Hong Kong Museum of Art faces Victoria Harbour, and the exterior wall includes floor-to-ceiling windows that frame up the seaside view.
2. The use of clear glass allows the introduction of sunlight and helps to bring nature indoors.
3. The building retains its original cubic shape and has been enhanced using modern design techniques to give it a refreshed feel.

West Kowloon Mediation Centre・Long Mei Beach
Shing Kai Road Refuse Collection Point

A Minimalistic Temperature

To begin our conversation about the West Kowloon Mediation Centre and the Shing Kai Road Refuse Collection Point, William Tsang humorously began by quoting Hong Kong film director Gordon Chan's interpretation of Hong Kong-made films. 'The price of leftovers, but the taste of a drumstick.' In other words, you get more than what you paid for.

The biggest challenges faced by these two projects were insufficient funding and time. Many works of architecture are built with money, but as the American postmodernist and deconstructivist Frank Gehry once said, light and air don't cost anything. There are many minimalistic and refined materials available, such as fair-faced concrete, but that requires fine craftsmanship. So, at the West Kowloon Mediation Centre and the Shing Kai Road Refuse Collection Point, William instead chose to build with simple materials – aluminum, corrugated cardboard and metal mesh.

Architecture is often designed to reflect its particular purpose. The red-coloured West Kowloon Mediation Centre, with its large garden, is of a Japanese-style design adorned with greeneries. Individual rooms are surrounded by a landscape of bamboo, rocks, stones and sand. Together with the courtyard garden, these spaces create a serene and peaceful atmosphere, bringing tranquillity to the senses. In addition to providing designated routes to individual rooms to protect users' privacy, such design also creates a harmonious atmosphere, making it easier for users of the centre to achieve resolution and agreement.

In the Kai Tak Development District, in addition to the use of brick walls and aluminium strips, the newly built refuse collection point on site 1J4 uses floor-to-ceiling glazing to maximise natural light. The building is like a glass box that gives people a comfortable working environment. For the smaller ancillary buildings nearby such as storage spaces and washrooms, prefabricated components such as corrugated panels and aluminium strips, and even bricks for the exterior walls, have been used to streamline the construction process.

William values the work process of his team and does not wish to burden the construction team with excessively complex design. While working for P&T Group, he witnessed first-hand how constant revisions could eventually lead to deviation from the original, intended design. He was convinced that as an architect, he ought to have an accurate understanding of construction methods when designing and selecting materials. He strives to produce the best results within resonable parameters, and at the same time be mindful of reducing the need for maintenance to improve sustainability.

William views the American architect Louis Isadore Kahn as his idol, and he believes that architecture should respect the local climate, culture and traditions. His use of geometry, repetition, light and shadow are important creative concepts which determine the materials, techniques and even the spatial appearance of an architecture.

The Tai Po Lung Mei Beach, adjacent to Tai Mei Tuk and Plover Cove Reservoir, is an artificial beach complete with service buildings and includes an observation deck and changing facilities. Sitting on the observation deck, one can take in a great view of the sunset. The beach was officially opened on 23 June 2021.

The design of the entire project strives to be open, airy and functional. The observation deck's design uses aluminium tubes to create an undulating roof that echoes the Pat Sin Leng ridgeline behind it, while the exterior wall is made of fibrous white clay panels using bamboo strips as templates. On top of the outdoor shower facilities, there is a triangular skylight that allows users to enjoy views of the mountains.

William remarked bluntly that prior to joining the Architectural Services Department, he had been engaged in residential design projects which wore out his passion for the art. He believed that had he maintained that same path, it would not have led to any changes or improvements for his career, and he would have eventually become much less energetic. His move to the Architectural Services Department was due solely to his wife, also an architect, who knew that he would get more room to showcase his talent there.

During his career, William has been moved by the spirit of the Japanese architect Tadao Ando, who approached each project as if it would be his last and as if he had to fight for it. This 'spirit' of architecture is reflected in Ando's signature pursuit of perfection, meticulously and consistently polishing rough materials into refined pieces through sheer hard work and dedication. William hopes that future architectural design can incorporate a touch more humanistic temperament.

1. The red-coloured exterior of the West Kowloon Mediation Centre has a large courtyard that helps create a harmonious atmosphere.
2. Brick walls and aluminium strips help to increase the transparency of the refuse collection point and invoke a sense of simplicity and neatness.

1   Tai Po Lung Mei Beach is the first artificial beach with a landscaped terrace and a long causeway.
2   The scenic platform and causeway on the beach echo the Pat Sin Leng Ridge in the distance.
3   The outdoor shower facility is topped by a triangular skylight built of fair-faced concrete, exuding a sense of simplicity.

Winner of the Flower Festival Photography Contest

Jao Tsung-I Academy

A Refined and Silent Nurture

Since the end of the nineteenth century, the current site of the Jao Tsung-I Academy has seen many different occupants. It has been a customs station, a labourers' dwelling, a quarantine station, a prison, a hospital for infectious diseases, and a psychiatric rehabilitation centre. Throughout its history, this place has met the changing needs of the society it served, each new incarnation adding to its unique story.

Shortly after completing the Jockey Club Creative Arts Centre, Humphrey Wong partnered with P & T Group in the design of the Jao Tsung-I Academy. Jao Tsung-I Academy, formerly known as Lai Chi Kok Hospital, is a group of Grade III historic buildings. Built on a hillside, the buildings are divided into upper, middle and low zones, giving the complex a distinct sense of layering, much like the composition of a painting with a foreground, middle ground and background.

However, the site of the former Lai Chi Kok Hospital was not the first-choice location for the Jao Tsung-I Academy. 'At that time, the Hong Kong Institute for the Promotion of Chinese Culture approached me, because they wanted to apply for the North Kowloon Magistrates' Court to be part of the Revitalising Historic Buildings Through Partnership Scheme.' Humphrey told them bluntly that the North Kowloon Magistrates' Court was not suitable, whereas the Lai Chi Kok Hospital was the better choice. In his eyes, Lai Chi Kok Hospital was not merely a place or building complex but also a multi-level space that encompassed 'architecture and space, space and nature, nature and architecture', and the combination of different landscapes and elements allowed Humphrey to see a step-by-step connection between architecture and space. 'But they reacted quite strongly upon hearing my opinion on the matter, telling me that the Lai Chi Kok Hospital was very haunted!' It took Humphrey a lot of effort to convince them. At that time, the Savannah College of Art and Design, a well-known design school in the United States, was planning to set up a branch in Hong Kong, and it had also applied for the site of the North Kowloon Magistrates' Court but had not requested government funding. Humphrey knew that the Savannah College had a better chance of succeeding.

The Jao Tsung-I Academy was officially opened in June 2014. Post-revitalisation, it has managed to integrate both the old and new premises and brings together the essence of both Chinese and Western cultures, while still retaining the upper, central and lower building complexes. The Heritage Lodge occupies the upper zone, while the middle and lower zones consist of The Gallery, Heritage Hall and the Skylight Atrium where exhibitions are held from time to time. The original building complex is of traditional English red-brick architectural style, with a hint of Chinese influence in the roof tiles, wooden doors and windows. 'We tried not to interfere with anything that could be retained and to present everything in its most authentic form.' Humphrey believes that revitalisation or renovation of a building does not necessitate the full restoration of its original appearance. 'Leaving behind some traces is also tasteful.'

While taking in the view of the group of historic buildings, carefully hidden within nature, Humphrey explains that its unique cultural ambience can only be fully appreciated when one is immersed in it. 'Every year from March to May, when the Bauhinia Variegata is in flower, a truly magnificent scene unfolds as the hill bursts into colour with a sea of flowers in full bloom.'

| 1 | 2 | 1 | The Bauhinia Variegata on the hillside is in flower from March to May. The sea of blossoming flowers attracts plenty of tourists. (Winner of the Flower Festival Photography Contest).
| | | 2 | The historic buildings of the Jao Tsung-I Academy are hidden within nature.

Untold Stories

Jockey Club Creative Arts Centre
It All Starts Here

'It all started with JCCAC.' Humphrey Wong and Kenneth Tse, sitting on either side of a ping-pong table, were doing some deep soul-searching. They were looking for the source of the spark that had ignited their passion to actively participate in the historic building revitalisation project.

JCCAC, short for Jockey Club Creative Arts Centre, is a home to artists' studios and art groups. On 29 January 2019, they posted a message on Facebook: 'Meta4 is home! JCCAC L306B.' In the attached image, the words 'MDFA Architects' could clearly be seen.

Founded in 2001 by Humphrey Wong, Kenneth Tse, Steven Chu and Anson Tsang, MDFA Architects (Meta4 Design Forum Ltd, hereinafter referred to as 'Meta4') went through several phases before settling on its specialisation: revitalising historic buildings. Although Meta4 had been co-founded by four professionals, the four did not often work as a team. However, they worked together on JCCAC, in partnership with P&T Group.

The JCCAC was previously the Shek Kip Mei Factory Estate, the first entire factory estate building to be revitalised into an art village and art centre. Before commencing their design, Humphrey and Kenneth visited every unit in the building. It was filled with the shadows of rundown factories from the Fifties and Sixties. Some units had tools scattered around; others had been left intact. 'It felt as if time had stood still after the workers had suddenly left without taking anything with them.' Humphrey was moved when he saw this. He said it was as if he had seen the whole manufacturing process.

The toy factories in the building also caught Kenneth's attention, as they had a hint of familiarity about them. 'As a kid, when I was looking for ways to make extra pocket money, I would make handicrafts at home with my sister. It felt like I was not the only one.' Humphrey went on to say that one of the students whom he taught at university brought his father to see one of the factories. 'His father cried the moment he saw the old signboard.'

Having seen all kinds of historical traces in the factory building, Kenneth said, 'It carries the memories of different ages, and it would be good if we could do something to evoke or preserve those memories.' They agreed that revitalisation was not about demolishing the original structure and then rebuilding it, nor was it about building something grand.

The design of the JCCAC incorporated 'hide and seek' ideas. For instance, a snow-white wall has been built on the rooftop, 'It can be an ordinary wall, but it can also be used for movie-screening, exhibitions… We didn't directly tell anyone about it, and we didn't specifically determine the usage of the space.' As the inhabitants would no longer be factory workers but, rather, artists, they tried to provide a design that would allow the artists to explore the use of space.

'The four of us felt that what we were doing for artists would be different from what we would do for others.' Humphrey also enjoys doing creative work in his free time. While working on this project, he made the most of the creative opportunities available to him, pushing himself so that he would not be stuck in a rut.

Around the same time, Kenneth began assisting St. James' Settlement in preparing the design for its Wanchai Livelihood Place project before the Blue House Cluster revitalisation project even came into existence. After the opening of the JCCAC in 2008, Humphrey was similarly invited to help design the office of the Hong Kong Institute for the Promotion of

1		3	4
2			

1. Shek Kip Mei Factory Estate was built in the 1970s near the seven-storey building in the resettlement area to address the employment issues in the district and reduce the need for cross-district commuting. In 2008, it was revitalised as the Jockey Club Creative Arts Centre.
2. The revitalisation preserves the historical traces of the factory building, such as old signboards, machines and semi-finished products.
3. These spaces, with different orientations, light sources and proportions, are spread across the floors of the factory building, adding a combination of ergonomics and aesthetics to the façade of the old building.
4. The founding of MDFA Architects at the Youth Square began with the Chai Wan Youth Development Centre Architectural Design Competition in 1999.

Chinese Culture's office at the JCCA. This accounted for the subsequent follow-up ventures such as the Jao Tsung-I Cultural Centre, the revitalisation of the old Tai Po Police Station, and the restoration of Lai Chi Wo Village.

So, how did they come together?

'The four of us were university classmates, and we were also teammates for our course work. We were nicknamed "the weakest link".' The two couldn't help but laugh. The memories from university still seemed to be fresh. Without hesitation, and in unison, the two of them added, 'homework was often handed in late'.

After graduation, the 'weakest link' team participated in a design competition for the Youth Development Centre. They won. The Chai Wan Youth Square was their first architectural design in Hong Kong. And that was when Meta4 was born.

Untold Stories

Tsim Sha Tsui Promenade

Strolling by the Sea

On New Year's Eve, Raymond Fung asked where the best place was to go for the countdown. Almost immediately, two thoughts came to my mind: 'a sea of faces' and 'an impending cold spell'. Perhaps it would be better to just stay home and watch some TV, or even play a round of Mah-jong. I thought he would stay home, too, but he headed to Tsim Sha Tsui waterfront to experience a special New Year's Eve that would include the sound of bells that hadn't been heard for the past seventy-one years.

At six o'clock in the evening on 9 December 2021, the sound of a long-lost bell could be heard on the Tsim Sha Tsui waterfront. In the warm glow of the sunset and the gentle evening breeze, everything seemed so tranquil and beautiful. The next morning, Raymond posted a reflection on Facebook:

Don don don... The bell finally rings for the sixth time!

Perhaps, I am the most emotional person in the thousands of people at the site, not because of the merits from a 'hard earned victory'; words that imply any deserving credits, I have no need for them.

I am emotional because a peaceful sound much anticipated by the folks of Hong Kong has finally arrived.

I am emotional, because thousands of people are waiting to become witness to their city, though humble, yet heartwarming.

I am emotional, as this is the inflection point of communication between the government and the people; born and raised here, it is a resonance I share.

I would like to give thanks to my comrades with whom we have worked hard together to make this wish come true: Shun Chi Ming, Xinbao Ding, Lau Chi Pang and Cheng Cho Ming; and the unsung heroes who have worked together with us and with such dedication behind the scenes. The most heartwarming of all is seeing residents of this city filling the square to express their affectionate sentiments for Hong Kong!

Raymond is a romantic, yet he is wary of over-indulging in romanticism. His post did not have any rousing words, just plain and simple ones. However, between the lines, each word revealed his love for this city, and arriving at the phrase 'though humble, yet heartwarming' was akin to meeting Raymond in the flesh. The sustained tolling of the bell in Tsim Sha Tsui seemed to extend the narrative and assuage Raymond's past regrets.

The Tsim Sha Tsui Promenade Beautification Project, which ran in parallel with the Peak Improvement Scheme, included the development of the clock tower and the plaza in front of the Hong Kong Cultural Centre. While handling this project, Raymond, as usual, insisted that a spring cleaning exercise be carried out prior to adding on new structures or facilities. The design team, which included Stephen Tang, K.C. King, Daniel Chow and others all shared the consensus to make the Victoria Harbour scenery the main focus of this project. Thus, structures that blocked the views of the harbour were removed. The coastal archway was demolished; the bulky stone railings were replaced with glass balustrades; and reflective lighting replacing the street lights close to the sea. The original pedestrian bridge ramp was also replaced with a lift, thus freeing up space for leisure activities, and more than 200 Bauhinia

1	2 3 4

1. The design incorporates sculptures inspired by popular international culinary utensils to make the place more vibrant.
2. More than 200 Bauhinia trees were planted along the way, bringing shade to the summer days.
3. The minimalist design creates a sharp and clean stroke in the skyline.
4. The seemingly inconspicuous changes have removed the visual barriers and brought everyone closer to the waterfront.

trees were planted to provide much-needed shade. These facilities and changes have silently removed visual barriers, bringing visitors one step closer to the sea.

As for the abandoned seawater pump house, Raymond converted it into a promenade restaurant. He said it was inspired by the movie *An Autumn's Tale*, starring Chow Yun-fat as Boat Head, a character who had always longed to set up a restaurant by the sea.

In addition to the beautification works on the promenade, the HKSAR Government had intended to relocate the Star Ferry Bus Terminus and then extend the area of the Star House and make space for sidewalk cafés. On hearing Raymond talk about this, the eyes of those listening to him grew wider as they imagined how the square would look if the plan were to be implemented. 'Back then, a design competition had already been held and new locations for the bus terminus were selected. Unfortunately, this once-in-a-lifetime plan was scuppered by various interest groups...' After listening to him describe a square that could have rivalled London's Trafalgar Square, I could only shake my head and sigh.

The beauty of a city is not determined by the number of buildings designed by renowned masters but whether the existing buildings can preserve history and tell their stories. 'The lost historic buildings are beyond rescue, yet it is decent enough if we can recall the familiar sounds and nostalgic memories of the past, in this case then, speech is golden, while silence is silver.' Although Raymond is still brooding over the past, those who understand him will know that he is not one who gives up easily.

West Kowloon

New Territories East

Reading Guidance

The New Territories East is the most dazzling chapter of the seven regions covered in this book.

Starting with the urban area in Sha Tin, the Che Kung Temple Sports Centre, whether viewed from afar or upon visiting, often gives the first impression of being a museum. The temple is one of the many successful projects by Thomas Wan, who is known to be very passionate, dedicated and meticulous in his architectural endeavours. In addition to the Che Kung Temple Sports Centre, another of his masterful works in the same district is the GREEN@SHATIN at Shek Mun. As part of the government's efforts to enhance awareness for environmental protection, the Environment Bureau of the HKSAR Government has implemented the GREEN@COMMUNITY Programme and set up waste recycling stations in all districts of Hong Kong. Given that the Secretary of the bureau himself is also a professional architect, he has emphasised the importance of aesthetically pleasing designs for each station; and the GREEN@SHATIN serves as the inaugural project of the scheme. The positive response from the public towards these recycling centres demonstrates the willingness of Hong Kong residents, especially the younger generation, to actively participate in environmental protection.

Also located in the Shek Mun District is the Kitchee Academy, a project designed by Vincent Pang following his work on the West Kowloon Exhibition Pavilion. There is a story behind this pavilion. The West Kowloon Project did not originally include a pavilion, but the chairman of the board of the West Kowloon Cultural District Authority, Mr Henry Tang, had the sudden realisation that for such a significant cultural area in Hong Kong, there was a lack of engagement with the public and especially with young architects. He subsequently requested the addition of a pavilion, the design of which would be selected through an open competition offered to young professionals.

Amongst the hundreds of entries, and after several rounds of screening, Vincent Pang's design stood out. His experience shows that it is not easy for a small architecture firm to obtain a contract; however, building credibility through winning awards in public competitions is a viable way for start-ups to grow, slowly and steadily.

Apart from the admiration-worthy Che Kung Temple Sports Centre, the Tzu Chi Environmental Action Centre, a bungalow located at 5 Che Kung Miu Road, was designed by Ms Corrin Chan. Corrin is a compassionate individual who practises meditation regularly; she has dedicated herself to combining a simple lifestyle with environmental concepts while seeking truth, kindness and beauty from an alternative perspective. The City Art Square outside the Sha Tin Town Hall is a rare, large-scale outdoor sculpture square, with works designed by artists such as Zaha Hadid, Xu Bing, Freeman Lau, Barrie Ho, Danny Lee, James Law, Man Fung-yi, Sara Tse and Vivienne Tam. On the large stone staircase in front of the Sha Tin Town Hall, there is a set of red-painted installations designed by Ida Sze and Billy Chan. In Hong Kong, there is only a handful of full-time artists engaged in sculpture. Many of them have come from the architecture or design professions to create these sculptures, as a cross-disciplinary artistic interest. Similarly, some architects like to produce their own furniture, and there are also interior designers who love architecture projects.

New Architecture at the Chinese University of Hong Kong

The 137-hectare campus of the Chinese University of Hong Kong includes several buildings whose main feature is fair-faced concrete. When the campus was inaugurated in 1963, it was designed in a literati style chosen by Mr Szeto Wai. However, after years of use and maintenance, the exteriors of many older buildings are now covered with grey waterproof paint. Despite this, the campus features several newer buildings that still uphold the established aesthetic, with a grey base complemented by touches of vibrant hues to highlight the different personalities of each building. These include the Lo Kwee Seong Pavilion designed by Rocco Yim at the

Art Museum (of the Chinese University of Hong Kong); the C.W. Chu College designed by Liu Yikang; the Chung Chi Student Development Complex designed by Ivy Lee; the CUHK United College Student Hostel designed by Ida Sze and Billy Chan; the new wing of the University Library designed by Angela Pang; the AIT Building at the School of Architecture designed by Wallace Cheng and Yuet Tsang Chi; and the Morningside College designed by Frank Yu and Benjamin Wood.

Walking from the CUHK campus towards the Pak Shek Kok waterfront, the Hong Kong Science Park comes into view. The Charles K. Kao Auditorium, designed by Leigh & Orange Architects, looks like a golden egg floating in mid-air and is a rare form of architecture in Hong Kong. The waterfront of Pak Shek Kok has been mostly developed into a residential precinct for the middle classes, yet there is a small cluster of buildings that deserves everyone's attention. Although Hong Kong gives the impression of repetitive architectural design, these buildings on the waterfront of Pak Shek Kok that are the early works of Mr M.C. Chung, are eye-catching. They illustrate that there are still interesting, innovative and elegant works in Hong Kong.

The Most Beautiful Buildings are the Ones Raised for the Departed

Further north through the woods, one arrives at Wo Hop Shek. Perhaps walking along this

path that leads to a crematorium might send a slight chill down one's spine, but it is nevertheless a journey worth taking, as it leads to a series of beautifully designed buildings. There are two of them that reside within the Wo Hop Shek Cemetery: the Wo Hop Shek crematorium and columbarium. Those who have not visited these buildings in person may have actually seen them from watching one of Hong Kong's police and bandit themed movies. It seems that film directors in Hong Kong often do have a good grasp of where the most scenic spots are in the city.

It is also interesting to note that the more uniquely designed architectural projects in Hong Kong tends to be in the non-mainstream category. One possible reason behind this is that owners of these buildings typically have fewer personal requirements and seldom interfere or meddle with the design process, thus giving designers the rare opportunity for a greater degree of design freedom and leading to the creation of various exquisite works. The two non-mainstream buildings being introduced are works of two different designers, M.C. Chung and Ida Sze. There is also a beautiful columbarium within Poon Chun Yuen of the Lotus Association of Hong Kong located in Tai Wo in the Tai Po district. It is an Oriental-style building built out of pine wood. Its style is contrary to the existing traditional architecture in the surrounding area. Designed by Annette Chu with a modern oriental form, its roof retains

the traditional yellow glazed tiles, while the exterior walls comprise 120-centimetre pine strips alternating with glass and arranged in the shape of a comb. Whenever the sunlight shines through, the orderly projection creates a temple of melodious and peaceful beauty.

The Hong Chi Pinehill Integrated Vocational Training Centre located in Tai Po is a somewhat unknown place. It was introduced to me through word of mouth. The centre consists of several inconspicuous buildings hidden in the foliage, whose lively design features align with the Hong Chi Society's commitment to safeguarding the concept of 'serving those with intellectual disabilities and helping them realise their dreams'. From Tai Po to Plover Cove Reservoir, there are some uniquely designed New Territories Small Houses, some of which were built by Michael Ng in the early days. The Observatory Tide Gauge Station in Tai Po Kau is also a new design worth taking a look at. It invokes the concept of 'the tip of the iceberg'. Designed by Bill So and Kylie

Chan, it won the Tai Po Kau Tide Gauge Station Architectural Design Competition.

At Long Mei Beach, there is a series of geometric aluminum waterfront buildings that have been designed by William Tsang. In the same district, the Tsz Shan Monastery, another Tang-style building after the Chi Lin Nunnery, is a must-visit site for tourists, as well. The introductory guide to the Tsz Shan Monastery cites the inspiration for the architecture as the 'solemn and elegant styles of the Tang while integrating customs of both the ancient and the modern'. This indicates that it is not purely a Tang-style building but incorporates steel as the basic structural material while cutting back on the traditional practice of supporting eaves with *dougong* (the 'bucket arch' of traditional Chinese architecture). Nevertheless, the overall result still remains extraordinarily impressive. Since its opening, visitors to the monastery leave amazed that such a beautiful, elegant place exists in Hong Kong.

A Forgotten Ancient Village

Lai Chi Wo is a popular destination for tourists. Starting from Wu Kau Tang near the Plover Cove Country Park, it takes about two hours of walking through the mountains to get there. Lai Chi Wo is a Hakka village that still retains its 1950s style due to its having been abandoned by farmers who migrated to the UK. Because of access difficulties, it was difficult for the villagers to interact with the outside world and this has subsequently resulted in the loss of an active trading market for the village's small houses. Its remoteness also explains why it escaped demolition.

Years later, a retired nature lover named Mr Lam Chiu-ying began writing his book, *Stories from Afar*, and discovered a number of old photographs of the area. It turns out that in its heyday, there were more than 2,000 people living in the village of Lai Chi Wo, mainly as farmers. However, there are now only about twenty residents remaining. Lam believed that Lai Chi Wo had the right conditions for preservation and revitalisation and subsequently took initiatives to ensure its protection. Lam later received funding from the Hong Kong Jockey Club and worked with the University of Hong Kong to set up the Hong Kong Countryside Conservation Foundation'. He selected the first batch of fourteen relatively intact village houses in Lai Chi Wo and consulted with the owners to find conservation solutions that would bring the best of both worlds to create the Lai Chi Wo Hakka Life Experience Village. The revitalisation of the Hakka Village, which was jointly led by Humphrey Wong and Steven Chu, was the most challenging and difficult project the architects had ever faced due to the lack of transportation means and labour support. However, the preservation of the Hakka architectural style was made possible thanks to a dedicated and supportive team who became the driving force behind the entire restoration project. In 2018, the HKSAR Government set up the Countryside Conservation Office with the aim to first assist in the ecological conservation of Lai Chi Wo and Sha Lo Tung before extending its help in preserving other villages in the New Territories and bring life to these abandoned rural areas once again.

The Rear Garden of Hong Kong

Sai Kung is known as the 'Rear Garden of Hong Kong'. It includes Hoi Ha Wan in the Sai Kung West Country Park, which is home to a well-known coral sanctuary. The beautiful tourist centre in that area is yet another signature work of Thomas Wan. Using fair-faced concrete, steel I-beams, solid wood and glass to create a strong contrast between solid and void, and complemented by the picturesque scenery of Hoi Ha Wan, it is the cream of the crop of public architecture. Also located in the restricted area of the High Island Reservoir, the scenic Wong Shek Pier, the proud work of Ivan Ho, has a simple but wavy roof and sloping posts, conceptually signifying the natural beauty of wind and waves through deconstructivism.

I have left behind a number of architectural projects in Sai Kung, where I have lived for more than thirty years. One of them is the Sai Kung Visual Corridor co-created with K.C. King and Ida Sze, which was highly regarded by various government departments at the time as a model of an inter-departmental urban design project. The Tin Hau Temple forms the central axis, connecting the outdoor basketball court, the Man Yee Playground, the Sai Kung Waterfront Park and the Sai Kung Pier through five large bronze bells, hence the name 'Sai Kung Visual Corridor'. The Sha Tsui Road recreational space project was undertaken in coordination with the Highways Department to integrate the original footpath with the recreational area to provide a better link and improve the ambience of the outdoor restaurants there. This has now become a highlight of Sai Kung.

Another challenge for the Sai Kung Waterfront Park was the addition of beachfront restaurants, the first such establishments to be promoted by the government. One of the highlights of the park is the group of large sculptural paper boats that float in the centre of a pool. The boats were created using Anti-Japanese War newspapers. They commemorate the heroic deeds of the Hong Kong Independent Battalion of the Dongjiang Column and also reference the history of Sai Kung as a fishing port. Origami, a plaything for children in the past, carries a symbolic meaning. The paper boat installation has long been a favourite of the locals, who refer to Sai Kung Waterfront Park as the 'Paper Boat Park'.

Towards the end of the promenade in Sai Kung is WM Hotel, a Nordic style building designed by Aedas. The place has been described as a tasteful resort hotel. From my perspective, however, the most tasteful club and resort in the city is the Hong Kong Tennis Academy located in the same district. The Academy boasts a collection of retro-style structures with terracotta roof tiles and beige walls, the finest of the many buildings Robert Stern has designed in Hong Kong. The ambience of this place is reminiscent of the picturesque Avignon in the south of France.

However, despite Hong Kong having plenty of secluded landscapes, a magnificent coastline, a wealthy population and a large number of tourists, there is still a lack of interest for staycations. Nature resorts such as those found in Bali, Indonesia or Phuket, Thailand are still largely absent.

Besides Discovery Bay, Sai Kung is the most Westernised small town in the area and a popular residential community for expatriates. Inside its small bars, it is common for Chinese and foreigners alike to gather and relax. As more and more members of the middle class move in, another subtle transformation in Sai Kung is the emergence of more veterinary clinics and sustainability-related shops. Sai Kung has several SSSI[2] and four yacht clubs. It attracts many nature lovers, with cottages of different design styles scattered around Che Keng Tuk, Ta Ho Tun, Pak Sha Wan, Clear Water Bay and Sheung Sze Wan. Take a walk around these areas, and one is sure to find something interesting. In addition to public architecture, I have also designed two private houses in Sai Kung, named 'The Flower Box' and 'Archivilla', the details of which can be found in the interview chapters that follow.

Although Sai Kung has been viewed by many as a rural area, the dense estate of Tseung Kwan O is also part of Sai Kung. There are two schools in the estate. The Hong Kong Design Institute, designed by French architects Thomas Coldefy and Isabel Van Haute, has a design plan that was generated through an open competition. The appearance of the building is rather striking, and its style is considered as 'noisy'. It is a design the students are proud of, which indirectly enhances the image of the school; the second school is the French International School, which adopts a low-key style and is much smaller in scale. It was designed by Elva Tang and Claude Godefroy. The campus has become surrounded by a concrete-jungle. When viewed from afar, one can see the simple white squares that are permeated with vibrant colours, symbolising the lively and playful nature of children.

The Hong Kong University of Science and Technology campus is closer to the coast than the Chinese University of Hong Kong. It was designed by Simon Kwan & Associates and has a harmonious style overall. The grand plaza at the entrance surrounds the sculpture in the centre through a circular promenade, making it the grandest entrance of all the Hong Kong tertiary institutions. As the university continues to expand, new campus buildings have been gradually deviating from the original style. One of them, the Shaw Auditorium of the Hong Kong University of Science and Technology, is composed of several concentric circles, signifying the interaction of different functions. This is another building designed by Elva Tang and Claude Godefroy.

There are many bungalows in Clear Water Bay, with only a few being particularly ornamental. The most exciting example of architecture in Sheung Sze Wan must be the residence of Steve Leung, and there are also one or two

trendy small houses in Hiu Po Path. Amongst the mansions in the area of Kowloon Peak, there is a huge one owned by a celebrity. It is composed of large and small cubes, with neatly arranged windows that are uniform in size with horizontal wooden louvres. It is a wonder that there is a wealthy owner in Hong Kong who pursues the simplest of shapes!

The most unique feature of the Mount Pavilia Clubhouse, located on Clear Water Bay Road, is best appreciated at night, when it looks like an especially eye-catching, translucent lantern. From the interview with the project manager Edwin Chan, one learns that this is one of the few residences in Hong Kong that promotes art as its selling point, targeting residents who are looking for quality of life. Designed by Korean architect Minsuk Cho, the visual effect of brick stacking tests not only the skill of the brick masters but also the sensitivity of vision of its viewers. It is indeed an exquisite architectural craftsmanship.

Notes

1. Hong Kong Countryside Conservation Foundation: The Hong Kong Countryside Foundation Limited was established in 2011 to create a medium for people interested in caring for the long-term well-being of the people of Hong Kong. It is a place for them to come together and turn their dreams into reality; by owning and managing these natural assets and related land and providing funding to promote conservation education to the public.

2. SSSI: Site of Special Scientific Interest.

Hoi Ha Visitor Centre
Che Kung Temple Sports Centre

Picking Chrysanthemums Under the Eastern Hedge

Located in the Sai Kung West Country Park, the Hoi Ha Visitor Centre was originally a barbecue site. Taking into account the pre-existing slope of the terrain, the overall design centres around the existing lawn, and the original large trees have been retained. A traditional village layout has been adopted, and the design employs a simple wood tone. Along the adjacent path, visitors can take a ten-minute walk to the nearby Hoi Ha Wan Marine Park, where they can canoe, stand-up paddleboard or snorkel to catch a view of the marine life and corals.

Thomas Wan and Peter Lau of the Architectural Services Department led the design of the Hoi Ha Visitor Centre. Their shared design concept was 'Adaptation to local conditions', with the aim of closely connecting people, architecture and nature, in line with the original ecology of the place. The building is equipped with multi-purpose rooms, a reception desk, an administrator's office and a staff rest area. There is also a central lawn and a multi-purpose outdoor covered space. With a little close observation, it is not difficult to detect the architects' thoughtfulness in its design.

The design of the lavatory is relatively open, allowing wind to penetrate and provide natural ventilation. The buildings are connected by a central lawn, allowing children to have a larger space to move around when they are outdoors. The multi-purpose outdoor covered space can be used for group activities or study sessions, and has been designed to provide a quiet place for visitors, allowing them to connect with nature, meditate and practice *zazen* freely. The centre is surrounded by trees of different heights, and the entire structure is a courtyard that integrates with the surrounding natural beauty. At the same time, the Hoi Ha Visitor Centre features an exhibition hall where, from time to time, exhibitions on the theme of marine ecology and environmental protection are held. The Hoi Ha Visitor Centre can be said to encompass art, lifestyle, nature, architecture and humanities all at the same time.

Peter Lau joined the Development Bureau in 2010 and was responsible for the Sichuan Redevelopment Project before moving on to the Architectural Services Department. When asked about the most important part of the design for the Hoi Ha Visitor Centre, he remarked, 'Each project has different needs. For example, some projects are born from the environment, and some are driven by the needs of users. As this visitor centre was built to match the beautiful surroundings of Hoi Ha Wan, the first thing to do was to think about how to integrate the architecture with the natural environment'.

Thomas Wan has always used Oriental elements as his personal style, and the Hoi Ha Visitor Centre exhibits such characteristics. The courtyard elements serve to bring man and nature closer, 'My goal was to create a community in the Hoi Ha Visitor Centre. A work of architecture is not just an object, nor is it just a small house. In addition to considering its appearance, I hope this place can bring cohesion to everyone as if they were in a small village, and enable them to view nature from different perspectives as well as to sing its praises.'

Visitors can participate in leisure activities in the middle of the Hoi Ha Visitor Centre, or simply take a seat and appreciate a moment of peace. Perhaps this atmosphere, which amplifies the blossoming vitality of nature, truly reflects Thomas Wan's philosophy. In the midst of this place, the pure beauty of Hong Kong can truly be felt.

The design concept of the Hoi Ha Visitor Centre draws inspiration from the beautiful countryside of Sai Kung. The building is centred around the existing lawn and the multi-purpose rooms are designed as glass pavilions that look onto the central lawn, thus connecting the indoor and outdoor spaces.

1. The building and the surrounding cloisters and gardens are tightly intertwined, reinterpreting the ambience of the traditional settlement and town.
2. The layout of the gymnasium is progressive, introducing the mountain into different spaces. Facilities and public spaces are arranged along the promenade. The promenade serves as a pedestrian corridor connecting different functional spaces and slowly introducing the natural landscape.

Completed in 2020, the Che Kung Temple Sports Centre in Sha Tin is a grey four-storey structure built against the mountains. Thomas Wan designed the Sport Centre with simple lines and colours and with exterior walls of mostly fair-faced concrete, presenting the beauty of building materials without concealment – avoiding decorative materials to reveal the original, as-constructed concrete. The two concrete walls next to the entrance of the Sports Centre have wooden panels added to them, creating an eye-catching 'pitting' effect and projecting a sense of 'natural, yet rugged'.

Che Kung Temple Sports Centre introduces the outdoor mountain into different indoor spaces through layers of perspective, integrating with the surrounding landscape, to preserve the tradition of villagers worshipping Fengshui Shan (the practice of Chinese geomancy). The design aimed not only to create a diversified recreational facility but also a natural and comfortable common space for public leisure. The centre incorporates green elements and features open passages, a central courtyard and terrace gardens, allowing ample natural lighting.

Another consideration was the large area required for a sports centre. To reduce the total footprint required, Thomas made the ticket office smaller and arranged for a structural design that would allow a more open layout.

The essence of public space lies in sharing. Thomas designed the building with multiple entrances but kept signage to a minimum so that visitors could wander freely. The centre is connected by a long corridor and staircases, thus allowing visitors to shuttle through the different floors, facilities, gardens and terraces from multiple directions, creating a true sense of leisure.

The most prominent features of the building are the long staircases at the front and rear that give one the feeling of ascending a mountain. (There is an alternative, less-strenuous path to the top of the building.) The rooftop garden overlooks the adjacent Chun Shek Estate. Thomas took good advantage of the surrounding nature by giving many of the indoor spaces floor-to-ceiling windows and incorporating open spaces to create a natural and inviting environment enriched by lush foliage. On the opposite side, there are tall windows that allow a view of other activity rooms, creating visual connections and enhancing user interaction.

Slats of artificial wood made of eco-friendly plastic have been incorporated into the building's fabric to meet the current fire protection regulations and elevate the environmental friendliness and safety of building materials. Materials, colours, spaces and functions are intertwined within this building, and square and circular columns hold the different views tightly together. Thomas remarked, 'A master architect once said that nature only becomes a landscape when it is put into a picture frame.' He adapted the building to the local environment by designing an open-air stairway to the rooftop garden that merges into the slope, thus integrating with the environment.

The overall design of the Che Kung Temple Sports Centre brings to the table a slight sense of Oriental Zen-like elements. Thus, it is different from traditional gymnasium architecture; all of its elements have been studied from a multi-faceted perspective: 'Framing yourself & others.'

The façade of the building is inspired by the *Baizi* cabinet (Chinese cabinet with multiple drawers), and the decorative shelves, blue bricks and wooden screens added to the building act as a modern interpretation of traditional craftsmanship. The layout of the library suggests several Chinese courtyard houses stacked vertically, and the atrium is tightly intertwined within.

Wo Hop Shek Crematorium
Pak Shek Kok Promenade

The Art Museum at the End

The Wo Hop Shek Crematorium and Memorial Garden, located in Fanling, New Territories, was completed in 2013. It is not only the largest crematorium in Hong Kong, but it also has a most unique design that combines its dynamic forms and various elements into the mountain as if it were a well-designed art museum.

A large pool and reclining lawn come into view as one walks into the Wo Hop Shek Crematorium. The ambience bestows a sense of peace onto its visitors. The entire structure redefines the image of a Hong Kong crematorium. In the past, the design of crematoria was based on functional needs, and they would often seem cold, sad and insensitive to the emotional needs of their users. However, through careful consideration, the designer, Mr M.C. Chung, broke out from the traditional, miserable design scheme that had thereto been synonymous with crematoria. The primary design intent of the Wo Hop Shek Crematorium was to provide comfort to the bereaved. A reflection pool at the entrance allows mourners to cleanse their minds and prepare for the ceremony, and it allows their hearts to be purified.

The mourners are led past the large lawn and pool, spaces designed by the architect to signify letting go. The incinerator is located under the lawn in an echo of the traditional burial ceremony and to symbolise ancestors entering the earth. M.C. Chung designed a bamboo forest courtyard as a background, echoing the symbolism of bamboo in Chinese culture: integrity, gentlemen's humility and refined pre-eminence. The crematorium is not only about functionality; it also takes into consideration the sentiments of the bereaved. As the mourners enter the auditorium, healing words come into view against a backdrop of feather pines.

The various circulation routes in the crematorium have been carefully designed, with separate entrances and exits, lavatories and paper money-burners to avoid the taboo of 'backtracking' (encountering with the next grieving family) during Chinese funeral rites. After leaving the hall, the deceased's relatives can also walk directly into the central landscaped area and take a short pause, which also helps to avoid encountering family members of any other deceased. The exit from the hall leads to a lawn with a lotus pond that had orginally been planned to be filled with the characters of the hundred family surnames. However, controversy over the plan prevented it from being implemented, and, instead, a continuous bubbling effect was created, symbolising the birth and rebirth of human life. Instead of intimidating symmetrical forms, the design makes use of powerful asymmetrical forms to symbolise diverse and difficult lives, and weathered steel has been used to symbolise the journey of life.

The Pak Shek Kok Promenade located in Tai Po in the New Territories, another project of M.C. Chung, also exudes the beauty of tranquillity. The two-kilometre-long promenade allows pedestrians and cyclists to enjoy the scenery of Tolo Harbour on the way to Tai Po, where the architecture and facilities are the equal of the innovative style of Hong Kong Science Park. M.C. Chung has turned wooden boxes into a pavilion with a lively yet relaxed style. A mirror fixed to the door of the public lavatory enhances the sense of space. Along the way, there are also park management offices, bicycle rental and snack kiosks, sidewalk cafés and refuse collection points.

1	
2	4
3	

1. The texture of the fair-faced concrete exterior wall matches the atmosphere of the crematorium, and the irregular building layout and bamboo stalk-shaped window openings create a natural and relaxed feel.
2. A backdrop of bamboo for the altar in the Chinese hall brings both solemnity and a natural atmosphere to funeral ceremonies.
3. The roof of the crematorium is designed as a reclining lawn and a small park. Families can seek serenity and calm on the rooftop lawn.
4. The innovative architecture is nothing like the traditional crematorium. The entrance pool serves to cleanse the minds of funeral attendees.

1 Geometric shapes and clean lines express a sense of simplicity.
2 The variety on show in the facilities of the Pak Shek Kok Promenade demonstrates M.C. Chung's emphasis on architectural diversity.
3 The buildings and facilities here complement the innovative style of the Hong Kong Science Park, with a focus on simplicity.

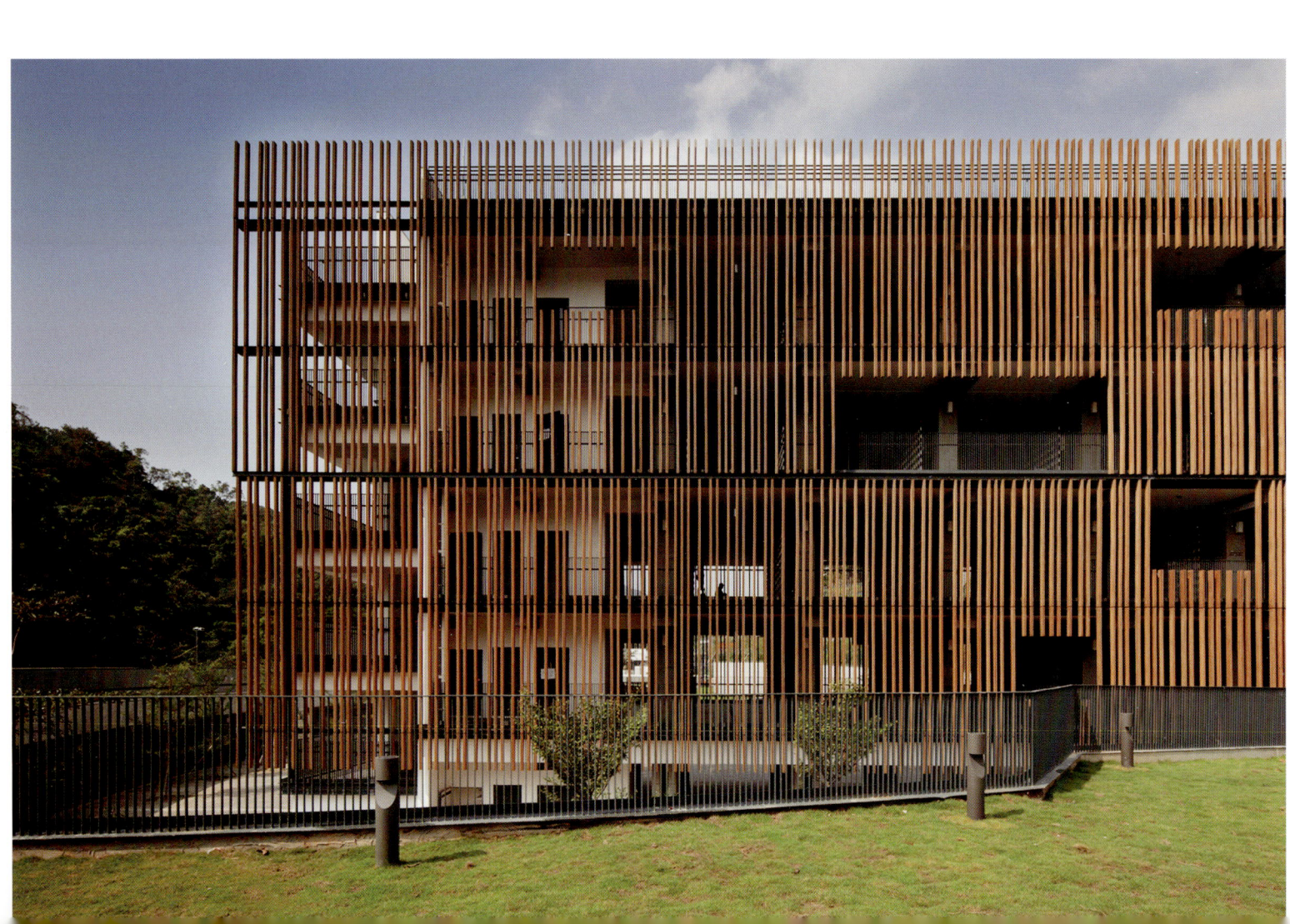

Wo Hop Shek Columbarium

The Land of Reminiscence

It has been said that the soul weighs twenty-one grams, and that when it leaves, the body becomes lighter. Where does the soul go after it leaves the body? The Buddhist interpretation of life and death is that there are six reincarnations after death, while for Western religions there is heaven and hell. Ida Sze did not think much into the afterlife or the cycle of life and death; she was more curious about the meaning of the cemetery and niches. 'The architecture of death is the purest architecture that allows people to stand between heaven and earth, allowing them to connect with nature and find themselves.' With this in mind, Ida began her design of the Wo Hop Shek at Kiu Tau Road Columbarium.

Regardless of your mood, when you step into Wo Hop Shek and are touched by its breezy, calm atmosphere, your emotions will at once become pure; whether you feel a trace of sadness, or annoyance, or nervousness, you will nevertheless feel it in its purest form. Along the curved path ahead, wooden screens partially conceal bamboos that rustle in the breeze. The pond at the entrance is mirror-calm, rippling only when the occasional bamboo leaf falls.

The Wo Hop Shek Columbarium is located in a valley with a quiet and spacious environment. 'Actually, the original site chosen was a car park close to the village, but villagers viewed that as a taboo, and so the plan was never approved.' Death has always been considered a taboo in Chinese culture. As the demand for cemeteries and memorial niches in Hong Kong far exceeds their supply, this caused much dissatisfaction within society stemming from the sense that people were dying 'graveless deaths'. Ida recalled trying to locate another site with her supervisor, Ms Alice Yeung. 'Finally, we found this valley near the parking lot on Google Maps.' When they visited the site, they discovered that it was the site of an abandoned cemetery overgrown with weeds – an ideal site for transformation into a columbarium.

Although the site available for the development of the columbarium was large, the valley topography would mean that fog would be persistent during the spring and autumn worshipping seasons. Ida threw convention to the wind and designed a tall, single main building with a large podium. The form of the building is softened, warmth is added, and the coming and going of visitors partially obscured by wooden screens that shroud the building. These screens create a sense of privacy and a space to mourn. 'Connection and separation are important elements in this design.' However, the screens are open enough to let in natural light and create a sufficient sense of transparency, as well, that allows the building to blend in with nature.

The main building can accommodate more than 30,000 niches, and the building's lifts provide access to the adjacent terraced slopes, which contain 4,000 outdoor niches. The building's podium contains a visitor centre, incense-burning facilities, car parks, lavatories and other supporting facilities. It is connected to the hillside, leaving a wide view for the eyes. 'The starting point for the entire design was to have the least number of buildings and as much nature as possible; followed by having enough negative space in the building to allow for people to breathe and feel, so that the peacefulness of nature can give comfort to their hearts.'

Ida had been working for the Architectural Services Department for six years, and she resigned before the completion of this project. Did she consider leaving only after completing the project? Ida did have her

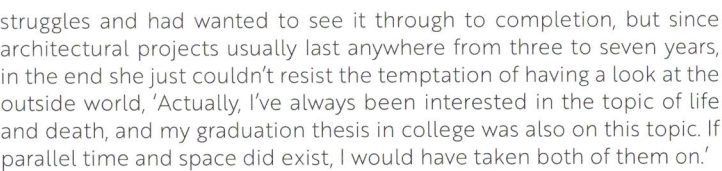

1. The design has economised on the number of buildings to provide for more activity space. The place resembles a grand park, with a large podium and a rectangular building. Worshippers walk through winding paths in the platform to the central stepped plaza to reach the columbarium. The building is connected to the terraces containing outdoor niches on the adjacent slopes.
2. The podium houses memorial halls, furnaces and lavatories. The rooftop terrace is like a large meadow in the jungle. It serves as a place of respite for people, especially during the ancestral worship period in spring and autumn.
3. A reflective pool sits at the entrance of the park, with visible reflections of the clear sky and clouds, giving reference to the beginning of the cleansing of the heart.

struggles and had wanted to see it through to completion, but since architectural projects usually last anywhere from three to seven years, in the end she just couldn't resist the temptation of having a look at the outside world, 'Actually, I've always been interested in the topic of life and death, and my graduation thesis in college was also on this topic. If parallel time and space did exist, I would have taken both of them on.'

After Ida's departure, the project was taken over by M.C. Chung. 'He basically utilised the entire original design and added more meaningful landscape elements to add depth to the design.' The main building is not located at the entrance; as one passes through the aforementioned pools and paths, accompanied by the breeze and the bamboo leaves along the way, one's mood cannot help but be slightly lifted. The pool seems to have no edges. According to Chung, this symbolises the deceased looking back on his or her life. In addition to the main building, there is a memorial garden on each of the hillside steps on the east and west sides; The East Wing is inspired by Chinese culture and features a three-storey memorial garden themed around bamboo, plum and willow, three plants with distinct Chinese characteristics. The memorial garden to the west is predominantly of Western style with stone carvings of animals and themed monument walls, adding a touch of art to the space.

'Many of the remarkable architectural works of the world are columbaria, because these places can be very pure and spiritual.' Ida was pleased with not only the design but also the feedback she received. A good friend of Ida's had her mother settled there. 'Every time she visits her mother, she will send me a text message thanking me that she felt at ease and could let go whenever she is there.'

For designers, the completion of a project does not always mean the end. On the contrary, meaning only begins at the moment of its completion. If the moment of death is the end of life, then it follows that funerals, cemeteries and ashes may be the comfort and thoughts being left behind for the world.

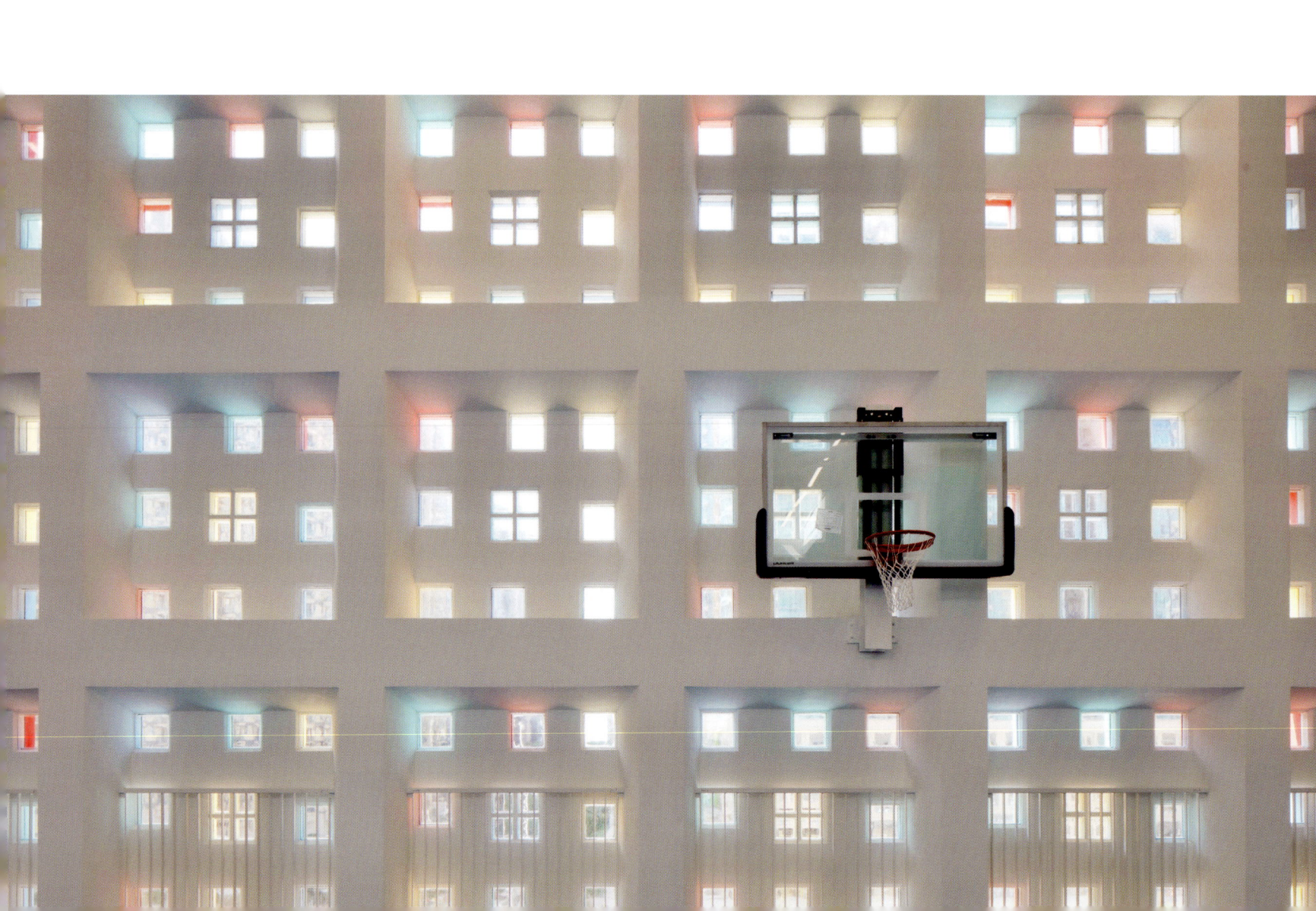

French International School · Shaw Auditorium,
Hong Kong University of Science and Technology

No Going Back

The skyline of a city is always mingled with the silhouette of its architecture. Walking unhurriedly into an urban jungle and looking up at the concrete, steel and glass edifices that rise straight out of the ground, I am hit by the realisation that the body which carries our consciousness is rather insignificant.

Elva Tang once stood in the middle of this jungle, 'besieged on all sides', and imagined what the French International School might look like if it were to be built here. As a partner and design director of the Danish architecture firm Henning Larsen Architects, Elva had previously worked on projects in exceptional environments – in stark contrast to densely populated Hong Kong. However, in this city now stands a building that is minimalistic but not simple and whose appearance turns the heads of passers-by who cannot resist a second look. From a distance, the building's neatly arranged, multi-coloured lattice windows stand out against the surrounding rows of houses. This is the newest building of the French International School in Tseung Kwan O which was officially opened in 2018.

Tseung Kwan O, one of Hong Kong's new towns, used to be full of construction sites; thus, it was no wonder that parents were sceptical when they first heard news of a school being built there. Elva described being 'besieged on all sides' by the shock of it. 'How do you build a work of architecture that is *sui generis* in a place full of high-rises? How do you create an oasis in the city? How do you design this place to have its own character and appeal?' Elva remarked bluntly that the project was challenging in many ways. 'Time was the biggest challenge. We had only about two and a half years after winning the competition for this project.'

Although the environment surrounding the school is multifarious, once you enter the campus, you begin to experience a world of its own. To minimise the impact of noise, acoustic design was crucial for this project. 'We hired a world-class acoustic designer.' The sense of silence encountered by visitors is not only auditory but also visual. Elva had adopted an open concept throughout the campus design and spared no expense to increase the height of the campus and enlarge its sense of space, in her own words, 'using open space to deal with being besieged on all sides.'

In addition to increasing the sense of space, the design aimed for flexibility. A kindergarten, canteen and lecture hall are located on the ground floor. There is a play area within the campus with a blazing colour scheme and a 400-metre-long running trail ('The Loop') that winds through the play area and gardens. 'There are few play areas this large in Hong Kong.' The play area is used as a drop-off zone at certain times of the day. It can accommodate forty school buses shuttling 1,150 students to and from the school. It is due to this flexible design that traffic issues were resolved and that was one of the reasons why they won the design competition, 'Turning problems into opportunities is a daily training for architects.'

The French International School is divided into French and international departments, and teachers and students in both departments typically had little opportunity to interact. 'They didn't know one another even though they were on the same campus.' Elva's design of the new campus ensured a break from the status quo. The design provided movable partition walls that allow teachers to switch easily between open spaces ('villas') and conventional classroom areas. A 'villa' space is

| 1 | The south façade of the school building is made of 627 small windows set deep within brightly coloured frames. In addition to attracting attention, the colorful exterior also symbolises the school's vision of supporting multiculturalism and its forward-thinking international educational mission. |
| 2,3 | The French International School abandons the traditional classroom model and fosters creativity and teacher–student interaction with open learning spaces. In the Junior School, traditional enclosed classroom spaces can be merged to create large, open spaces. The middle corridor can be used as a shared space for more than one hundred students of the same age to learn together. A good school campus design can bring bliss to both teachers and students. Space and lighting can transform the learning experience and bring joy to the children. |

large enough to accommodate an entire year-level of students. Not only can the students learn in a large group but the setting also encourages communication between classes. 'When English-speaking and French-speaking play together, their language skills will naturally improve.'

Nordic architectural design always carries with it the purity and temperature of nature. Just like a ray of sunshine in the morning, it does not generate a feeling of blazing heat but, instead, a comforting warmth. This gentle atmosphere can also be felt in the French International School. 'Sunlight and wind come from the east, so if the classroom faces towards the south and the north, it can avoid direct sunlight but still have sufficient natural light.' At the same time, the windows have been designed with deep frames that allow for natural light to enter the room while blocking direct sunlight.

The eye-catching and colourful lattice wall is made up of 627 red, yellow, blue squares framing small window openings. It has been neatly arranged and gorgeously coloured, just like a movie by American film director Wes Anderson, exuding a sense of childlike fantasy. There is a gymnasium behind the wall, and natural light with a candy-coloured tint seeps into the gymnasium through the deep-set small windows in the wall, making summer seem gentler and less scorching.

When asked to define good architecture, Elva said, 'Respond to the society, to the weather and to the users. Certainly, personalities can be added in, but only if you can strike a balance on all fronts.'

When the French International School invited bids through an open competition, most of the architecture firms that took part in it were from France. At first glance, engaging a French architect to design a French international school had seemed logical. However, switching to a different train of thought, their lack of experience in local construction practices put them at a disadvantage to local architects – although, in fact, this was Elva's first project in Hong Kong.

'I wanted to become a doctor, but my elder brother beat me to it.' When asked about how she and architecture had crossed paths, she unhesitatingly admitted that architecture wasn't her first choice. 'I was never artistic to begin with. Neither did I know how to draw nor build models.' Then one day, during a lecture at school, the speaker told the students that if they liked making decisions and wanted to be leaders, they should become architects. 'And that was how I was drawn to the idea of it.' She spoke frankly and bluntly. Elva was direct with her words, never beating about the bush. She spoke a little too quickly, and, though she was petite, there was vigour in her every word and movement. There was no time to relax when chatting with her.

After graduation, Elva did not enter the workforce immediately. Instead, she took her scholarship money and travelled around the world to expand her horizons. When she was a child, her family had not been well-off; thus, she had never travelled abroad. During her second year at university, she travelled to Beijing on her own for an internship with Mr Chang Yung Ho. She remembers him encouraging her to travel abroad. She and I first met after she had returned from her trip and then joined the Architectural Services Department. 'You would often tell us about the hardship you went through while trying to make a living and

1 The Shaw Auditorium is oval in shape and appears to be composed of three coaxial white rings. A glass curtain wall is set between the rings, allowing people to have a glimpse of the Sai Kung Bay. The opening of this auditorium signalled the addition of a world-class event venue to Hong Kong.

2 The Shaw Auditorium is a flexible, multi-purpose space with high-quality acoustic design. The picture shows the opening performance of the Hong Kong Philharmonic Orchestra.

complete your architecture studies in the United States; and I thought to myself, was it possible for me to experience the same thing, too?'

Curious and unafraid of failure, she was determined to experience the unknown. She began to enrol in schools abroad. 'My family knew nothing of my plans. Everything was done in secret. I also applied for scholarships at the same time.' She later received an offer from UC Berkeley, with the university also offering her a partial scholarship. 'My brother, who had just begun his career as a doctor, sponsored part of my tuition fees.' Once she was in the United States, Elva had to work in three different jobs every day to get by. 'I also enrolled in Landscape design for a double bachelor's degree. Do you know why I read Landscape design? Because there were scholarships – win – win!' she said unabashedly.

During her studies, Elva won a study tour scholarship. In 2002, she returned to Hong Kong and spent two months at the Office for Metropolitan Architecture to begin her research project. 'I met my husband there.'

Mr Claude Bøjer Godefroy, Elva's husband and also her partner at work, is of English and French descent. It is common to see husband-and-wife partnerships within the architecture profession. She uses the word 'complementary' to describe their relationship, but, as blunt as she is, sometimes disputes have been unavoidable. 'We've been together for more than a decade and are still learning to get along; We both know what's on each other's mind, but we don't necessarily agree on everything.'

A year later, Elva returned to the United States and continued her studies while Godefroy returned to Paris and later ended up in Copenhagen. Returning to Hong Kong was not the first thing on her mind after graduation. 'It was so hard to leave [home]; of course, I was going to stay abroad for a little longer.' However, she didn't think about looking for Godefroy in Copenhagen. Instead, she moved to the one city that had been on her mind and which she thought it necessary to work there at least once in her lifetime: New York.

The United States is not very far away from Denmark, but the distance between New York and Copenhagen still made her feel like she was at her 'intersection of life'. After staying a year in New York, she decided to quit her job and bought a one-way ticket to Copenhagen, not knowing what to expect. 'Just follow your heart.' Her speech slowed noticeably when she said that.

It was 2003. Not long after arriving in Copenhagen, she joined Henning Larsen Architects. 'Back then, the company wasn't very international. I was the only Chinese.' She and Godefroy later got married, but even after that, they couldn't escape the fate of a long-distance relationship. 'My husband found working on a construction site rather boring. He returned to Paris and worked for Ateliers Jean Nouvel.' So, did she follow him to Paris? 'Nope. I spent a year or two in Copenhagen before moving to Paris.'

Elva and Claude later set up their firm in Paris, in cooperation with Henning Larsen Architects. 'We won a big project through a competition back then which helped us to kick-start a new chapter.' Unfortunately, it was 2008, and the financial crisis had caused defaults in payments owed to Henning Larsen Architects, and it almost went out of business. 'They said to us, "Try solving the Foshan project on your own!"'

So the two of them were on their own. From the Foshan Grand Theatre to the Yuhang Theater in Hangzhou, all the way to the French International School and the Shaw Auditorium at the University of Science and Technology, the team has grown from two to several hundred people. Her hand has sustained repetitive strain injuries due to her work: 'I basically can't draw now, and it feels very difficult to use the mouse for even half an hour.'

Looking back, she said candidly that she hadn't been all that lucky. Although the Foshan project was a turning point, it was also the most bitter and tiring period, but, fortunately, she learned a lot from it. To date, some of the fees for that project are still outstanding.

In 2013, as business for Henning Larsen Architects was gradually improving, it was a natural progression for Elva and her husband to lead the Hong Kong branch. The Foshan project brought her back to Hong Kong, and the French International School was her first project on her own turf. 'Going round in circles and back again, just like a home run.' Although Elva still believes that not many opportunities exist on the Hong Kong architecture scene, and despite the difficulty of breaking into the market, being as unafraid of failure as she is, she won't compromise, even with the market. 'I will do whatever I can.'

The 45-year-old says this is the golden age of her career. 'Of course I don't have the energy I had ten years ago, but I am smarter now, and know that I should put thought into what I can still achieve.' Life is full of possibilities. Whatever new journeys or challenges await her, her husband and even her son, it seems that the phrase 'It is a must to succeed, there is no going back' will accompany her all the way.

Lai Chi Wo Hakka Life Experience Village

Mr Reclusive

'In the past, why would anyone visit the countryside?' said Humphrey Wong in a slow and muffled voice while pushing his round-framed glasses further up the bridge of his nose.

Two years have passed since the outbreak of the coronavirus pandemic and the day of the interview. During these days when we were unable to travel abroad, we have had to focus our attention on our local surroundings. Very often, one would hear this remark: 'Nowadays there are more people hiking in the countryside on weekends than people shopping in Mong Kok.'

Humphrey is very fond of the rural lifestyle and enjoys living in a low-rise, 'I don't even feel comfortable living on the fifth and sixth floors.' Ideally, the surrounding area should be empty. If one were to describe it with a word, it should be 'remote'! Humphrey not only prefers living in a low-rise, but he also has no interest whatsoever in the towers usually sought after by many architects.

In 2018, Wang Weijen curated the local exhibition for the *16th Venice Biennale International Architecture Exhibition*, and the theme was 'Tower'. 'Come to think of it, I really haven't designed any sort of towers.' While everyone was talking about height, Humphrey was so immersed in the countryside that he felt a little out of place, and this was when we quipped that he was the 'the architect on the fourth floor.'

At the outbreak of the pandemic, Humphrey began working from home. Returning home from his office in the city, he was elated. 'I can go out to my garden anytime and play with my pets, pick flowers, pull weeds out of the lawn and have a meeting while basking in the sun.' Listening to Humphrey describe the beauty of working from home, a poem suddenly came to mind: 'Do not let that spectacle go to waste, embrace fine wine and poetry in your prime.'

Although Hong Kong was once described in 1841 as a 'barren rock' by fromer British Foreign Secretary Lord Palmerston, the barrenness of this rock has long disappeared. Standing below row upon row of towering skyscrapers and gazing at the gorgeously illuminated Victoria Harbour, one could imagine, were it not for the 24-hour convenience store nearby, one would be looking at a scene after nightfall: 'With all fretful stirrings of the world now hush, the chirping sound of a cicada now permeates into the stones.'

In the New Territories and the outlying island areas, there are more than 600 villages of various sizes, located far from the hustle and bustle of the city and offering a peaceful and tranquil retreat. Amongst them is the over 300-year-old Lai Chi Wo village. Without the Closed Area Permit, it will take more than an hour to ferry from the Ma Liu Shui Ferry Pier to Lai Chi Wo; If you hike through the mountains, it will take more than two hours from Wu Kau Tang, passing through Kau Tam Tso, Sheung Miu Tin, Ha Mui Tin and Sam A Tsuen. Some describe Lai Chi Wo as a secluded and ancient village.

In its heyday, Lai Chi Wo Village was home to more than 200 households with over 1,000 inhabitants. The villagers made their living through fishing and farming, enjoying bountiful rice harvests. It was the liveliest of the seven Hing Chun Yeuk villages in the Northeast New Territories. However, since the 1960s, there has been a steady decline in the village's population.

By the 1990s, all that remained were empty village houses and weed-filled fields.

Who would have thought, then, that this lonely village, abandoned for decades, would later be ranked fifth amongst the 'Top 10 places to visit in Asia' by Lonely Planet in 2016. In 2020, it won the UNESCO Asia-Pacific Awards for Cultural Heritage Conservation, and it was awarded the AIA

Hong Kong Citation 2021 by the American Institute of Architects Hong Kong Chapter. Since the summer of 2022, people can visit the village and even stay overnight in restored dwellings to experience the simple leisure and traditional Hakka culture offered by this historic village and to better appreciate what life was like in Lai Chi Wo.

'I don't think this would have happened without Mr Lam Chiu-ying and the late Dr Ng Cho-nam.' Humphrey continued the story in his steady voice. Lam Chiu-ying, a former director of the Hong Kong Observatory and now the chairman of the Hong Kong Countryside Foundation, enjoys hiking in his spare time and it was an unintentional encounter that led to the various opportunities down the road. He and Dr Ng, a Research Fellow of local environmental studies, were close friends. Their shared concern for Hong Kong's environmental and rural conservation led to the birth of the current Sustainable Lai Chi Wo Programme.

Blessed in gifts of nature, Lai Chi Wo is situated within the Yan Chau Tong Marine Park of the Hong Kong UNESCO Global Geopark, with Mangrove forests along the shore intertwining with looking-glass trees and white-flowered derris that have given the place an extremely high ecological value. The village houses in Lai Chi Wo are located under a lush fung shui forest. The tiled roofs of the houses are painted in alternating grey and white. An enclosure built outside the village provides an example of the quaint style and features of a Hakka village.

The Hong Kong Countryside Foundation leased its village houses from their owners for twenty years, during which time it was responsible for their restoration and revitalisation. The project was funded by the Hong Kong Jockey Club in 2017, with Humphrey being given the responsibility of restoring the village houses of the Lai Chi Wo Hakka Life Experience Village. During the first phase, fifteen village houses are to be revitalised into homestays and other multi-purpose spaces, with the ultimate goal of renovating twenty-five village houses.

The word 'revitalisation' is usually associated with the act of demolishing buildings and then rebuilding them. However, Humphrey remarked that 'Revitalisation is not just about the renovation of buildings; it is a return to the most basic way of life.' Thus, in the Sustainable Lai Chi Wo Programme, recultivation, not restoration, was the first step. 'Turning wasteland into farmland and creating livelihood – only then will residents be attracted to return.'

Differing from other holiday accommodation on the outlying islands, the homestays in Lai Chi Wo provide an experience of traditional Hakka rural life with different thematic experience activities such as farming and Hakka food culture. 'Many have come from afar to visit this place to experience the lifestyle it offers.' Only through participation will one reap a greater sense of engagement. In the process, of course, there have been voices of doubt: 'Have you tried living there?'; 'You are used to the comfort of the air-conditioner, would you know how to deal with it?' Humphrey smiled, as he recounted this and told me that when he heard questions like that, he would think to himself, 'I know when the mosquitoes will come out and when they will return.'

From recultivation to restoration and, finally, the resurrection of the village, everything was unfolded one step at a time; and although throughout the process many were sceptical, along the way there was never a lack of support and promotion from those who cared. While sharing the bits and pieces of his story, Humphrey still expressed his admiration for the foresight of Mr Lam Chiu Ying and the late Dr Ng Cho-nam. 'This is their vision.'

The population of Lai Chi Wo today consists of not only indigenous residents but also families who have relocated from the city to participate in the recultivation project through the setting up of small farms and cultivating local produce. From time to time, Lai Chi Wo produce, such as coffee beans, rice, turmeric powder and vegetables, can be found in supermarkets. It is as if Tao Yuanming's fable 'The Peach Blossom Spring' has been projected onto twenty-first-century Hong Kong:

> The land was flat and vast, with residences arranged in good order; the fields were fertile with beautiful ponds, bamboo groves, mulberry trees and paths criss-crossing the fields in all directions; the crowing of cocks and the barking of dogs were within everyone's earshot; and within the fields were villagers planting seeds, with men and women clothed in strange ways with their yellow hair in long tufts, and they seemed joyful and happy.

1. Conservation design does not necessarily mean restoring old structures to their original state. Rather, it is carried out to adapt to the different conditions of each village house and the expectations of the owner.
2. There are more than 200 Hakka village houses in the Lai Chi Wo Village built at different times. They are arranged in a three verticals and nine horizontals pattern, following the principles of feng shui, thus providing valuable references for the entire project.
3. The four connected ancient village houses in the Hakka Experience Village have been damaged to varying degrees. The most serious one has only the outer wall intact, thus, there is a greater degree of freedom to add new elements.

Archivilla · The Flower Box

House of the Rising Sun

In the chorus of their hit 'Empire State of Mind', Alicia Keys and Jay-Z sing, 'New York, concrete jungle where dreams are made of. There's nothing you can't do. Now you're in New York...'

Once Raymond was done listening to the song, the words New York lingered long in him and could not be forgotten. His mind was suddenly filled with a fantasy and a yearning for that place 'where dreams are made of'. Raymond had a dream – but it was not the New York dream, which he dared not dream about; at least, that's how he had described it.

Raymond was born more than half a century ago in the Year of the Dragon. In line with traditional Chinese culture, Raymond's mother had hoped, as would any other parent, that the future of her child would become just as golden as the dragon. He attended Maryknoll Convent School for his primary school education. Occasionally, American military personnel would perform at the school, and that was how his yearning for the US developed. Every Wednesday, an American propaganda film would be shown on Duddell Street. 'I would walk over from Hollywood Road to that place every week. I rarely missed it.'

In his autobiography, *Untold Stories of Raymond Fung*, he wrote, 'I fall under the horoscope sign of Gemini, pro-American in elementary school, aspired to all things foreign in secondary school, anti-establishment in university and entered the officialdom after graduation.' This short statement encapsulated a life experience and mindset that had undergone many twists and changes. In the 1970s, Raymond travelled alone to the United States – not to New York but a small town in Louisiana. 'Although I was already very frugal back in Hong Kong, I was simply disappointed once I got there.' Taking in a shabby scene in front of him, and recalling his mother's hard work selling jewellery and doing odd jobs to scrape together the money for his one-way ticket, his heart, which was previously fired up with hope, suddenly turned cold. 'When my relatives and friends heard I was heading to the States, they thought I was somebody. I didn't dare tell them anything!' He didn't tell them which town it was, but the impression in his mind of that shabby scene made him determined to change his circumstances.

Initially, Raymond was studying communications at the Baptist College. However, his determination and passion for architecture propelled him to take the bold step of going abroad to the United States. He was prudent every step of the way during his application process and yet, things didn't go as smoothly as he would expect. The letter of acceptance from the Louisiana State University arrived half a year late; it turned out that the university had no idea where Hong Kong was. 'If my mother hadn't sent me that letter of acceptance, I would have remained clueless.'

Armed with the letter, Raymond was determined to pursue the subject of his choice, in which, of course, he succeeded. 'Fortunately, I achieved excellent grades and won a four-year scholarship at the Louisiana State University.' In addition to his studies, Raymond was also working all hours at several jobs: wood-treatment factories, Chinese restaurants, washing dishes and waitering, which kept a large part of his life occupied. Money earned was spent prudently, and during his third year he bought a flat for his mother in Hong Kong, 'We were living under someone else's roof for a while and we wanted to have a home of our own.'

The previous generation did not often speak openly about love. Raymond did not have an emotionally expressive relationship with his mother, but he did recall his mother staying up late and keeping him company as he studied. 'I used to be quite mischievous and would start getting to my studies only after dinner. I would study through the night until three or four in the morning, and my mother would sit next to me, sometimes dozing off. Occasionally, she would make me a glass of salt water to replenish my strength.' On his first birthday in the United States,

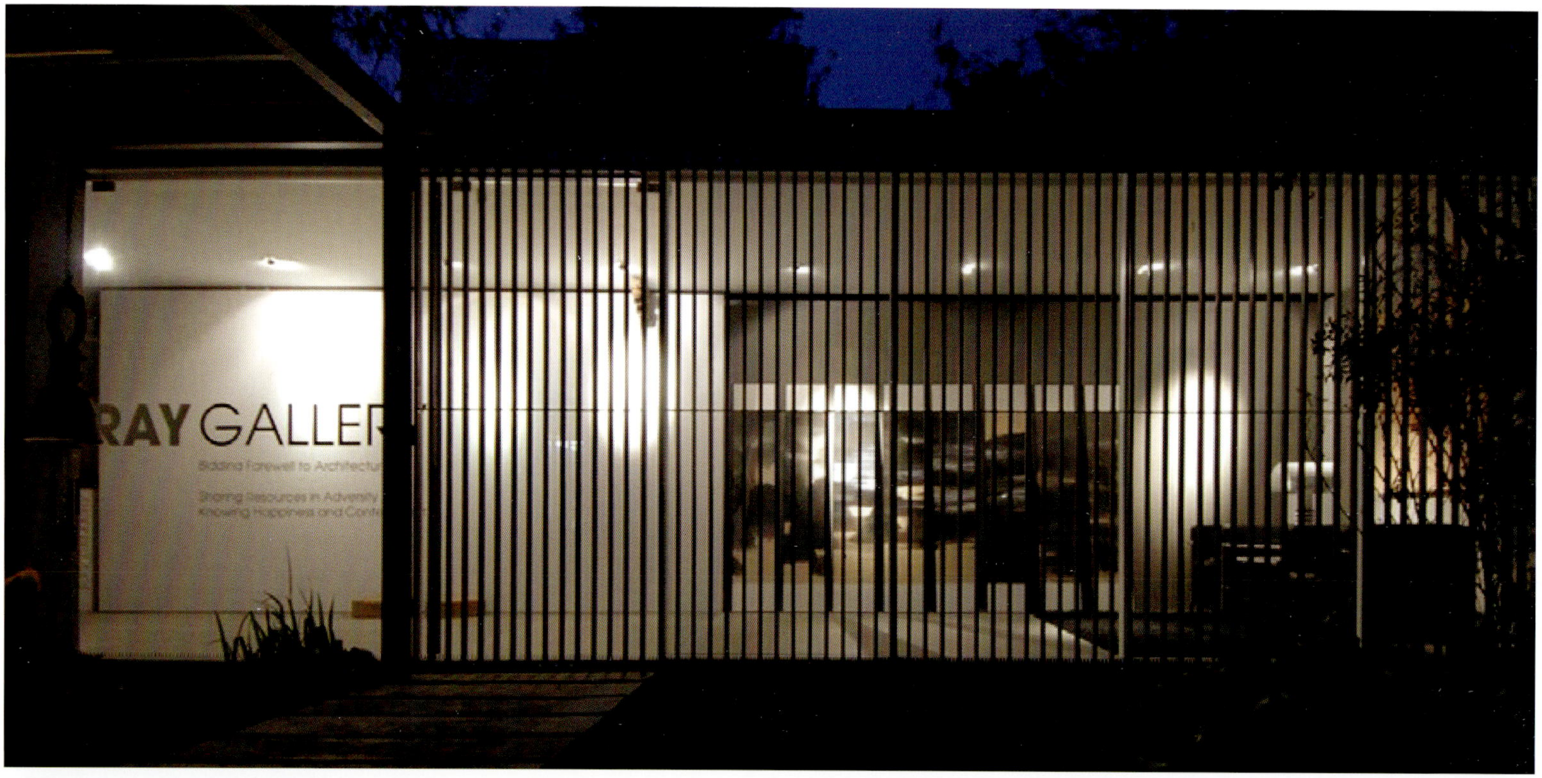
RAY GALLER
Bidding Farewell to Architectu
Sharing Resources in Adversity
Knowing Happiness and Conte

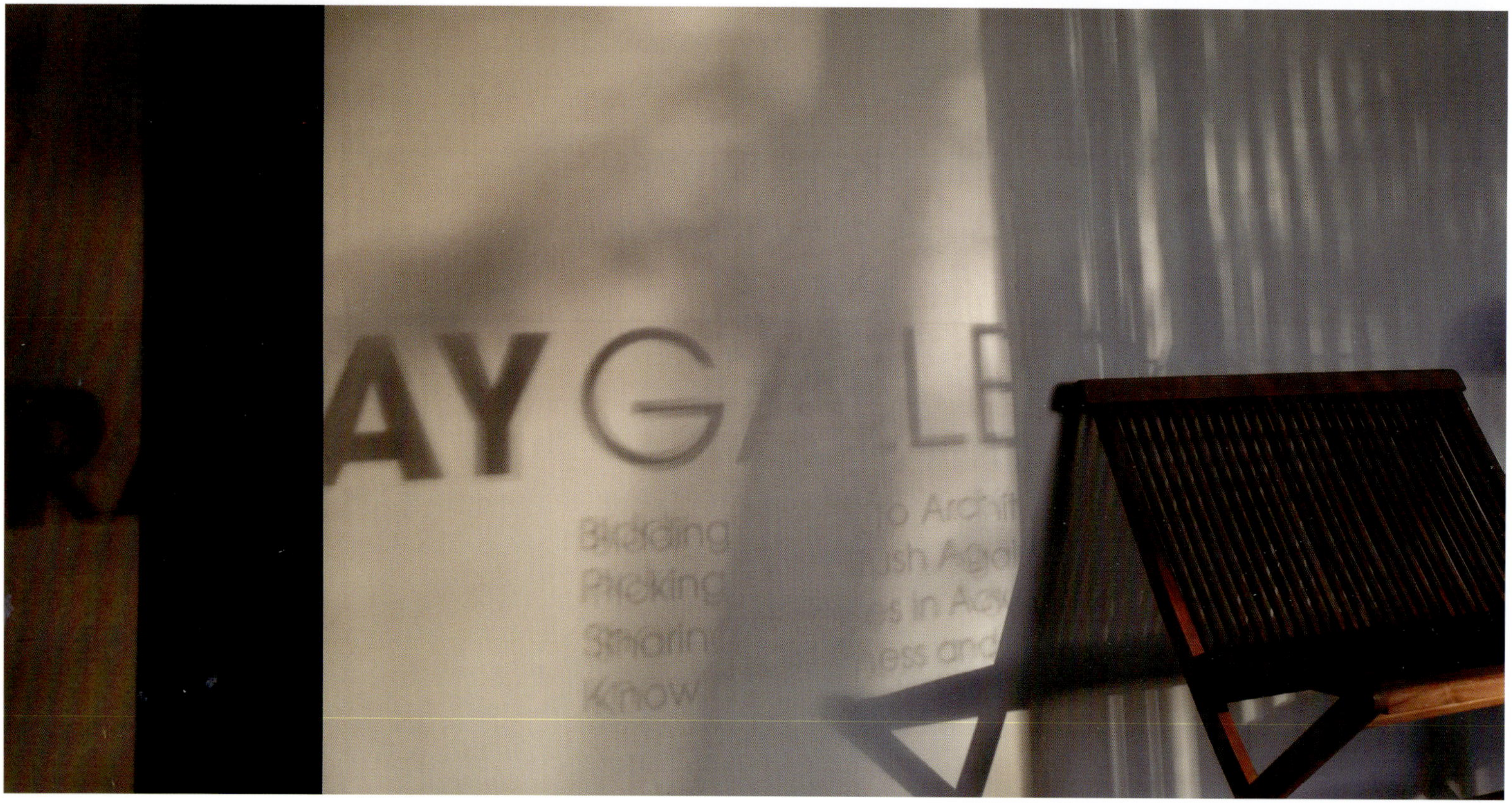

1,2 A studio in Archivilla, featuring a poem on a glass wall. Every time the sun rises, the poems are projected on the warm white walls, echoing a folk song that the owner has a profound feeling for. *House of the Rising Sun* outlines the trajectory of anticipating the coming of light and better days ahead.

3 The main feature of the entrance to Archivilla is the vitality of the white façade wrapped in abundant plants. The silhouette of the iron plate in front of the door symbolises the architect's silent protection of the humanistic spirit here.

1 2 3
4 5 6

1. The rear block is built of fair-faced concrete that seeks to create a youthful taste for the children of the owner. The front and rear buildings are connected by a corridor, the wall of which has a large opening-and-closing blind for not only controlling the amount of light and heat coming in but also maintaining privacy.
2. The mansion consists of front and rear buildings. The mainly white front building is shared by the whole family. The contrast between the white space and the dark-grey gate accentuates the purity of the building. The front garden is composed of Chinese grey bricks arranged in chevrons, permeating the quaint Chinese style of oriental architecture.
3. There are eight Chinese characters cut into the steel plate of the garden pool. 'The garden is as calm as it is pleasant; so let not your glorious years be disturbed.' Every day at around noon, the characters can be seen reflected in the sunlight on the surface of the pool.
4. The front façade of the Flower Box is designed to suggest a large gift box. It consists of a metal mesh with large flower patterns on it.
5. The Flower Box penetrates the small atrium on two floors. The ground floor and the exterior deck are constructed of the same materials.
6. The side of the Flower Box is adorned with extensive glass walls, inviting the outdoor landscape and allowing in abundant natural light.

Raymond spent twenty-five cents on a cake to celebrate alone. Thinking back on this decision, believing at that time that he had burnt all his bridges, he became emotional and started tearing up.

'I questioned myself from time to time, was Baptist College not good enough? Why have I put myself through all these hardships just to be here?' During his five years in the States, what Raymond saw was not the crème de la crème of society but something far from it that was never shown in the American propaganda films he watched in his childhood. It was the most authentic America. 'Discrimination against a black man, with the white man being viewed as superior. The Chinese? They were not important in American society.' Racial inequality; the sorrow and hopelessness of it; and the search for short-term sustenance by those discriminated against, for whom survival was a daily struggle. Even now, whenever Raymond listens to *House of the Rising Sun* by The Animals, he will still shed a tear thinking about how deeply uncertain the future was back then.

After enduring those five long years, Raymond wasted no time in returning to Hong Kong upon graduation. He later worked at Tao Ho Design Architects then Wong Tung & Partners Ltd before entering officialdom and participating in public architecture projects of various scales. Even as life began to improve for him, he worked hard without slacking. In 1991, he had the opportunity to further his crafts abroad and he chose I.M. Pei's architecture firm in New York, without the slightest hesitation. The late I.M. Pei was his idol and his appreciation for Mr Pei had not just been confined to his marvellous design but also the fact that he was a Chinese renowned in a Western society; that fact had a huge impact on Raymond. 'I may never be as great as I.M. Pei, but I do ask myself, "Can I be better?"'

To struggle is human. Coming from a poor family who had little, he was driven by his longing to have his own home; and coupled with his architect's complex, he hoped that he could be the master of it. He named his residence 'Archivilla', which essentially means 'a residence for architects to play around with'. The house exudes a simple yet elegant feel. The white exterior wall is clothed with an abundance of plants, and traces of vitality penetrate through in its undertone; and the steel plate in front of the door incorporates silhouette elements – Raymond's favourite imagery technique – traversing between light and shadow while silently guarding the humanistic spirit found within. The house is open and well-lit and is surrounded by greenery. This is the type of place where one gets up at sunrise and works until sunset. A key focal point of the design is a glass curtain wall in the studio with a poem written on it.

As light from the rising sun shines through the gradually dissipating fog, the words of the poem are projected onto the warm, white wall. This echoes squarely with the song that so moves him – House of the Rising Sun – which, for him, suggests the trajectory of anticipation of light and better days ahead. 'This view gives a strong sense of vitality, which uplifts my spirit and rejuvenates my motivations on a daily basis.'

Other mansions designed by Raymond include the Flower Box and a house on Wiltshire Road. The Flower Box was inspired by the artistic concept of 'Commune by The Great Wall'. The floor-to-ceiling glass windows extend from ground level to the top floor, thus allowing ample natural light into the room. The changes of light and shadow throughout the day suggest the blooming and fading of nature within the house and, also, the continuation of life. The interior of the house penetrates the small, double-height atrium, and, from a vantage point within, one can view both the internal and external treatments of the ground-level wooden platform. As the surrounding landscape at the main entrance of the Flower Box was not as calm as the forest landscape next to it, Raymond decided to move the main entrance to the side facing the forest. He also boldly employed industrial materials as shade barriers, decorating them with floral patterns in a greyish-purple colour tone. This served to not only break away from its industrial feel but also added a touch of romance.

The mansion on Wiltshire Road consists of front and rear blocks. Raymond employed the colour scheme of white and grey for each of them. The front is painted in white with a large, dark-grey gate, which expresses a sense of simplicity and neatness; while at the rear is a fair-faced concrete building, which exudes a kind of unpretentiousness due to its original and natural texture. The garden has been adorned with Chinese grey bricks arranged in a herringbone pattern, expressing the simple and elegant style of Oriental architecture. The steel plate on the pool has eight Chinese characters cut out of it, translated as: 'The garden is as calm as it is pleasant; so let not your glorious years be disturbed.' At noon, these characters will reflect off the surface of the pool in the sunlight.

Whether it is the Archivilla, the Flower Box, or even the mansion on Wiltshire Road, it is obvious that Raymond enjoys integrating variations in light and shadow to present nature's romantic and poignant journey of life.

Learning Garden, The Chinese University of Hong Kong University Library

The Difficulty of Determination Lies in Challenging Yourself

Many would often view architects through the same lens as they do artists ('What is the style of your architecture?'). While it is undeniable that many world-renowned architects have their own unique and personal architectural styles, a work created under such 'personal' style does not necessarily mean that it is a good piece of architecture, nor that its creator is a good architect.

When designing the Learning Garden at the Chinese University of Hong Kong University Library, Ms Angela Pang wanted to create something different for the university. However, she was aware that 'A style being a style in and of itself, is meaningless.'

The Chinese University of Hong Kong (CUHK), perched on the mountainside, adjacent to Tolo Harbour, stands distinct and majestic. Within its campus, lush greenery and the melodious chirping of birds abound, offering a tranquil and pleasant ambience reminiscent of a hillside retreat. It exudes a refreshing and vibrant atmosphere, reminiscent of the nearby islands, creating a stark contrast to the bustling vibe of a downtown-based university.

In 2009, the CUHK planned to expand the University Library, which is located at one end of The University Mall. The Beacon, a popular student forum space, is positioned at the main entrance of the university and on which sits *The Gate of Wisdom*, a sculpture by Mr Ju Ming. The sculpture itself is both a landmark and legend of the CUHK.

Rumour has it that if one passes through the Gate of Wisdom in the direction of the library, one would graduate with first-class honours; conversely, passing through in the opposite direction would result in failure. Although there is a wide spectrum of opinions regarding this, it nevertheless adds a touch of intrigue to the campus. Next to it, there is also the Romanesque fountain square named the Forum. Collectively, they form an immovable part of the unique features of CUHK which carry with them memories and stories of this place.

Without damaging the original appearance of the campus, the university set out to develop a basement. 'During the initial design phase, I wanted to incorporate elements of nature.' When Angela first laid her eyes on the site, it was extremely chaotic, and the space that was covered with concrete had rendered the environment very dark. She described it as needing a lot of imagination when she was conceiving its design. However, the environment of CUHK reminded her of mountains, trees and rocks.

As one of the libraries on campus that is open twenty-four hours, the Learning Garden does not have the serious atmosphere of a traditional library. There are no study-room-style desks and chairs that would make one feel the pressing need to work hard. Instead, it is a simple, bright and open space with creatively designed tables and chairs. Upon entering the library, one feels relaxed and at ease.

Although the library is located in the basement, the bright and open space is not created by purely shining pale lights onto it. The glass pool in front of the Forum, directly above the library, acts as its skylight, introducing natural light. Sunlight passing through the pool ripples in sympathy with the water, creating a swaying interplay of light and shadow, so that, even while indoors, one can still 'feel' the breeze that caresses the water's surface while the sun hides behind the clouds.

Another eye-catching feature of the library is the S-shaped table, which looks both like a piece of ribbon and an intricately winding path that traverses the library. The tables are of varying heights, and users can

The library is located in the basement, but it is bright and comfortable. The open space design incorporates natural and humanistic elements, allowing students to immerse themselves within it.

choose to sit on conventional chairs or bean bags. 'I am rather lazy, so lying down for me is more attractive than sitting upright. I asked myself, "What should be the ideal height of the desk if I were to lie down?"'

The Learning Garden has been described by some as a heaven for students. It is the best spot for burning the midnight oil while conducting student council business, completing coursework or studying for finals, which is why it has also been dubbed 'the Learning Accommodation'.

Design is something fancy for many, but sensationalism is not what Angela believes in. The multi-faceted approach of the Learning Garden is to allow students to find a learning mode that best suits them. 'Let the project speak for itself.' Instead of making it the way you want it. 'It is more important to first understand its essence. The single face of a wall also has its own meaning,' Angela said.

Angela has her own very strongly held views on architecture. However, architecture was never her first choice to begin with. When asked why she studied architecture, Angela spat out the answer in her thin voice: 'Actually, my father wanted me to study architecture. It was not my initial choice. I wanted to be a war correspondent.'

Having developed an interest in art and photography at a young age, she has watched quite a number of documentaries. Amongst them was a social photographic documentary named *The Workers* by Sebastião Ribeiro, which was the source of her inspiration to become a war correspondent. The documentary showed her a world she had never seen before: one segment covered a gold mine in Brazil where thousands of workers were seen digging and sweating from every pore; another

1. The study and reading space added to the library of the Hong Kong Polytechnic University, inspired by free reading. A series of pavilions in the Study Landscape were later designed to allow students to find a mode of study that suits them best.
2. The design of the Lingnan University Library includes a new floor named the Platform of Knowledge, which provides students with a space to expand their minds, metaphorically speaking.
3. The S-shaped table is a 'learning path' that weaves together the vast space, and its subtle changes in height, width and shape provide a path for students to develop new ideas.

segment showed a textile factory in Sri Lanka where, one after another, tanned-skin female workers were processing fabrics day in and day out. Growing up in Hong Kong in the 1980s, Angela never came across such images. What struck her was the realisation that 'there are many people in the world whose lives are different from mine.'

It was a trend in Hong Kong in the 1990s to send children abroad to study. When she was thirteen years old, Angela took a plane to the United States to attend a boarding school. She brought with her luggage three times her size.

'Father' to Angela, was a man who was smart, hardworking and good at maths. 'He really wanted to study in a university; however, he just didn't have the conditions to do that.' Her father started out on the construction site and later founded his own contractor company. 'To him, being an architect was a very respectable role.'

Falling in line with her father's expectation, she became an architect. Although she has now taken on a different role, did the feeling of wanting to make a difference in society still remain? Angela gave no answer right away and was silent for a moment, after which she began speaking slowly. 'Behind that sense of purpose, a lot of persistence and effort are needed...' She continued to share some of her work experiences in recent years, including some in which she was very invested in creating a good design, but to no avail. With regard to those instances where much sweat and blood had been put in but had bore no fruit in the end, she still felt a little helpless and aggrieved when talking about them. She described herself as similar to the protagonist, K, from Kafka's novel *The Castle*, who was summoned and went through such hardships on his way to the castle, only to still be denied entry in the end.

Regardless, as Kafka wrote in *The Castle*,

> K knew that there was no threat of actual compulsion, he had no fear of that, especially not here, but the force of these discouraging surroundings and of the increasing familiarity with ever more predictable disappointments, the force of scarcely perceptible influences at every moment, these he certainly did fear, but even in the face of this danger he had to risk taking up the struggle.

Angela thought the same. 'I wouldn't say that I have this same sense of purpose in changing the world, but at least I do the best I can while being sincere both in heart and with my abilities.' What will you say to yourself should you encounter setbacks in the future? 'Just work hard and don't give up.'

The Lee Shau Kee Architecture Building,
Chinese University of Hong Kong

Isn't it Delightful to Roam Within

The minimalistic texture of fair-faced concrete makes the CUHK School of Architecture (Lee Shau Kee Architecture Building) feel unpretentious, without a sense of fanciness or exaggeration – just like Wallace Chang and T.C. Yuet: real and grounded.

CUHK held a long-overdue design competition in 2008 for the design of the School of Architecture. More than forty international designers took part. The requirements stipulated that each participant could submit only only three design drawings. Wallace's and T.C.'s design was selected in the final six. T.C. recalled that Rocco Yim, who was one of the judges, posed this question to them: How can I tell from your design that this is an architecture school?

Upon hearing this, T.C. imitated the solemn answer he gave back then: 'Our architectural design inherits the tradition of the Chinese University of Hong Kong – modesty. The interior of the building can be used as a school of architecture, and so there is no need for anything iconic on the outside.' Wallace had then chipped in with, 'This is just another campus building.' T.C. recalled thinking that Wallace was very bold. 'They asked you for its special features, and yet you actually gave them such an answer – and in an official setting.' Although their response had been a little out of line, a few months later, they received a letter carrying the unexpected good news.

In addition to being the designers of the School of Architecture, Wallace and T.C. were also its users. During the design process, the two of them did not start from their own perspective; instead, they sought to understand the perspective of the users. They asked the students for feedback on their design. 'We have this belief that architecture should not be extravagant; we prefer it to be real and grounded.' The School of Architecture is like a big tree under the shade of which students and teachers and even people from different disciplines can absorb, create output, interact and learn from one another. T.C. remarked that this concept had come from the American architect Louis Kahn's interpretation of a School of Architecture – 'Communal ground. One big roof.'

So, being real and grounded is what you understand as aesthetics? 'The word "aesthetics" originated in the West. The Chinese refer to it as the study of the heart, not necessarily of physical beauty. At least, it was not until the era of Mr Hu Shih that aesthetics began to take form...' Standing nearby, Wallace suddenly interrupted, 'He was asking you what you thought of aesthetics, not what Mr Hu Shih had thought of aesthetics.' The two burst out laughing, and T.C. continued. 'Aesthetics is to some extent related to the sense of sight, and Hong Kong's aesthetics sits somewhere between inclusiveness and complexity, so I would see aesthetics as an environment in which it sensationalises your sense of sight.' Wallace then added. 'To sum it up in a few words, isn't it delightful to roam within?'

Ever since the two met in university decades ago, they have been at each other's side. 'He was very quiet and didn't talk much back then,' said T.C., looking at Wallace. Recalling their university days, their memories were still as fresh as ever. It was their mentor, the late Mr Chang Chao-Kang, who had brought them together.

Chang Chao-Kang took pleasure in the study of Chinese residential architecture and culture. During their university days, Wallace and T.C. would follow Chang Chao-Kang out to the countryside to study the Fujian Tulou (traditional earthen dwellings found in the mountainous areas of Fujian province, China). 'He was basically one of the first Chinese architects to pay attention to folk dwellings; these are buildings filled with vitality and they are able to keep pace with the changing times; not to mention they are people-oriented and friendly. However, architecture

1. In addition to designing studios, libraries and other facilities, the soul of the entire building should emphasise the concept of 'A man under a tree, in nature, reflects on life', as advocated by architecture educator Louis Kahn.
2. Lee Shau Kee Architecture Building, The Chinese University of Hong Kong.
3. A place where ideas are exchanged freely, blurring the lines between teacher and student.

schools would not consider such ideas at that time, because there was a global trend towards postmodernism.'

After graduation, Wallace taught at CUHK and founded Arch Design Architects Ltd, and T.C. joined him shortly after. During the early years of the new millennium, the company was plagued with difficulties with no projects and staff and, with only the two of them at the office to stare into the eyes of the other, together with their secretaries. Even then, payroll became a problem. 'I didn't want to make them redundant so I paid them through my salary from teaching at the university.'

After listening to Wallace's recollections, T.C. lamented that this dire situation continued for such a long time. 'We weren't on the payroll for about ten years, give or take. While he depended on his salary from the university, I was running a French restaurant with my high school friends. So I ran the company during the day and changed clothes and headed to my bartending job when the evening lights were lit.' T.C. later joined the teaching staff at CUHK as well, and the two have been inseparable brothers ever since.

On the topic of satisfaction, T.C. explained it thus: 'Both of us were taking one solid step at a time. If looking at it from the perspective of money, there was absolutely no satisfaction; but, as architects, our sense of satisfaction is derived from being able to honestly take ownership for the works designed by us. The worst thing for an architect is not daring to take ownership of a project.'

It has been thirty years since they graduated, and over twenty years of that time has been spent teaching. 'Honestly, we will be sixty years old in a couple of years, but we still feel young and enthusiastic!' Although being a professional architect and a teacher at the same time has not been easy, being able to teach is something they both feel fortunate about. 'From a humanistic angle, going through life with students feels a little more noble and pure than conforming to societal norms.'

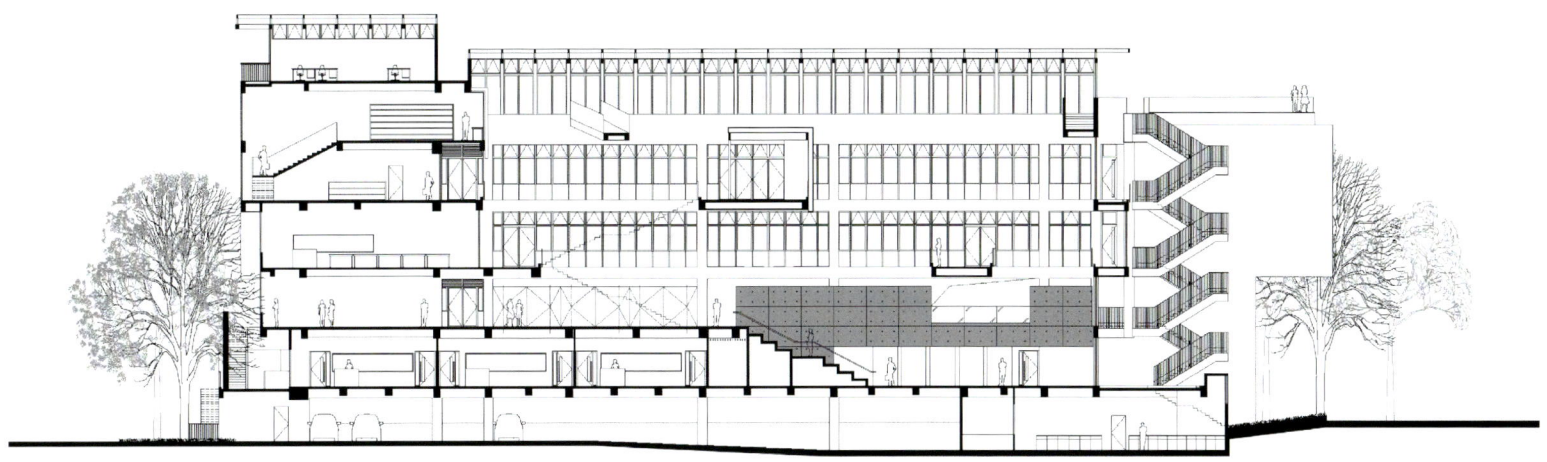

Morningside College,
Chinese University of Hong Kong

Runway

Frank Yu has sported a buzz cut for many years. Perhaps that hairstyle is easy to manage – after all, it keeps its shape even after wearing a helmet. Coupled with his tanned scalp, his entire presence exudes a polished and sharp impression. When one sees him, your gaze will naturally be drawn to his face, locking eyes directly with his distinct black-and-white monolid eyes.

At the time of the interview, Frank was in blazing hot Thailand. Despite his busy schedule, he had made time to speak on a Friday morning. Frank used to accompany his father to construction sites when he was young, and that was how his fated encounter with architecture came about. 'I thought the study of architecture was an easy task when I was in school – something you graduated from just by doing some drawings.' Frank recalled this beautiful misunderstanding with a smile while on the other side of a screen.

At the Pratt Institute, where he read architecture, the professors had very high expectations of the students. Because of the intense competition, Frank survived on only three or four nights' worth of sleep per week. 'Even on normal days, I would just be getting a few hours' sleep.' Recalling his university life of over thirty years ago, he appreciated that his initial belief of architecture being easy was a beautiful delusion. However, he would never forget the gratitude he felt towards his mentors. 'I really do have to thank them, really.' Just as every child has to go through the process of growing up and will only understand the meaning behind the well-intentioned and earnest advice of adults once they have grown up.

New York in the 1980s was a prime place and time for architecture. After graduation, Frank joined the biggest architecture and construction company, Ellerbe Becket, and worked in the Design Studio led by Peter Pran. To make up for his lack of experience, Frank learnt from his teachers while also taking part with his peers in many competitions. He was winning them, too, including one at John F. Kennedy. 'I was taking part in those competitions together with Norman Foster and Zaha Hadid.' Recalling his old days, Frank couldn't hide the delight on his face, and he described them as some of his happiest years. 'Not only was it fun, but after winning a competition, you could also actually materialise your design into a real piece of architecture.'

In the early 1990s, as the Chinese market began to grow, he chanced upon an opportunity to return home. Back in Hong Kong, he founded Gravity Partnership with Mr Claude Wong. Wasn't it the same year as the outbreak of the severe acute respiratory syndrome pandemic? 'Exactly. We were quite the bold and ambitious entrepreneurs!'

In the early days, Frank had quite a traditional mindset. The firm didn't engage in any marketing or advertising. 'I felt that if we had a good reputation, people would naturally come looking for us.' Gravity has now been in business for twenty-one years as at 2022. Frank's work has included residential, commercial and public architecture and even integrated projects. Some of his projects include the Chengdu ICC, Beijiao Cultural Centre and the UpperHills. Most of his projects have been Mainland-based, but he firmly believed that as long as he produced quality work, opportunities would naturally come from other places.

In 2006, Frank collaborated with Studio Shanghai on the design of Morningside College, CUHK, his first project in Hong Kong. Morningside

| 1 | 2 | 1 | Morningside College is a cluster of buildings located on a small hill.
| | 3 | 2 | The bridge between the two dormitories strengthens the overall relationship of the two buildings.
| | | 3 | The building complex is divided into high and low levels, echoing the terrain and protecting the view of the surrounding buildings. In front of the entrance is the central square, which provides a large gathering space for teachers and students.

College, built on hilly terrain, was completed in 2011. The campus consists of the Tower Block residing on higher ground as well as the Greenberg Building on the lower ground. The square between the two buildings, a comfortable, quiet place which has become a meeting place for students, commands a scenic view of the distant Tolo Harbour. The exterior colour scheme of Morningside College combines brown and grey, with elements of lightly coloured fair-faced concrete and bricks that echo the typical style of CUHK.

With regard to architectural style, Frank remarked that he had not gone after any specific design elements. 'Every place has its own characteristics, just like you would dress accordingly for different occasions.' To him, his greatest sense of satisfaction from architecture comes from the satisfaction of his users. 'I have done a lot of things not for myself but for others. If I was doing it for my own sake, it would have been easy in the sense that every project would just need to reach a similarly acceptable standard. However, if a user comes back to you and says, "Thank you, I really enjoy being here" – that would bring me the greatest sense of satisfaction.'

His Chinese name is Siu-fung. Those two strong characters, when put together, amplify his aura, yet when he speaks, his gentle words put you at ease. Frank is not just an ordinary architect; he is also a professional race car driver who has raced for Aston Martin, Porsche and Mercedes-Benz. He has even stood on the winner's podium – his first time was at the 2010 GT Asia race. Speaking of racing, the spark in Frank's eyes was no less than when he talked about architecture. He has always enjoyed challenges, and both architecture and racing satisfy him in that respect. Although the two pursuits are quite different, to him, whether it is the start of a project or a race, it is a brand new venture, challenge and practice. What follows depends on how well he handles himself and his ultimate performance.

Sai Kung Visual Corridor

Not Just the Rear Garden of Hong Kong

As soon as I arrive at Sai Kung, the 'Rear Garden of Hong Kong', the pleasant sight of rustic fishing villages and the oldest hiking trails in Hong Kong comes into view. Along the way, there are coastal mountains, clear water and blue sky, and the moss on the mountain slopes gives off the smell of greenery and soil. Suddenly, the roar of the metropolis has been cut off.

To Raymond Fung, Sai Kung is more than the rear garden of Hong Kong. The 2003 severe acute respiratory syndrome pandemic brought about a depressive atmosphere. The then Financial Secretary of HKSAR proposed a promotion of the local economy, and Sai Kung was selected as the first testing ground. Raymond led a team that included K.C. King and Ida Sze. The leading department for the project was the Tourism Commission, whose primary intention was to design several kiosks and stalls along the waterfront to enrich the community. But how could a project remain that simple if it was entrusted to Raymond?

Starting from the pier and strolling towards the visitor centre, one is greeted by welcome signs in ten different languages. A little further in is the Sai Kung Waterfront Park, which everyone refers to as 'the paper boat park'. As the water of the shallow pond ripples in the gentle sea breeze, paper boat sculptures, inspired by the origami boats of childhood, sit motionless on its surface. They are printed with text from newspapers published during the period of the War of Resistance Against Japanese Aggression. They tell the stories of Sai Kung's past as a fishing port and commemorate the heroic deeds of local residents who joined the Hong Kong Independent Battalion of the Dongjiang Column during the war.

'The park has always been there. We actually did not rebuild anything, but we did make a few minor modifications.' To open up the entrance and reduce the sense of alienation that the original layout induced, Raymond and his teams relocated the engineering room and lavatories from the entrance to the side. As a result of this added sense of transparency and openness, the park now interacts more with its surroundings. It is now a more inviting and restful place for visitors.

The night breeze that blows gently across the coastal park gives the place a sense of tranquillity that has sparked the idea of waterfront restaurants in Raymond's mind. However, matters relating to restaurants were the concerns of the Food and Environmental Hygiene Department while the park itself fell under the management of the Leisure and Cultural Services Department. With interdepartmental cooperation being a rarity, it resulted in a not-so-smooth outcome during the first round of tender from the restaurants. So for the second round, instead of submitting just formal documents, Raymond, together with his teammates K.C. King and Ida Sze, opted to organise an exhibition to provide a comprehensive explanation to the public regarding the project. 'It sure did break some of the usual practice; very seldom do architects engage in this sort of marketing activity.' While some may consider this to be a little out-of-line, Raymond just had a quick laugh when recalling this incident. 'Even K.C. King thought I was crazy.' The restaurants now make the place more lively than before. Raymond even initiated contacts with the restaurateurs to organise a children's painting competition and set up a make-shift exhibition space that displayed the entry pieces, thereby bringing some warmth and a sense of belonging to the place.

Upon closer examination, one would notice the towering bronze bells along the way. According to Raymond, the inspiration for these bells came from the Sai Kung Town Tin Hau Temple Complex, an old temple complex built in the hope that the Goddess of the Sea would bestow blessings of protection and safety on fishermen and their boats. The

 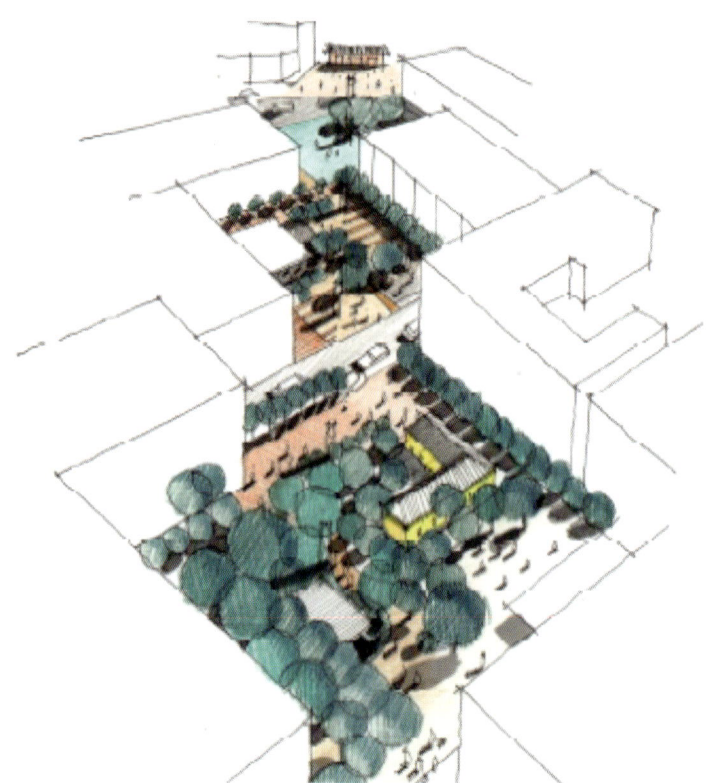

original plan was to install thirteen bells, one for each of the temples scattered around Sai Kung, thereby referencing the relationship between the temple and the bygone fishing village culture. All thirteen bells were meant to be installed along a route stretching from Tin Hau Temple to the pier and passing through the basketball court, Man Yee Playground, the bus terminal, the minibus station and the waterfront park to create a continuous line. However, such a proposal would have required the repurposing of land usage, and unfortunately, the bus terminal and minibus station were difficult to relocate, resulting in the installation of only five bronze bells. In Wei Jen Wang's words, 'Raymond has successfully combined architecture, landscape and urban space with environmental art in the public square.'

As an architect, Raymond is well aware that whereas art can live for itself, architecture cannot do the same. Over the years, he has insisted on the idea of 'Building less for more' while taking bold steps that have been considered 'out of line'. Recalling his work on the Sai Kung Visual Corridor, Raymond has had to deal with a wide range of issues with the Civil Engineering and Development Department, Food and Environmental Hygiene Department for the restaurants, Leisure and Cultural Services Department for the parks, and even the Highways Department for the roads outside of the sidewalk cafés. He left no stone unturned in his pursuit of harmony, even specifying paving bricks to match the bricks used for the restaurants and stalls.

'The architects lead not just the architecture itself, but also the activities of the entire community.' Later, the government even used the Sai Kung project as a demonstration project for urban design. 'I have lived in Sai Kung for years, and this place I call home has always been close to my heart; especially when hearing about the opinions of everyone around, whether they be good or bad, it does create a very special relationship between the architects, users and the city.'

Being here, the roar of the city falls on deaf ears, but not for the whispers of life. Perhaps as Mr Lin Yutang once said, 'The best architecture is one where being within makes you wonder where nature has ended, and where art begins.'

| 1 | 2 | 3 | 1 | Hand-drawn perspective of the Sai Kung Visual Corridor.
| | | | 2 | Hand-painted perspective of the aerial view of the Sai Kung Visual Corridor.
| | | | 3 | The original plan for the Sai Kung Visual Corridor included the relocation of the bus terminal and the installation of thirteen bronze bells. Unfortunately, it has not been fully realized.

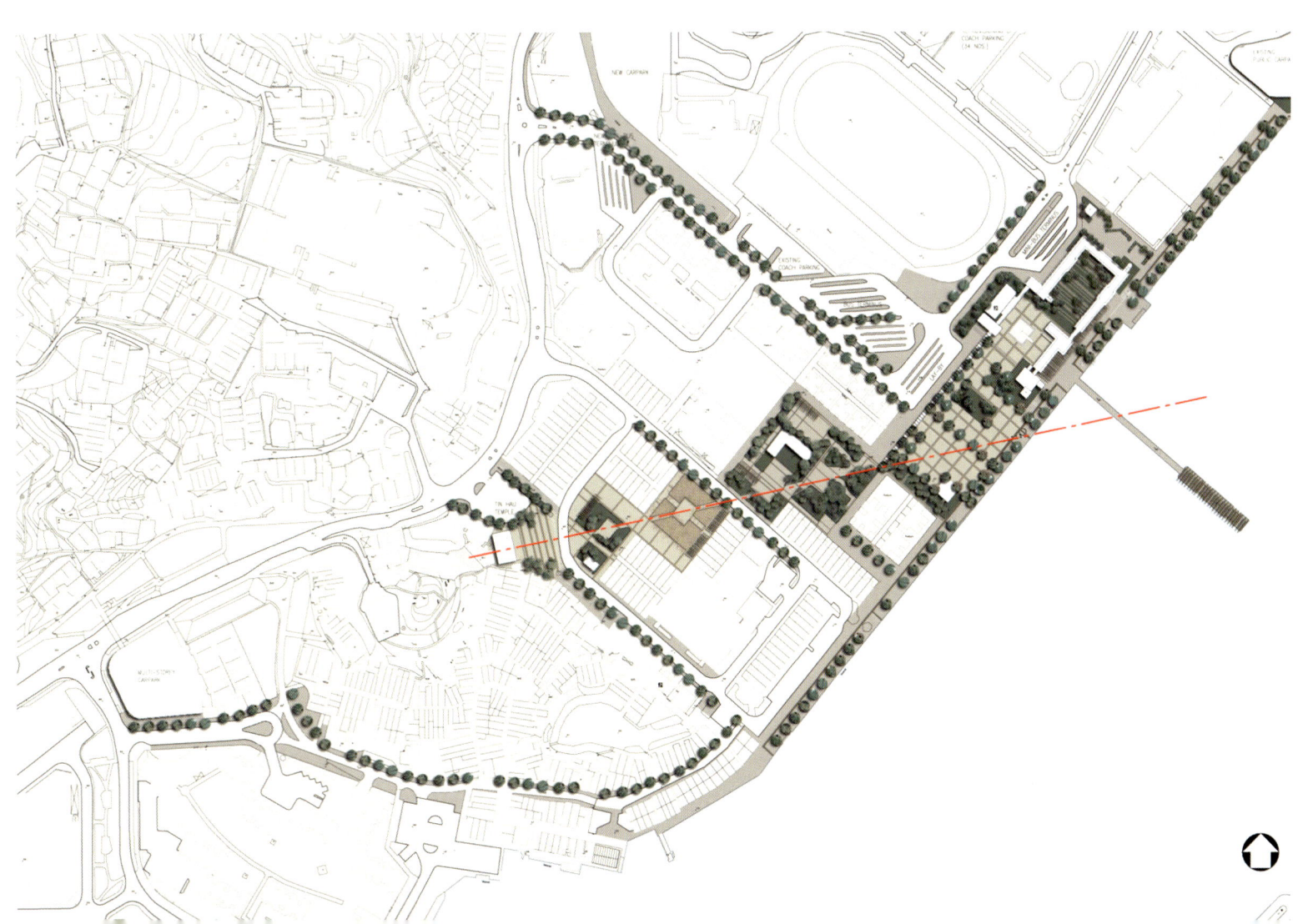

| 1 | 2 | 3 |
| | | 4 |

1 The flags beside the gazebo in the waterfront park greet tourists from all over the world in multiple languages.
2 The design team organised a children's drawing competition. The entries were displayed amongst the gazebos.
3 Paper Boat Park.
4 Free-spirited cows break through the boundaries set by man.

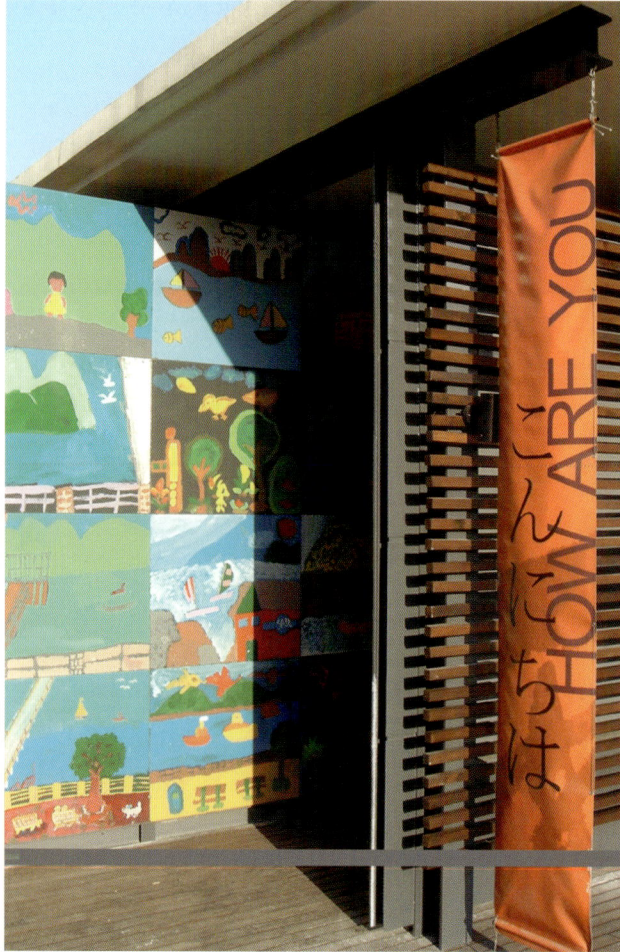

1		
		3
2		

1. The architects worked hard to ensure the introduction of sidewalk cafés at the Sai Kung Waterfront Park.
2. A gazebo and a bell were installed at the Sha Tsui Road Playground. The bronze bells were installed to represent the temples of Sai Kung. The original idea had been for the bells to be rung at noon, but they currently remain silent.
3. The waterfront pier is characterised by a natural, light-transmitting roof and display boards in multiple languages. It uses modern design techniques to highlight the youthful vitality of Sai Kung.

New Territories West

Reading Guidance

How would one define the New Territories? In the past, Boundary Street separated Kowloon and the New Territories, but the distinction has now become ambiguous. The area of New Territories West generally refers to the districts of Kwai Chung, Tsing Yi, Tsuen Wan, Tuen Mun and Yuen Long.

Kwai Chung is mainly populated by industrial buildings, with good architecture in short supply. In contrast, the Tsing Yi Municipal Services Building on the Tsing Yi island, completed in 1991, is a masterpiece by Mr Anthony Ng. With its white grid pattern and the skillfull interplay of solid and void spaces, it was the most elegant municipal services building of its time; and even from today's aesthetic standpoint, it still retains its timeless charm. Eighteen years later, another masterpiece was erected on Tsing Yi island. The exterior of the Tsing Yi Southwest Sports Centre, designed by Mr M.C. Chung, is composed of clean geometric lines with an indescribable tension. It stands tall on the square as if it is a monument. Its interior presents a pleasantly surprising contrast with strong visual elements.

There is also a crematorium in Kwai Chung, designed by Mr Benny Lee and Mr Paul Mui. This building joins the other funeral-related architecture presented in this book whose designs are amongst the most distinctive examples of Hong Kong architecture. It is a smaller piece of architecture with a minimalistic undertone and a streamlined, quiet and simple design that penetrates through the glass and the lotus pond. Benny and Paul have won numerous public art competitions, which serves to illustrate that many young architects begin with designing outdoor sculptures before developing into architecture projects. I believe this is a positive, step-by-step approach for young professionals.

Also of note are Ms Sarah Mui's designs of the rooftops of two car parks at Tseung Kwan O and Tuen Mun. The designs include some unique basketball courts, which, instead of the traditional line markings, uses varicoloured lines, breaking away from the common basketball court design.

The Tseun Wan Yi Pei Square Playground and the Portland Street Rest Garden have undergone a major transformation from their original states of disrepair. The development of the parks came about as part of the Play is for the People initiative, one of the projects spearheaded by the Design Trust Futures Studio organised by Ms Marisa Yiu.

The initiative uses art and design to transform dilapidated public spaces or parks in the city into pioneering miniature parks, giving these places a new look filled with colourful and positive interactions.

In Tsuen Wan, there is a trendy new location named The Mills, which sits on the site of the former Nan Fung Cotton Mills. Following the decline of Hong Kong's industrial sector, the third-generation owners have preserved this industrial building and transformed it into a new and trendy cultural centre to attract the younger generation. Perhaps other third generation owners could take a page out of this book in terms of the cultural role they could play in Hong Kong; they are both contacts and creators, and not just mere receivers. Little by little, they could change the trajectory of this new era of Hong Kong. The Mills contains an exhibition hall that

showcases the history of the Nan Fung Group, as well as a large exhibition space available for hire by professional curators. A team including Mr Ray Zee, Mr Boris Lo, Mr Gary Ng, Mr Billy Tam were collectively responsible for its splendid design. Another revitalisation project that has achieved similar results to The Mills but through different means is the Luen Tai Industrial Building in Kwai Hing. A local project by Ms Lucia Cheung, it has transformed the originally unassuming factory building into a dynamic and trendy shopping mall. With many industrial buildings in Hong Kong now waiting to be transformed, if projects of such nature are matched with suitable architects who dare to be creative in their approach, it will surely entail a win-win situation.

Along the coast of Tuen Mun – another similar industrial district – a new, brightly coloured building with a distinctive appearance and a red clay tone catches the eye. Designed by Rocco Yim, the campus of Chu Hai College of Higher Education has undergone several relocations before finally settling on its current, stunningly beautiful form. This achievement is attributable to both Rocco's effort and the vision embodied by the school. I concur with the notion that a beautiful campus can instil a greater sense of pride in its students. This has been evident in my interactions with the students there, whose joy and anticipation could be felt throughout our conversations. Paradoxically, although Rocco graduated from HKU and has designed several university campuses in Hong Kong, he has designed very few buildings for his alma mater. Most of his works were designed for CUHK. Elsewhere in this book, Rocco discussed his work on the Graduate House project for HKU. In addition, Mr Paul Chu, head of the architecture department at the Chu Hai College of Higher Education, has been instrumental to the success of the department. Originally a full-time architect, in 2008, he changed course to take up a teaching position there.

Another prestigious educational institution is the Lingnan University located at Fu Tei. P&T Group designed the original campus. Subsequent additions of premises and facilities, including the Lingnan Institute of Further Education, have been co-designed by Wei Jen Wang, AD+RG Architecture Design and Research Group Limited, as well as the Lingnan University Library designed by Angela Pang. Wei Jen Wang from Taiwan has designed numerous cultural architectural works in the Mainland, including in Chengdu, Hangzhou and Shenzhen. His designs have demonstrated a special affinity for traditional Chinese architecture interpreted with a modern approach. This is particularly evident in his design of the Lingnan Institute of Further Education, which takes its inspiration from Chinese Siheyuan (Chinese courtyard houses) and gives it a modern reinterpretation. It is indeed a place worthy of admiration.

A lesser-known masterpiece designed by a world-renowned architect is the Maggie's Cancer Caring Centre Hong Kong in Tuen Mun, designed by Frank Gehry[1]. Amongst Frank Gehry's works in Hong Kong, the most well-known would be the Opus Hong Kong, which has been nicknamed 'the Hong Kong Bauhinia'. The building showcases a skilful form of distortion that defies the orderly style typical of Hong Kong's residential buildings.

It is very unusual for such a minor building as this cancer centre to have been designed by such a world-famous architect. The likely reason for this circumstance is that the principal donor is related to Frank Gehry. The building looks like a large European mansion, and has been designed with the needs of the users in mind to create a restful environment specifically tailored for cancer patients.

There are many new, high-quality pieces of architecture in Tuen Mun. 'T. Park' is a self-sustained waste treatment facility that not only serves as an educational centre but also as an experimental ground for the waste-to-energy initiative. Interestingly, the park also offers a free footbath for its visitors. This modern building has a streamlined, wave-form exterior that highlights the surrounding natural landscape and topography. The design also utilises the elements of sunlight, natural ventilation and green roofs to reduce energy consumption, setting itself as a leader in green buildings. The architecture is by renowned French architects Claude Vasconi[2] and Thomas Schinko[3].

'The Miami of Hong Kong', is a long embankment lined with palm trees and a spacious lawn on Ho Wo Street, Tuen

Mun. Visitors come from afar to enjoy this temporary getaway from the city.

Yuen Long in the New Territories has always been a rather traditional town. Since the introduction of the West Rail Line, travel time from Kowloon has been drastically reduced, leading to the town gradually becoming a new spot for the young to frequent. This growing popularity has brought with it new and exciting developments. For instance, cycling has become an increasingly popular pastime. The government adopted a very minimalistic style in the design of a bicycle station and adjacent public lavatories, both located under an elevated highway. This style has now become the standard in Yuen Long. Another building of note in Yuen Long is the new wing of the Yuen Long District Community Services Building, which was designed by Mr William Liu. Its exterior of corrugated squares decorated in lively colours epitomises new, modern architecture. This piece of architecture gives encouraging evidence of the ongoing rejuvenation and modernisation of Yuen Long's cityscape.

Frank Lui's career trajectory, from a rugged beginning to his later development, provides a salutary lesson for young architects. The first encounter I had with him was through his projects in Shenzhen, where he designed a lot of distinctive public architecture. This begged the question of how someone from Hong Kong could achieve such a breakthrough in the Mainland. As it turns out, what made it possible was the open tender policy adopted by the local government of Shenzhen. In contrast, even as a born-and-bred Hong Kong local, Lui had little chance of finding someone who appreciated his talent; except for a chance encounter with a friend who later invited him to design a Small House (a village house belonging to an indigenous male) in Yuen Long. The Vice Versa House is well worth a visit.

Hidden Utopia of Hong Kong

The Hong Kong Golf Club, established in 1889, is situated in Kwu Tung, Fanling and covers an area of 170 hectares[4]. Prior to my visit, I couldn't have imagined such a stunning natural park existing in Hong Kong. Upon my arrival, I was delighted to discover the elegant charm of British-style architecture,

409 valuable old trees, and vast stretches of grassland. Particularly captivating is the rare sight of a magnificent grove formed by layers of Melaleuca trees, rivalling the renowned beauty of London's Hyde Park and New York's Central Park. It was a delightful revelation that Hong Kong has long been home to such breathtaking scenery. However, few residents in the city are aware of this hidden utopia, reminiscent of Scotland, that lies within their own city. The continuous and devoted cultivation efforts undertaken by the Hong Kong Golf Club has been pivotal to the existence and upkeep of this charming place; and it is this mutually dependent relationship that deserves much admiration and respect. Should the grassy expanse of this golf course be one day transformed into a 'Central Park' for the residents of Hong Kong, while preserving all the existing gardens and waterways, it would undoubtedly be a source of pride for the city.

Not far from the Hong Kong Golf Club is the Tai Lung Veterinary Laboratory. Its appearance deviates from the ordinary mundane laboratories. Its exterior showcases a contrasting effect of yin and yang with a white spray paint finish. This accentuates the geometric interaction between circles and square boxes, revealing the meticulous arrangement by its architect, Mr Daniel Chow. It stands as a masterpiece of architectural brilliance.

The No-Longer-Sad Tin Shui Wai

Tin Shui Wai is a new town that is densely populated with housing estates. During its early years, the town lacked basic amenities

with our work and notified us to proceed with the design and planning for Phase 2. That was where the real challenge began. The creation of a sixty-hectare leisure and scenic area with a 10,000-square-metre main exhibition hall, branch halls and bird hides; the construction and commissioning of a geothermal heat pump system and many other unique green measures. And towards the end came yet another episode of drama: the discovery of a saltwater crocodile in the Ng Tung River! It took a city-wide crocodile hunt over several weeks to catch 'Pui Pui', who was later gifted to the Park and had a luxurious residence built for him – this new friend of ours.

largely due to its narrow social structure. The resulting dreadful conditions in this community earned it the nickname 'city of sadness'. Eventually, the government began to develop residential and public facilities, such as the Ping Shan Tin Shui Wai Leisure and Cultural Building designed by Thomas Wan. The building has utilised many different materials to create interesting spaces, with the special and bold design feature of having an exterior constructed of weathering steel, giving it a rough texture. This is the first time such a construction material has been employed in Hong Kong.

To enrich the quality of life in Tin Shui Wai, the Leisure and Cultural Services Department set out to construct the Heritage Conservation and Resource Centre, thereby creating a cultural landmark in the district. In addition to being a repository, the centre also features public exhibition areas, providing residents who are distanced from downtown cultural facilities with an opportunity to engage with art. P&T Group is leading the design of this building, whose construction is expected to be completed in a few years' time.

Why Was the Wetland Park Built?

The Hong Kong Wetland Park nearby is yet another landmark in Tuen Mun. It traces its origins back to the year 1999 when many cities in the world were looking to complete a new architectural statement to commemorate the arrival of the new millennium. Beijing built its World Art Museum, London celebrated the occasion with the completion of the Millennium Dome, and Chicago built its Millennium Park. The HKSAR government, too, undertook a screening process to determine a suitable piece of architecture to be built for this special occasion. At that point in time, the only piece of cultural architecture nearing completion was the Hong Kong Heritage Museum in Sha Tin. However, due to reservations about its appearance, the government came up with the idea of advancing the construction of the Hong Kong Wetland Park, hoping that its first phase could be completed by the end of the year 2000. The design work for Hong Kong Wetland Park was initially intended to be entrusted to a private architectural consulting firm. However, due to the tight construction schedule that required completion within a few months, many firms had politely declined the invitation to submit a proposal. Therefore, Mr Michael Li and I had no choice but to undertake this millennium project.

Our team, along with Mr Kevin Li, took on the first phase of the project, encompassing its construction, interior designs, exhibition areas and landscaping, with the goal of completion by the end of December of the new millennium. Then came September, when the initial confidence of the team was dampened by consecutive thunderstorms. When senior officials from the HKSAR government visited the site, they deemed that the proposed schedule would be unachievable given the conditions. They silently gave up this millennium celebration project. However, our team did not. Sparing no effort, we managed to complete it in mid-December.

After the completion of Phase 1, the owner – the Agriculture, Fisheries and Conservation Department – expressed their satisfaction

Notes

1. Frank Owen Gehry: American postmodernist and deconstructivist architect who won the Pritzker Prize in 1989.

2. Claude Vasconi: French architect who, in 1964, established his own office in Paris, France, and designed the Forum des Halles.

3. Thomas Schinko: French architect who founded the Vasconi Architectes by Thomas Schinko in 2010 that serves as a continuation of his former partner, French architect Claude Vasconi, who passed away in 2009.

4. On 1 September 2023, the Hong Kong Golf Club has returned 32 hectares of land from the Fanling Golf Course to the HKSAR government upon the expiration of its lease. Approximately 22.5 hectares will be used for conservation and passive recreational use for public enjoyment, while the remaining 9.5 hectares will be used to construct public housing as intended by the government.

The Hong Kong Wetland Park

Building Less for More

What should retirement look like? Soaking up the sunshine while passing each day leisurely? Raymond is not a big fan of the heat, and he is not one to slow his steps either. So his retirement is actually more like a full-time job, with a packed daily schedule; he works, painstakingly, day in, day out. He appears to have become busier since he retired.

Raymond is a typical Gemini: he multitasks; he can't seem to stop; and he is always looking for perfection. However, romanticism flows in his blood like a Pisces; otherwise, he wouldn't have chosen to resign on a special day.

On 14 February 2008 – Valentine's Day – Raymond chose to leave his 'lover'. At least that was how he had described leaving the Architectural Services Department where he had worked for twenty years. He handed in a resignation letter that contained just sixteen Chinese words ('Parting with architecture and picking up the paintbrush; having been through humble circumstances together, I am forever grateful'). 'But my superiors and colleagues didn't believe I was doing it for painting. They just couldn't understand why I was throwing all that fame and fortune away and thought I had other plans.' Every time the topic of his resignation came up, he raised his voice a little.

Perhaps most would come to know Raymond as an architect first, then an artist after. However, looking back, it seems that he had already been in love with art prior to his encounter with architecture. During my first interview with him, I recall him mentioning that the unfavourable family circumstances when he was young made it difficult for him to discover and cultivate his interest. But he had known since then that he was responsible for his own survival. 'Strangely, I thought it was rather easy to paint back then. And I was actually quite good at it.' When he was eleven, he began to submit his paintings to the 'Children's Corner' of the *South China Morning Post*. 'Back then, for every successful submission you would get a cash prize of ten dollars.'

Raymond was a kid who grew up without being spoiled. Such an upbringing cultivated in him his sheer drive and determination. Upon his resignation, he started putting his thoughts back onto that long and narrow rice paper. He continued to tell his stories, this time through ink painting. Since the beginning of the millennium, Raymond has painted many pieces themed around the city of Hong Kong; from the natural scenic spots of Tolo Harbour, Pat Sin Leng to Hebe Haven, Double Haven and Hoi Ha Wan; these ink paintings effortlessly express his deeply rooted sentiments of love and a sense of place for this city. Although there are no apparent traces of architecture within these paintings, Raymond's architectural ideals are evident through the strokes of his brush and the colours of his ink; islands are clouded by smoke and mist from heaven, while migratory birds soar high in the sky. Such masterful depiction in his ink paintings makes it an easy association to the concept of unity of nature and man displayed in the Wetland Park.

In a corner of the New Territories, that patch of wetlands of more than sixty hectares stands in sharp contrast to the bustling pace of the city. Its serene and picturesque beauty are paradisiacal, washing away all the dust and glamour. It is yet another rarity in Hong Kong to have such an elegant garden adorned with an abundance of natural beauty. Laying one's eyes on the tens of thousands of birds soaring and passing by in the sky, it looks more like a paradise for migratory birds to forage and inhabit than a mere backyard.

The main architectural work of the Wetland Park is a 100,000-square-feet exhibition hall and visitor centre built with unpainted fair-faced concrete. The design reveals a rough external texture but with clean lines that seem to draw a clean stroke across the skyline.

Confronted with the enchanting beauty of the Wetland Park, both Raymond and project architect Michael Li were reluctant for the architecture to overshadow the surroundings. Hence, they employed a sloping design, adorning the roof and exterior walls with climbing plants and covering them with lush foliage. In doing so, they concealed this 100,000-square-feet exhibition hall within the park. From a distance, all that remains in sight is a crescent-shaped 'birdcage', devoid of any ostentations, as if it emerged naturally from its environment.

'As an architect, every completed piece of architecture means a certain area of public space has been physically occupied, which will no doubt have an impact on the cityscape; and for better or worse, this is a direct result of the architect's personal orientation.' As with everyone else, Raymond loves beauty. However, beauty should not simply be interpreted on its own; rather, it has to complement and reflect its surrounding environment. The four wooden posts standing sentinel in the middle of the lake have become a resting place for birds. One could observe the graceful white herons descending gently, unruffled and composed, as they leisurely enjoyed the wetland surroundings. Inadvertently, they seamlessly and effortlessly intertwined with the underlying theme of the Wetland Park: embodying the unity between nature and man.

The modernist architect Ludwig Mies van der Rohe was an advocate of 'Less is more'. Raymond has interpreted that as 'Building less for more'. He is passionate about his work, and in the hundreds of projects he has managed, it is easy to see that 'building less for more' has been his guiding philosophy. Rocco Yim once described this period of time as a 'noisy era', with most of the media inclined to celebrate and publicise examples of exaggerated architectural designs and dazzling visual effects, in the process ignoring the true value of architecture. Raymond has described his own work as being a splash of refreshing spring water amongst the noise; while it may not be exhilarating, it will, nevertheless, leave an unforgettable, lingering aftertaste.

Switching course at the half-century mark was a bold decision, and one he was only able to make after a journey to better self-knowledge. Looking at the sixteen words he had written in parting, he couldn't help but ask himself again, 'In fact it was just another five years before my then official retirement, so why didn't I wait?'

'I had this feeling that while my journey with art had not reached its destination, my path in architecture was nearing its end and there wasn't much room for further breakthrough.'

The breakthrough he mentioned was a reference to the 'noise' Rocco Yim had spoken of. 'In today's world, it would be hard to make your mark without making noise. And that doesn't fit well with my personality, so I suppose it was about time I let go.'

Untold Stories

| 1 | 2 3 4 |

1. Hidden beneath a large lawn lies a visitor centre measuring at 10,000 square metres. As the visitor centre is served by a geothermal heat pump system, there is no need for unsightly exterior air conditioning plant.
2. Origami-shaped sculptures represent six of the natural inhabitants of the Tin Shui Wai district: jinga shrimp, mudskipper, Romer's tree frog, dragonfly, black-faced spoonbill and fiddler crab.
3. Screen walls for privacy are a characteristic feature of traditional Chinese architecture. Visitors are welcomed by the copper duck sculptures next to the wall.
4. Lawn and trees planted on the sloping roof and water features help to make visitors feel closer to nature.

Within the birdcage-shaped semicircular visitor centre, the typical order of things is reversed; the birds are free while humans are in a 'cage'.

1	2	
3	4	5

1 The gentle flowing water at the entrance allows visitors to immediately immerse themselves in the natural ambience as they step into the park, while also masking the hustle and bustle of the nearby road with its soothing sounds.
2 The birds perched quietly on the four wooden posts in the artificial lake, becoming an unobtrusive centrepiece that runs through the entire structure.
3 There is a skylight at the top of the lobby to introduce natural light as well as to provide green energy.
4 The oyster shells in the murals are sourced from the local area and have been re-presented as an art form.
5 The composition of blue sky, white clouds, grey walls, and clear water resembles that of a carefully crafted print, yet it is the façade of the exhibition building at Hong Kong Wetland Park.

Chu Hai College of Higher Education

Though the Sparrow is Small

Rocco Yim designed the Chu Hai College of Higher Education's new campus to facilitate the College's move from its old campus in Tsuen Wan to Cafeteria Beach in Tuen Mun. Work had already begun on the building's foundation when Rocco took over the design. The project had originally been awarded to OMA (founded by Rem Koolhaas), the winner of the College's design competition.

The new Chu Hai College campus sits on a plot of land measuring only 1.6 hectares, a rather small area compared to other educational institutions. The challenge for Rocco was to create a miniature community in a short time frame with the design concept of 'Though the sparrow is small, it has all the vital organs.'

The Chu Hai College is an eight-storey building complete with classrooms, a theatre, an indoor stadium, a library and a staff dormitory. 'This place is like a miniature city with a wide range of functions including education, interaction and recreational activities; basically everything a university needs.'

It took three years to complete the new campus, and despite having a tight project timeline, Rocco was grateful that his ideas and visions were appreciated. He described how the owner was very respectful towards the directions as well as the solutions proposed by the design team in dealing with architectural challenges, considering the increasingly restrictive building regulations in Hong Kong. For instance, areas under the roof-overhang were included in the calculation of the gross floor area. However, rather than fully utilising every square inch of area in the pursuit of function, the College sacrificed some usable floor area to allow the full achievement of Rocco's design. 'They had a certain expectation for architecture and art. Things tend to go along much smoother when you come across owners who think alike.'

In terms of design, Chu Hai College cleverly connects the East and West wings by spanning the library bridge and the student union bridge over the grassy slope. This ingenious gesture forms a symbolic gateway and creates a sense of transparency, allowing for a clear view of the distant Castle Peak Bay and Lantau Island. It is a minimalist yet sophisticated approach.

Rocco has used the word 'rustic' to describe his feelings towards the campus, reflecting his design philosophy of: 'Not engaging in the unnecessary or excessive and, to the best of my ability, not designing for the sake of decoration and visual effects. Everything that exists here shall do so with its purpose, either functionally or symbolically; this is a form of honesty, an authentic representation.'

When asked about his views on design competitions, he replied, smiling, 'Competitions happen frequently, but winning isn't always guaranteed. What's most importantly is to engage in self-reflection.' When faced with the disappointment of not winning a bid, he would often try to comfort himself, 'Sometimes losing doesn't necessarily have anything to do with how hard you've worked. Thinking this way brings some comfort, just like in recent competitions where I lost and couldn't quite understand why.' He just laughed it off. 'But that's just the way it is, you win some, you lose some.'

1 The library connects the east and west wings above the central platform of the campus.
2 The library floats over the central grass slope.
3 The corridor of the teaching block takes advantage of the form of the building to introduce natural light from above and also facilitate natural ventilation.

1   A hand sketch of the design concept for the Chu Hai College. Is it an building, or a miniature city?
2   A college condensed into a single building, combining all the teaching, research, living space and recreational functions required by the college, and creating a series of diversified communication and interaction places through the interlocking outdoor and indoor spaces.
3   The library links the east and west wings, allowing a full view of the Lantau Island.

The Mills

A Place for Sharing Inspirations

In recent years, Hong Kong has seen the revitalisation of many of its historic buildings such as the PMQ, Tai Kwun and the Central Market. In their revitalised states, these historic buildings assume different roles but continue to tell their stories. The Mills in Tsuen Wan is another such example.

Established in 1954, the Nan Fung Cotton Mills was one of the largest cotton producers in Hong Kong and bore witness to the golden era of the Hong Kong manufacturing industry in the 1980s. However, as manufacturing gradually declined in Hong Kong, the Nan Fung Cotton Mills also lost its former brilliance.

In 2014, the Nan Fung Cotton Mills underwent major revitalisation work and upon its completion in 2018, it became a place of history and culture. The building now houses an exhibition hall and displays of cotton products and photographs that depict the history of the cotton industry. The Mills's plain and low-key exterior has remained largely unchanged. Amongst the high-rises, it represents the mark and history of another era.

The Mills consists of three factories of different heights. The architects who participated in this project include Mr Ray Zee, Mr Billy Tam and Mr Gary Ng. The intention of the revitalisation was to preserve its original façade as much as possible and, on this basis, the three factory buildings have been combined into one by using bridges as links. Perhaps the most thoughtful aspect of the revitalisation is that, without having to alter much of its appearance, the architects have given visitors the experience of an entirely new sensation the moment they enter.

Stepping into the Mills, one finds it to be quite people-friendly; the design follows an industrial style, with artistic and cultural elements brought into the mix. Local artists have been invited to create graffiti and murals representing the history of the cotton mills and elaborating on its stories. Structurally, The Mills has become a fusion of the old and the new, with significant reconfiguration made to its interior spatial layout. For instance, the previously inconspicuous rooftop has been transformed into an industrial oasis, providing a place of leisure for visitors. On the rooftop is a gigantic mural detailing the development and history of the Hong Kong textile industry. The mural has been created using more than six thousand pieces of aluminium that sway gently in the breeze like pieces of cloth.

Ray Zee speaks fondly of Ms Vanessa Cheung, who is the Group Managing Director of Nan Fung Development Limited and Founder of The Mills. It was Vanessa who initiated the preservation as well as the subsequent revitalisation of the place. With the lofty ceilings and vast space of the cotton mills, Ray expressed the tremendous potential for creativity and further development. Following the renovation of the main atrium, the increased transparency and vast sense of space make it exceptionally suitable for holding exhibitions. He described The Mills as a place for everyone to share their inspirations.

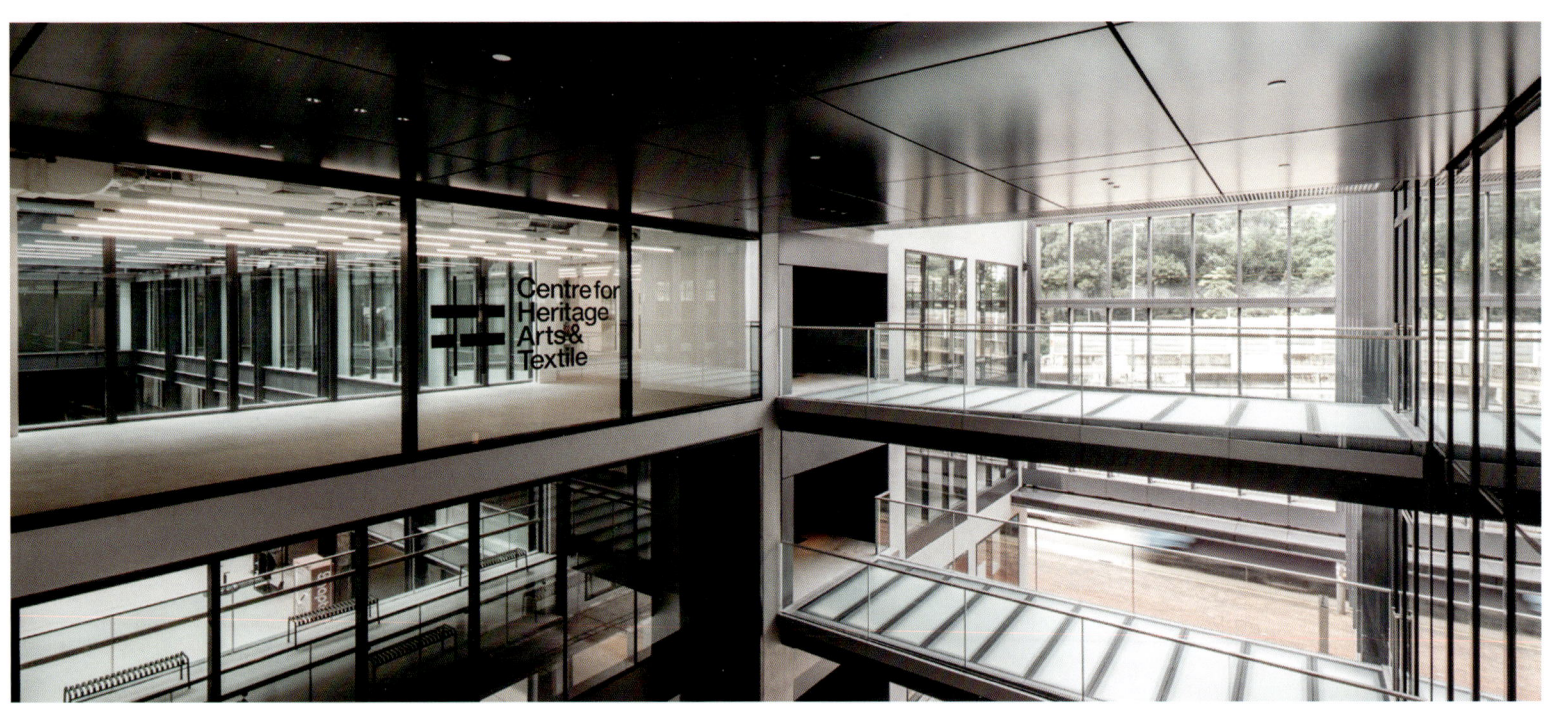

1. The glazed, connecting bridge spanning across the main entrance of the Mills.
2. The Mills Fabrica is committed to promoting creativity. The spacious atrium within is well suited for a variety of creative endeavours.
3. Upcycling old objects.

1 The colours of Hong Kong's past have been preserved in the stairway of the factory building.
2 Portuguese artist Vhils has interpreted the rich history of the cotton mills through large-scale portrait wall carvings.
3 The Hall is the heart of the Mills. It serves as a temple to the once vibrant textile industry in Hong Kong.

Untold Stories

Tsing Yi Southwest Leisure Building

Between Strength and Gentleness

Located halfway up a hill, the Tsing Yi Southwest Leisure Building provides a place for neighbouring residents to socialise and enjoy recreational activities. A public square in front of the building helps guide pedestrians into the complex, where they can access different activity rooms. An elevated walkway with a dynamic folded roof provides a connection to the Chung Mei Road pedestrian bridge, thus giving the residents of neighbouring housing estates direct access. The building houses a main arena, a dance room, a multi-purpose room, a children's playroom, an outdoor rock climbing wall, an indoor swimming pool. The interior design style has been based on the concept of 'dynamism'.

One prominent feature of the Tsing Yi Southwest Leisure Building is the presence of an outdoor lawn. M.C. Chung often witnessed children freely cartwheeling on the grass during his travels abroad, a sight rarely seen in Hong Kong. Recognizing that cartwheeling can be considered a form of exercise, he decided to create a grassy area on the platform of the sports centre, providing a space where children can indulge in cartwheels to their hearts' content. Chung remarked earnestly that he would always aim to bring new elements to his projects. In addition to grassed areas, he also paid careful attention to the interplay of natural light and shade. For instance, the steel elements integrated into the lobby represent the resilience and strength needed in sports while the sculptures in the lobby symbolise the lines of the pulses. Sit-up benches have been placed outdoors for users to engage in simple warm-up and stretching exercises. Above the swimming pool, a giant suspended sculpture references the dynamics of a swimmer's butterfly strokes.

The appearance of a building affects everyone's perception, but M.C. Chung prioritises meaning over considerations of function and appearance. While balancing the three will always require trade-offs, architects ultimately need to identify what they truly want in a project. Whenever Chung is assigned a new project, he hopes to bring to it new ideas without any repetition or limitation; and he doesn't shy away from working on small projects either. He believes that raising the bar for himself compels him to fight for his ideals and not just to be satisfied with a 'pass' or merely being 'stylish'.

While learning his craft at Ho & Partners Architects Engineers & Development Consultants Ltd, Chung was impressed by the strong innovation and management capabilities present there that allowed for continuous experimentation. He believes that the best architecture is all about 'balance', where appropriate elements are harmoniously integrated into the architecture. Even in innovative designs, the focus should lean towards considering the intended message of the architecture and its inherent craftsmanship, placing emphasis on attention to detail rather than imposing a fixed style onto all types of architecture.

A beautiful piece of architecture often reveals a 'personal touch'. However, when architects attempt to make breakthroughs in spatial design, it doesn't necessarily mean pursuing unconventionally bizarre designs. For instance, creating an open space and a grassy platform on top of a leisure building can bring about unexpected functionality. M.C. Chung hopes that, post-retirement, he can be engaged in more voluntary work with different architecture firms, so that he may continue to create freely and enjoy the pleasure that comes with it.

Untold Stories 300

1	
2	4
3	

1, 2, 3 The gymnasium's design incorporates the dynamic features that complement the energy of sports activities, such as the seating outside of the dance hall, the decorative wall at the entrance and its ceiling, reflecting the dynamism of sports. Outside, a grassy platform provides the children with an area to engage in outdoor sports activities with their families.

4 The sculpture suspended from the ceiling over the swimming pool is inspired by the dynamics of butterfly stroke. Simple straight strips are arranged to suggest the shapes of waves.

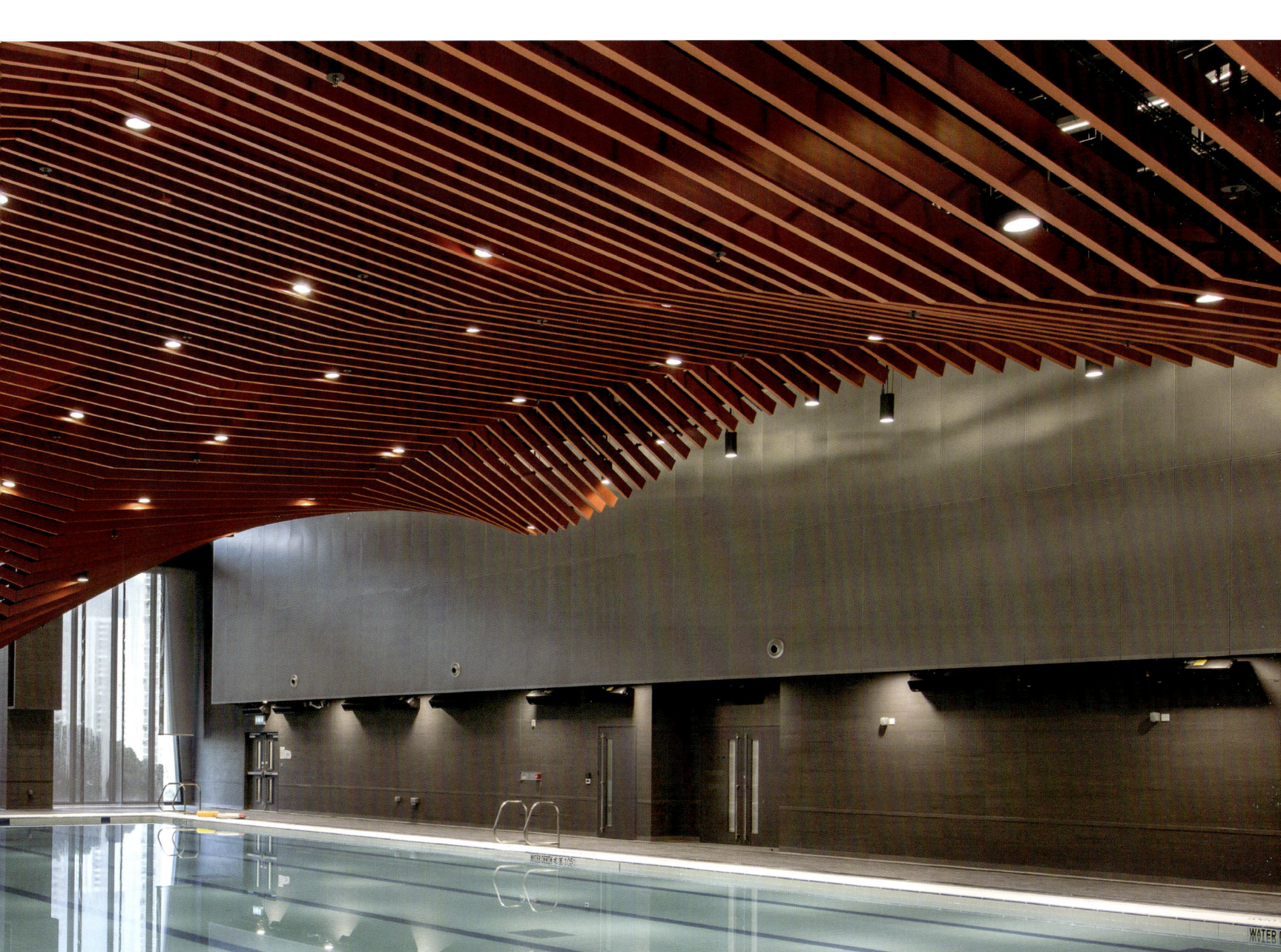

The Community College at Lingnan University

Revitalising the Siheyuan

Wei Jen Wang obtained his university degree in his hometown in Taiwan before pursuing the study of architecture at UC Berkeley, after which he continued working in San Francisco. Throughout his architecture and design career, Wang has always taken a special interest in the design of Chinese cities. In 1997, Wang took up an invitation to teach at the HKU, eventually becoming the head of the HKU Department of Architecture. Later, He founded Wang Weijen Architecture and participated in the preparatory project for the Energizing Kowloon East initiative. He was responsible for integrating research data and materials for Kowloon East, including those that related to the reorganisation of urban space and the conservation of historic buildings along the Kwun Tong promenade. He also proposed the low-cost option of utilising cargo containers as exhibition halls, which was later adopted.

Since Wang Weijen Architecture is a sole proprietorship, it is not easy for it to undertake large-scale public or commercial projects in Hong Kong. As a result, Wang has primarily focused on designing college and university campuses in Taiwan. In recent years, however, he has chanced upon an opportunity to participate in the design of the Chinese University of Hong Kong, Shenzhen. He pays particular attention towards the advantages of garden landscape and garden architecture and has, through his involvement in designing the Community College at Lingnan University, introduced the iconic architectural design of 'Siheyuan' (also known as Chinese courtyard houses or Chinese quadrangles), bringing in sources of light into the building through interactive means and transforming it into a contemporary urban architecture. Although Wang had previously experimented with this design technique in Taiwan, being able to realise the spatial relationship of traditional Chinese courtyard houses amongst densely packed high-rises in Hong Kong is indeed a challenge and a breakthrough. In order to seamlessly integrate elements of Chinese Siheyuan into the architectural context of Hong Kong, Wang tailored his design accordingly and created a conjoined courtyard space using an interlocking pattern.

Wang's extensive experience in design is evident in his utilisation of multi-storey public spaces. The traditional Siheyuan design requires a large amount of space, but due to scarcity of land in Hong Kong, constructing a cluster of buildings on flatland would be rather difficult. In view of this, Wang had adopted a flexible approach towards his Siheyuan design by connecting the courtyard houses into the main cluster of the campus and sequencing them according to different heights, forming several connected courtyards and developing them into a series of interlocking atriums. This way, the lower-level space is introduced into the open courtyard, while penetrating the upper-level landscape to increase the layering of the campus configuration. These interlaced and overlapping high-rise courtyards not only provide a modern experience of traditional spaces, but also increase air circulation through the staggered arrangement of the floors, thus contributing to the overall success of the design.

To integrate environmentally friendly elements, Wang deliberately did away with the installation of air-conditioning, save for the classrooms, where it was unavoidable to do so. He placed emphasis on introducing sunlight and stimulating natural ventilation, echoing the interactive relationship between nature and the design of Siheyuan. Continuing the traditional concept of being 'people oriented' and having a 'natural ecology' serves to shorten the distance between people and space, as well as people and architecture. Wang believes that a courtyard architecture is not a mere structure, but one that connects with its surrounding. Standing in the middle of the atrium and looking up at the sky, one cannot help but feel the versatility of nature. Just as the moon is subject to waxing and waning, so shall leaves eventually return to their roots.

In recent years, Wang has been more involved in Urban-Rural Development projects in the Mainland, and he has been deeply touched by them. The first layer that warrants consideration in Urban-Rural Development is the people, as villages are where they live. The second layer is the materials, such as soil, wood, bricks and tiles. By understanding these materials and their uses, deconstructivist architecture is no longer an abstract concept. Wang wishes to bring in a variety of plants to every architecture project, hoping to bring ecology and water into the design. During the interview, I could feel Wang's respect for nature and his concern for conservation. He will be participating in research on the architecture of country parks in Hong Kong and will continue to explore the relationship between architecture and nature.

1. On the lower level of the courtyard of the community college, the chapel is visible as the focus of the two visual axes; the landscape of the stepped platform reflects the original topography of the site and retains the native trees that were growing there.
2. A bird's-eye view of the northeast façade of the Community College at Lingnan University. The two-storey classroom modules are superimposed and staggered to form a multi-layered courtyard and platform space.
3. The Hong Kong Polytechnic University College of Professional and Continuing Education combines the sky garden platform between the classrooms and the public stairs to transform into a campus space that embodies the concept of a vertical urban courtyard.
4. The west-facing façade of the Hong Kong Polytechnic University College of Professional and Continuing Education building is adjacent to the Princess Margaret Road flyover. The towers are modularised with four-storey classrooms to form a series of sky courtyards that rise one step at a time.

Vice Versa House

As Within, So Without

'Frankie, If I were to own a house in the future, would you help me design it?' Who would have thought that a lighthearted joke at university would bring the two of them together again sometime in the future?

Less than a week after his return to Hong Kong from the United States, Frankie received a phone call. It was Henry, the medical student who had lived next door to him when he was reading architecture at the University of Hong Kong. He clearly remembered Henry asking that question in 1996. Now, years later, he heard the same question.

Like most people who graduated from the University of Hong Kong with a master's degree in architecture, Frankie Lui went straight into the torrent of life and worked for about six or seven years. When his friends and colleagues around him were starting to purchase houses and cars and start families, he decided to head to New York, alone, to pursue knowledge. 'I have always had a dream of going abroad to widen my horizons.' He quit his job and applied for the master's programme in architecture and urban design at Columbia University to pursue his second master's degree.

Prior to his journey to New York, Frankie already had a stellar résumé under his belt. He had worked for Aedas Global, Ronald Lu & Partners and Hellmuth, Obata + Kassabaum, and he had even won the HKIA Young Architect Award in 2003. Around the same time, the Asian Cultural Council awarded Frankie a scholarship and sponsored a field trip to the United States, where he also visited I.M. Pei and Frank Gehry. Upon his return, he thought to himself, why not expand my horizons by studying abroad?

'I recall telling my mother back then that I might not be able to provide for two to three years.' Fortunately, his mother and his wife were very supportive and helped him through this difficult period.

Frankie has been the family's breadwinner since he was young, and especially so after graduation. 'That was why even after working for six to seven years I had very little savings – only enough for my studies.' Some even commented that Frankie's decision to study in New York so soon after getting married – and their subsequent separation – meant that he and his wife might as well be divorced. That didn't happen, of course; he returned home soon after completing his programme.

When Frankie arrived at the Shan Ha Tsuen in Yuen Long, there were still some Chinese brick houses and tenement houses in the village, and there was a large wood-burning kitchen which would become lively during festive seasons. Today, Shan Ha Tsuen is still a single-surname village of the Cheungs, and is very much a micro-community within the city. 'In fact, this kitchen is a social gathering place.' Looking out into the open space, Frankie appeared deep in thought.

When Frankie was reading architecture and urban design at Columbia University, he had this idea: If the everyday life and relationships of the streets could be condensed into an architecture, what would it look like?

Next to an open space is a house that belonged to the owner's father – and to his father before him. As the family's eldest son and the current owner of the ancestral home, he had a cheerful and outgoing personality and was the glue of the family's relationships. 'Could we create a sense

of cohesion through this house and unite all of the family members and relatives?' In the end, two houses were built on this vacant lot, one for the owner and the other for his younger brother.

The two houses are predominantly white, and contain many light-transmission elements. The glazed exterior allows the owner to see the houses of his grandfather, father and younger brother when using the stairs, thus allowing a visual dialogue in the process. 'The children enjoy sitting on the stairs and reading in the sunlight and greeting their grandfather when they see him.'

There are also many secret passageways within the house that are linked to the garden and common area by sliding doors. Even though they live in their separate and different spaces, there is one less barrier standing between them while they go about their daily chores and activities. 'They don't even have to call. Just take a walk outside and they will be able to see everything.' By turning everyone's daily interior activities into an extension of communication between different families and, at the same time, relocating outdoor social activities into the interior, Frankie has shaped the concept of 'the streets of the walled villages residing within the house'. In acknowledgement of this, the house has been given the name 'Vice Versa House'.

Prior to taking on this project, Frankie had chosen to start out on his own and founded Atelier Global. However, he was caught in a dilemma. 'If I were to swim against the current and do something based on ideals, can I survive?' As a born-and-bred local, Frankie had always been grateful for the favourable conditions that Hong Kong had given him – though they also came with corresponding burdens. 'These burdens include how everything is so taken for granted here, including the values of this city, the goals of whose residents have always been about buying a flat and buying a car.' It may be difficult to change the customary values of a society on our own, but sometimes the environment changes people. 'That's why you have to place yourself in the right environment. Think about it; if you were to be placed in an environment where you could concentrate and contemplate on architecture, your craft would no doubt improve in due course.'

He also pointed out that 'The advantage of Hong Kong is that the tracks of architecture and business come together seamlessly. This is where I started learning about this industry. Every year there are two to three projects where I could explore a little, though these projects may not necessarily be profitable.' While the world is a kaleidoscope of countless choices, it is also about trade-offs. If he hadn't chosen the path of entrepreneurship, Frankie remarked he might have given himself to education or research. 'Regardless, survival will be certain.'

1. The living room on the first floor fully considers the elements of lighting, ventilation and interaction between each family.
2. Within the 'indoor streets' of the 'walled villages', the circulation of daily life is akin to the streets of a village, linking up with the open spaces.
3. The outdoor layout is similar to the streets of the surrounding village, connecting the shared spaces to the houses of the father and younger brother in all directions.

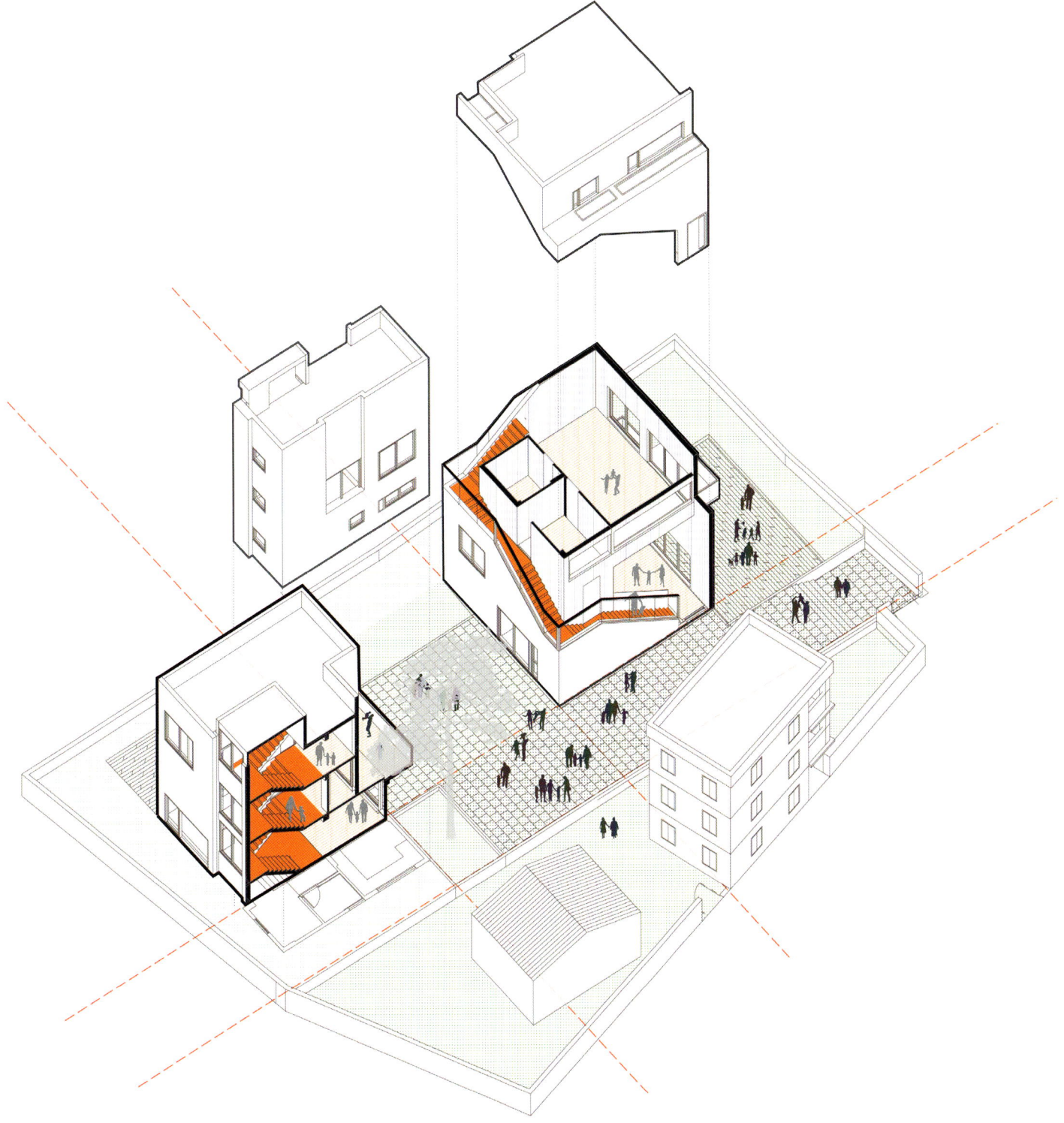

Outlying Islands

Reading Guidance

Those who have never visited Hong Kong may have the impression that this city is only about shopping and gourmet; but for those who have, they will no doubt have experienced the density of this city and, at the same time, been drawn rather quickly to its unique charm. In addition to the city life, the beauty of Hong Kong is evident in the world-renowned Victoria Harbour, which is adorned with undulating hills on both sides, the winding coastline, and the harbour valley formed of more than 200 islands. However, its natural, scenic beauty has been overshadowed by the notorious reputation of Hong Kong being solely a concrete jungle. Such prejudice has meant that many tourists have missed out on the opportunity to visit Hong Kong's beautiful nature reserves.

The Origins of the Country Parks

The poetically stunning natural places of Hong Kong are a source of pride. We owe much to those before us who had the foresight to enact the Country Parks Ordinance long before any significant development took place in Hong Kong. After the Second World War, the suburban environment had been greatly improved after fifteen years of restoration and expansion of forestry in Hong Kong. In 1963, according to the then Forestry Officer, Mr P.A. Daley, about 10,000 acres of government forest and 2,000 acres of village plantation had been completed. However, due to the rapid increase in population, a reduction of land supply, a decline of available labour for forestry work and the annual increase in wildfires, it was necessary for the government to rethink Hong Kong's forestry policy. Daley had attached great importance to the value and significance of forest planting to modern cities, and had suggested that forestry should provide society with recreational, conservation, scientific research and educational opportunities. Daley's unremitting efforts brought about the 1965 consultation report of Lee M Talbot and Martha H Talbot, which pointed out that the population growth of Hong Kong had accelerated urban development, including the new towns of Kwun Tong, Tsuen Wan, Sha Tin and Tuen Mun, which were being built at that time. The report also cautioned that if a system was not established soon enough for the parks of Hong Kong with the aim of preserving nature, the people of the city would likely come to regret that omission.

In 1971, Sir Murray MacLehose, who was known to have a fondness for the countryside, took office as the governor of Hong Kong. In the same year, an important convention relating to the conservation and use of wetlands, known as the Ramsar Convention, was signed by the international community in the city of Ramsar, Iran. In 1972, the Commonwealth Ecological Conference was held in Hong Kong, and, in response to the call for global conservation during that same period, several rural conservation policies were gradually introduced. In 1973, Hong Kong established the Sports Bureau and proposed that mountains and beaches should belong to the public. In 1976, the Country Parks Ordinance was enacted, providing Hong Kong with numerous conservation districts. This move not only protected water sources and nature but also provided outdoor leisure areas for the public. Hong Kong's high green ratio has been attributed solely to its country parks, of which there are currently twenty-four, with an aggregate area that accounts for 40 per cent of Hong Kong's land area. The one-hundred-kilometre MacLehose Trail was completed in 1979. Lantau Island, the largest island in Hong Kong, has two country parks located in South and North Lantau that, together, occupy most of its area, turning it into a tourist island of Hong Kong. There are also other tourist attractions on the island, including Disneyland, Inspiration Lake, the Tian Tan Buddha, Wisdom Path, Ngong Ping 360 Cable Car and the Tai O Fishing Village.

Six interviews were arranged for this chapter. The Jockey Club Mong Tung Wan Hostel was an early work by Rocco Yim. It was a small project, but it was nevertheless the best place for him to start his career. The youth hostel was constructed using a combination of geometric forms and façades. It earned him architectural awards and countless opportunities well into the future.

Many youth hostels with a taste for design have been going out of business one after

Untold Stories

another, due mainly to their limited capacities and a lack of amenities, which have made their operations challenging. However, in recent years, these youth hostels have been relocated from the countryside to the city, with their operations moved to Shek Kip Mei in order to attract a different sort of clientele. Under such circumstances, many young architects have thus lost good opportunities to hone their skills and practise their craft through these small projects.

Ever since my collaboration with K.C. King began, the Wisdom Path has been the most demanding project. Every step of the way has been marked with stories of hard work, from the search for suitable block mass and giant logs to overcoming the hurdles arising from transportation, as well as installing thirty-eight huge wooden pillars from the Gabonese Republic using indigenous methods. This extraordinary endeavour, now regarded as a blessing for Hong Kong, had already encountered many setbacks, starting with problems with site selection. Further challenges have included working to avoid the triggers of relevant environmental legislation, overcoming the constraints of complex terrain and handling public and media scrutiny. These challenges will be discussed in the interviews contained in this chapter.

Tai O Fishing Village is a Touristic Treasure

As the famous villages of Zhouzhuang, Wuzhen and Zhujiajiao are to Shanghai, the Tai O Fishing Village is the pride of Hong Kong and a testament to the preservation of our roots. The stilt houses of the village may not have been designed by architects but they have been preserved by Mr Gary Yeung. The results of his research led to *Above and Below the Stilt Houses*, which was published to

promote Hong Kong's unique characteristics to overseas readers. The resulting publication increased awareness of Tai O has helped maintain its tourism value and allow for the continuation of its legacy.

Another attraction, the old Tai O police station, is a successful product of the Revitalising Historic Buildings Through Partnership Scheme. An important consideration when applying for the revitalisation of historic buildings is that the applicant must be able to suitably utilise the historic building without effecting alterations to its appearance or unnecessary additions. Hong Kong has always been lacking in tasteful boutique hotels, however, a delightful encounter with the Scheme resulted in the creation of the Tai O Heritage Hotel. The historic building resides on a fitting location and was of an appropriate size; coincidentally, the applicant also had the necessary experience in hotel operations, thus when coupled with the intelligent design of Mr Phillip Liao, the resulting work was indeed a blissful endeavour. The design of the hotel exhibits many well-thought-out details. For example, to facilitate access for the disabled, the hotel has elevators designed to operate on a steep hill, the installation of which greatly reduced the engineering work that would have otherwise been required on the hillside. Phillip has also preserved the original exterior walls of the historic building; glass structures housing the restaurant section have been added sparingly, creating an elegant effect overall.

The Elegant Architecture on the Airport Island

Terminal 1 of the Hong Kong International Airport has been recognised as the most beautiful and accessible airport building in the world. I hope that the Airport Authority will retain as much as possible of Norman Foster's perfect design which has won international praise for Hong Kong. During the time when the new airport at Chek Lap Kok was built, many elegant structures were being built on the island (also known as the Airport Island), including the backup flight control centre designed by Mr Daniel Chow, the airport fire station and several radar stations built on the deserted islands.

These buildings are all of sharp and modern design but are difficult to reach on foot; thus, not everyone has had the opportunity to

appreciate these examples of Hong Kong's minimalist architecture.

The Tung Chung New Town located near the airport has also been developing rapidly. Within the town there are several buildings worthy of admiration, including the Citygate and Tung Chung Post Office designed by Mr Anthony Ng and the Tung Chung MTR Station designed by Rocco Yim. My biggest discovery here is the temporary quarantine centre in Penny's Bay built in response to the coronavirus pandemic. The centre has a youthful design and it is the result of the combined efforts of Wong & Ouyang Ltd, Leigh & Orange Limited and Ronald Lu and Partners under the Design-Build method. For those who had to spend two to three weeks in the quarantine centre, perhaps the lively

design may have brought them some small element of delight during their stay.

Initially, I was hesitant to select the new campus of Zheng Sheng College as the subject of one of my interviews. According to the information I had on hand, there was no chance of me getting a sneak peek at the design of the new campus. However, on learning of the touching story behind the college, coupled with the insistence of the principal, Mr Alman Chan, our team was getting more intrigued by the day. This project was known to have been overwhelmingly tough during the early stages of its reconstruction, as it was expensive and difficult to carry out the project on the outlying island off Chi Ma Wan: the Peninsula. It was no easy task to hire construction workers, either. However, if Mr Anderson Lee, with his heart of gold, was willing to contribute towards society and undertake this project, how could we give up on this meaningful interview?

Lamma Island has always been a favourite amongst foreigners. Rumour has it that the owner of the Banyan Tree Group had lived in Yung Shue Wan when he was young and was captivated by the big banyan tree there. Inspired, he later named the hotel after the banyan tree. I have long admired Steve Leung's residence in Acacia Bay; as I began to press for more answers, he showed me pictures of two attached houses that he had designed. They both looked extraordinarily attractive, like the villas built on the Aegean coast of Greece. But, in fact, they were his designs on Lamma Island. As the romantic gazebo stretches out towards the sea and fishing boats and egrets are at rest, and with the sunset and evening mist as a backdrop, it is an enviously beautiful sight to behold.

Hong Kong is fortunate to have numerous outlying islands. They provide the residents of the city with room to breathe and a quiet, alternative getaway from the stressful life of the city. On the island of Peng Chau, there is a little-known art village nicknamed the Secret Garden whose origin traces back to artists who relocated to this hidden location from the city due to its unbearably high cost of living. I have had the pleasure of speaking with the young people who have given up the hustle and bustle of the city life in pursuit of their dreams, and their persistence for art is indeed admirable. Peng Chau is a relatively quiet island, and on this island sits

a boldly designed three-storey house built using fully frosted transparent materials. It is the brainchild of a team of international architects named BEAU Architects. In Ham Tin, Lantau Island, there is a village house with a unique contour that is different from the rest, designed by William Liu, a British-born indigenous villager. A special design feature of this village house is its large platform on the second floor, breaking away from the general flat box shape of village houses. Further, a large piece of glass interacts with the white-painted wall that matches with the garden of nature, giving off a pristine, Wizard-of-Oz impression.

What is the Relationship Between the Village Houses in Hong Kong and Spain?

There is no lack of design opportunities for detached houses in Hong Kong, especially for Small Houses owned by male indigenous villagers. With each floor measuring at 700 square feet, that is, three floors with a total area of 2,100 square feet, it is not restricted by the Buildings Ordinance of the Buildings Department and, thus, the designer is freed up to unleash his creativity. Unfortunately, Small Houses belong only to the indigenous villagers of the New Territories, and their owners have always held the belief of building at the lowest possible cost. Following the early years of discussions between the Heung Yee Kuk N.T. and the government, specifications were produced to match the Chinese village houses. Most of these Small Houses originally had pagoda-style roofs built with ceramic tiles. However, over time they have evolved into a somewhat far-fetched interpretation of the 'Spanish-style' villas due to the local villagers' changing demands for amenity. Small Houses of similar style have kept the construction costs low, but since the design fee component is a negligible portion of the cost, there is no incentive for an architect to be involved in their designs. Some owners have tried different methods when constructing these village houses, but the thought of the extra cost incurred by engaging an architect has deterred most of them. Hence, tens of thousands of 'Spanish-style' village houses have been built in the New Territories. In recent years, due to the increasing costs of these Small Houses, along with the influx of a new generation of owners with specific needs and preferences (architects amongst them), the aforementioned circumstances have seen some changes with more varied and uniquely designed houses gradually being built.

Some may have heard of the Roman bath located in the drug rehabilitation centre in Shek Kwu Chau. However, not many will be aware that Mr Au Fai designed the new wing of the rehabilitation centre. Au found his first success with the design of a church in Huizhou, where he subsequently continued to develop his business contacts in the Mainland. However, his works in Hong Kong are far and few between. His first project was a

group of award-winning outdoor installations, followed by the new wing of the drug rehabilitation centre. Owing to the special purpose of Shek Kwu Chau, I am afraid that it may not be easy for readers to lay eyes on the Roman bath and Au's other works.

Cheung Chau Island, despite being the most populous outlying island, does not have buildings as impressive as those found on Lamma Island. The only notable building is the Caritas Chan Chun Ha Field Studies Centre, which was built more than twenty years ago. It was the first piece of architecture designed by Winnie Ho and it stands as the island's most beautiful and modern architectural achievement of that time. However, this will soon change with the completion of a newly designed community centre by the waterfront of Cheung Chau.

Cheung Chau Island is famous for its Bun Scrambling Competition – the more buns grabbed, the better the fortune for the grabber over the following year – but not many are aware the island is home to the Formosan cherry trees. However, the number of trees has reduced from the original forty to only just over ten now. I wonder: if people here will flock to Tai Tong just to admire the Sweet Gum Trees, or to Nam Cheong Park for the Yellow Poui – and some have even trekked to Ho Wo Street to admire its palm trees, why can't other districts also spend some time beautifying the environment with themed planting? I believe this will be the secret ingredient to attracting more tourists, and it is achievable with due effort.

Pondering on Lantau Island

Lantau Island is indeed a strange but huge outlying island. It is the largest island in Hong Kong with an area of 147.16 square kilometres, which is twice the size of Hong Kong Island measuring at just 78.59 square kilometres. If the British had chosen to settle on Lantau Island instead of Hong Kong Island, the urban outline of Hong Kong would have been completely different. If 90 per cent of Lantau Island had not been designated as country park back then, we would not be running short of land supply for residential usage. I have tried to analyse the underlying reasons from a broader perspective. The decision by the British to develop Hong Kong Island was based purely on its geographical advantage, while the reason for preserving the vast area of land of the New Territories North was so that a buffer zone could be established to block off Hong Kong from the Mainland. Lantau Island was not chosen for development as there was no need for doing so back in 1976 with all its inherent transportation issues. It was also for this reason that the British Hong Kong government allowed this vast piece of land to be dominated by a single property developer and developed it into Discovery Bay, a favourite amongst foreigners. Dating back to as early as 1923, there were already missionaries living in the twenty stone houses on Tai Tung Shan (also known as Sunset Peak).

Back in 1979, I was involved in the design of Phases 1 and 2 of Discovery Bay and the Discovery Bay Golf Club. Back then, Lantau Island was a vast piece of barren mountainous land. It was so vast, in fact, that it gave the impression that Hong Kong did not need to worry about the issue of land supply at all. Further, it was also a time when the city could increase land supply at will through unrestricted land reclamation; and, given that Lantau Island had no transportation infrastructure to connect itself to the city, and nor at that time was there any plan to develop the Chek Lap Kok Airport, it was just a matter of course to preserve the uniqueness of Lantau Island as a large tourist island.

Compared to the situation of Singapore, which has a total area of 718 square kilometres, Sentosa Island, which has been zoned for tourism purposes is measured at around 4.7 square kilometres. Hong Kong has a total area of 1,106 square kilometres, with Lantau Island having an area of 147.16 square kilometres. Although admittedly the functions of Sentosa Island and Lantau Island are different, Singapore gives an example of land being utilised in a balanced manner to solve the issue of land shortage. It is futile to imagine what could have been, but if Lantau Island had not been classified as a country park but was instead developed in the same way as Hong Kong Island, it would have already accommodated 1.5 million people. According to a proposal of the Planning Department, in the 1990s there was a plan to develop Lantau Island and connect it to the west of Hong Kong Island via a subsea tunnel. If such a plan had materialised, then perhaps the issue of land supply today would have been less challenging.

The above is just to let everyone understand the cause and effect of the matter. It is the consensus of the residents of Hong Kong to cherish nature and not easily give up their hard-earned country parks. Fortunately, Hong Kong still has many natural and beautiful scenic spots, which should be treasured.

OOAK LAMMA

Unwilling to Wait Ten Years for the Applause

While some have given their all in the hope of obtaining an architectural qualification but to no avail, Steve Leung had a change of mind not long after he had received his.

On the day of the interview, I arranged to meet with Steve at quarter to five in the afternoon at his office in Kowloon Bay. Even before stepping through the doorway, I could see a sculpture of a young female which, as it was designed during the pandemic, had been sculpted as if wearing a mask. I came across different kinds of artworks around every other corner. Not too many; not too few – just about the right number.

Steve was wearing black casual clothes which echoed the colour tone of his newly painted office (A few months prior, the office had been white). As soon as we sat down, he got straight into the subject. 'I am quite unlike the other architects. Most of them become practising architects right after obtaining their qualifications. I worked in different firms after I obtained mine, and upon gaining sufficient experience, I built up my own architecture and design firm.'

Steve graduated from the HKU Faculty of Architecture in 1981 and then worked for Wong & Ouyang, followed by the Buildings Department and Chevalier International Holdings Limited. In 1987, at the age of thirty, he founded an architecture and urban planning consultation company.

'From 1987 to 1997, I completed quite a number of projects, but I was only satisfied with a few.' As the saying goes, 'establish thyself at thirty, and cast away your doubts at forty.' However, despite having over ten years of experience in architecture under his belt, Steve became doubtful as he turned forty. Behind his trademark black-rimmed Maison Bonnet glasses, he knitted his brow and repeated the question he had asked himself: 'Steve, you are now forty. What do you actually want?'

Steve made a decision in 1997 that would alter the course of his life, at least that was how he described it. 'I loved doing interior design, and I would joke that I came from a background in interior design and product design.' After a decade of reflection, he decided he would pursue both architecture and interior design. He gradually transformed his firm into one whose main line of business was interior design and gave it the status it deserved. At the same time, he dived into the rapidly growing market in the Chinese Mainland to seize the explosive opportunities there.

'Shanghai was a great place to start.' As one of the first designers to enter the Chinese Mainland market, Steve captured the public's attention with his first show flat there. That sense of excitement was undoubtedly hard to replicate even with years of architectural projects. 'I thoroughly enjoy the process of being productive while mulit-tasking. Because for better or worse, the result would always be swift.'

Nowadays, architectural projects account for only about ten per cent of Steve Leung Design Group's portfolio; the rest consists of interior design projects. In the past, this split used to be reversed. At the same time, Steve has also begun creating a wider range of products that have made their way to the international market, including some that have made it to the Salone Internazionale del Mobile di Milano.

Not many architects would give consideration to both interior design and product design. 'We are jacks of all trades!' Listening to his views

Untold Stories   318

1. Inspired by the natural beauty of Lamma Island, the white walls, old wooden planks and turquoise furniture in OOAK LAMMA are all ingeniously intertwined with the surrounding natural environment, presenting the philosophy of unity between man and nature.
2. The white-painted house is in a secluded location that gives it a high degree of privacy. Embarking on the exclusive OOAK LAMMA yacht, one can depart from the bustling city and arrive at its private dock, commencing a comfortable stay.
3. Wooden planks from an old boat have been repurposed as deck planks on the private dock, interior wall panelling and interior steps. The texture of the planks adds to the ambience of its natural surroundings.

on interior design brings a sense of resonance. When asked if he would have picked interior design instead of architecture had he been given the chance again, he calmly swallowed his tea and then answered, 'No, I wouldn't. I have no regrets.' Architecture has always been something he has wanted to do.

Steve is always blunt with his words. With him, there are no euphemisms or prevarication, and there is nothing high-sounding. Between the lines, one feels that he is an easy-going person. However, after having been seated in his office for a while, and looking at the food and beverages menu with the SLD logo on it, one begins to appreciate his insistence on details and images.

One has to experience reading architecture to understand the hardship that comes with it. Burning the midnight oil to read stacks of books or construct models was the norm. However, during his university days, Steve was only willing to dedicate a third of his time to his studies. We couldn't help but ask: 'Busy chasing girls?' 'That was one of several important endeavours.' Steve continued. 'A third of my time was spent on my studies, another third was spent on my job, and the remaining time was spent on the sports ground.' Steve loved all sports, and he was proficient at many of them. 'I might not excel in all of them, but I am skilful at them all.' He was not one to take pauses, neither did he want to, and it was this restless yet focused personality of his that makes him a true Gemini, and sometimes more like a fiery Qilin (a Chinese mythical beast).

While many would skirt around the discussion of their own shortcomings, Steve has always been self-aware. 'Usually a person's strength is also his

OOAK LAMMA consists of two connected double-storey holiday villas. The architectural design is simple, and its seaside location allowed the designer to integrate his love for the natural beauty, culture and craftsmanship of Lamma Island, the evidence of which can be seen in the details of his design.

weakness. From what I understand, the weakness of a man is hard to rectify, as it relates to his personality; turning weakness into strength is almost impossible.' Once he has set his mind to a task, Steve will energetically – explosively, even – give it his all. The fact that he is more of an explosive athlete than an endurance athlete may shed some light on why he loves interior design.

He describes himself as a forward-looking person, as he will only set his sights on what is in front of him, not what is behind. 'That's the mentality an athlete should have. I know when it is supposed to start and when it will end. Besides, everything comes to an end eventually.' Having been through a period of doubt when he was forty, he is waiting for the year of destiny to arrive. The word 'legacy' keeps surfacing in his mind. 'It has been brewing in my mind for at least ten years, or maybe even longer than that, but I have started pondering on how I should be handing down my legacy ever since I turned fifty.'

Steve put down his cup of tea and continued. 'I want to become Robuchon.' The world-renowned chef Joël Robuchon has over thirty two-Michelin-star restaurants around the world. 'But there is only one Robuchon in the world, and he can't be in two places at once, so why is everyone still attracted to his restaurants?' He went on. 'Being hands on is not a bad thing, but it's not the only choice.' Steve believes that a system and a culture can influence and lead the company. In 2018, SLD went public on the Hong Kong stock exchange. 'Steve Leung Design is no longer an individual company; it has become a brand, just like Robuchon.'

From architecture to interior design, product design – and even yacht design! 'Few in Hong Kong can do yacht design, right?' Many have associated Steve with a smooth-sailing and successful journey, and while there is no denying that fortune has been kind to him, he remains grateful for all the benefactors who have come into his life. 'Yet I have been very hard working, and it has always been part of the plan.' Steve is as distinct as one can be, and his fiery personality makes him both likeable and unlikeable in equal measure.

He described his life as a plan, and there was a plan for each day. 'I will often be planning for the next day, next year, or even five to ten years later. I keep thinking about it, and I have never stopped making corrections to my general direction.' Naturally, the plan he has set out for himself is no easy task. 'That's how you stay motivated, but at the same time it can't be so difficult to the point of being discouraging; one step at a time will be the way to go.' Steve not only has a specific plan for each day, he is also prudent in managing his time. 'I start on time and end on time.'

Do you have any unrealised dreams? 'Maybe not big ones, but I would like to publish another book when I am sixty-five.' As we continued, he remarked that it seemed he was headed back to square one.

He is now engaging less in architectural design – not for a lack of interest; he is doing it more as a hobby – and he seems to be enjoying it much more. In recent years, he has begun creating his own projects, for example, the two village houses he bought in Lamma Island, both of which have been gifted to his children. These houses are located in a corner of Lamma Island, against the mountains and facing the sea.

Steve has an affinity for the sea. For the design of this house, he used wood salvaged from an abandoned fishing boat. 'Ninety-nine per cent of the wood used in the house has come from this fishing boat, with some even being kept in its original state.' During the renovation, the house was ravaged by Typhoon Mangkhut. Seawater poured into the living room on the ground floor. ' On principle, these wooden planks from the fishing boat should stand the test of seawater.' He later developed a breakwater to protect the house from being damaged again.

Steve's eldest daughter is a qualified lawyer but has a passion for cooking, and she dreams of becoming a chef one day. The house has been named OOAK LAMMA and it is both a holiday home and a private kitchen. 'I want to help her realise her dream. It isn't deliberate, but this has always been in my heart.'

Whenever the media writes about him, they describe his design as 'minimalistic', to which he says 'A style will do nothing but limit you. So, instead of calling it 'my style', I would say it's more like an attitude.' So what defines a minimalistic attitude? 'Do not engage in excess. Be on point.' Behind that pair of black-rimmed glasses, he did not hesitate, nor were any of his words redundant. He checked his watch and remarked, 'It's already time; I can't be too late.' At last, standing in front of the portrait that was gifted to him by graffiti artist and former colleague Gustav Szabo when he was sixty years old, he leaves behind a beautiful picture to mark the end of the interview.

The Wisdom Path

Behind the Contentment

As the first rays of the morning sun diffuse in the air, traces of darkness begin to retreat as all things gradually awaken under the gentle breeze. At this moment, a layer of gold gracefully covers the calligraphy treasure written on the Wisdom Path by Master Jao Tsung-I, the renowned master of Chinese academic research and art.

The Wisdom Path is located on Lantau Island in the southwest of Hong Kong. It is surrounded by luxuriant greenery and gurgling streams that run beside the roads. Situated near the Tian Tan Buddha and Po Lin Monastery, the Wisdom Path gazes at the sea from behind the mountains, and overlooks the Shek Pik Reservoir. Under the blue sky and thin clouds, and in an ever-so-gentle breeze, it is far from the commotion of the city.

The origin of the Wisdom Path can be traced back to 2002, a time when Hong Kong was hit by the Severe Acute Respiratory Syndrome pandemic. It was a depressing time of economic downturn. Master Jao Tsung-I presented the verses of *The Heart of Prajna Paramita Sutra* written in the form of giant seal script (a form of calligraphy often written on seals) with the hope of bringing blessings to the people of Hong Kong. These treasured scrolls of calligraphy were first donated to the University Museum and Art Gallery of HKU, and later to the steering committee of the Wisdom Path project, which transformed the calligraphy characters of the Heart Sutra into a large outdoor sculpture space composed of thirty-eight giant wooden columns. They were lined up along the mountain to form the character '∞', which bears the meaning of 'endless and infinite'. It is currently the largest outdoor installation of wood-carved Buddhist scriptures in the world.

Along the way, there is a serene and natural atmosphere that pervades throughout. However, such serenity should not be taken for granted. K.C. King and I were the architects in charge of this project. Recalling its construction, K.C. spoke of the serenity being earned through much sweat and tears. 'Although the project was small in scale, there were a lot of other stakeholders involved. From choosing the right location to procuring wooden materials, sculptures and transporting wooden materials up the mountain, all the way through to the laying down of the foundation and erecting and lining up columns sculpted with the Heart Sutra... Everything had to be completed within half a year.'

Altogether, there are 260 Chinese characters in the Heart Sutra. They have been carved by Mr Tang Jisheng, Mr Cheung Sing Hung and Mr Woody Lee, all of whom are experienced master sculptors, with Mr Tang Jisheng having close to twenty years of copy-painting experience with the works of Master Jao Tsung-I. The initial intention was for the words to be carved in granite; however, after an extensive search; no suitable granite material was found in Hong Kong. The rocks found were either too small or not flat enough, and transportation would have been problematic, as well. A bold suggestion was made to have the words engraved on wood instead, similar in style to ancient bamboo slip scroll carving. In fact, my inspiration had originated from the lumber yard in Sunny Bay, Lantau Island. I can still recall my chain of thoughts on the matter, 'There logs floating about on the water, so wouldn't it be better if the piece were to draw inspiration from the geographical relationship between cedars and Lantau Island?' Consequentially, not only would using wood as a substitute echo with the history of Chinese culture, it would also present the relationship between the Heart Sutra and nature, bringing the mind closer to a state of the 'unhindered mind'.

| 1 | 2 3 |

1   The wooden columns are arranged in the '∞' shape, which symbolises infinity.
2   Calligraphy has been engraved on the wooden columns in a manner similar to ancient carvings on bamboo slips.
3   In 1980, Professor Jao Tsung-I travelled to the Mainland and visited the cliff carvings of the Diamond Sutra in Mount Tai, Shandong, and was inspired to write a large-scale Heart Sutra.

The arrangement of the Heart Sutra also carries a profound sense of aesthetics. Drawing its meaning from the concept of infinity, the '∞' character is visible when viewed from above and from a distance along the ridge of the mountain. According to K.C. King, 'Back then, technology was not as convenient as it is now. To achieve this effect, precise measurements of the distances and heights between the columns were required.' The most observant viewer will notice that of the thirty-eight columns, only the twenty-third column has been left blank of engraving. As it turns out, this deliberate omission allows for a momentary pause during the recitation of the Heart Sutra.

The Wisdom Path undoubtedly brings about a feeling of serenity and peace. However, in this natural environment inaccessible by road, the task of transporting wooden columns that were eight to ten metres long along a mountain track of little more than a metre wide – uphill – was a significant challenge. 'In the end, the only practical and economic option was to use pickup trucks to painstakingly transport them uphill. Even the construction cranes had to be dismantled and carried in pieces to be used on the site.' The area is also of special scientific value. It is a protected nature reserve due to it containing the habitat of the unique Romer's tree frog, which is native only to Hong Kong and found on only four of its islands.

To undertake the project without unduly disturbing the frogs, construction had to take place outside of their breeding season, 'Which left only five months out of the year to work on it. It was undoubtedly a race against time.'

Although K.C. King spoke a little too quickly, he did have a steady answer in his heart as to what defined good architecture. 'This city doesn't require every architect to be as good as I.M. Pei; and, surely, not every building has to look like the Bank of China Tower.' He analogised this to Stephen Chow's movies: 'How do you set off the main character without supporting roles?' K.C. King has always been pleasant and hard-working; although he and I were part of the same team in the Architectural Services Department, with me being his senior, we shared a mutual respect and were both a good teacher and helpful friend to each other. 'Whatever you ask of me, I will do it without hesitation,' said K.C. King with a smile.

The Wisdom Path project has undoubtedly been a trial of patience and fortitude, with K.C. King and myself akin to a pair of twins, wielding our swords in unison. The project was achieved in under six months, yet its significance extends far beyond its timely completion, leaving a lasting impression on society. Each colossal column bears meticulously carved scriptures, their bark still clinging to them, as they endure the passage of time and the changing seasons. This evokes a profound sense of peace and contentment, bestowing upon us the wisdom of an 'unhindered mind'.

325 Outlying Islands

Jockey Club Mong Tung Wan Hostel

You Gotta Dance

Every architect should have a debut work off on the right path. Looking back at this debut project, however, it may not have been perfect but, nevertheless, it was special – like a first love.

We sat in Rocco Yim's office, a long wide desk between us, upon which architecture books and design drawings had been placed in an irregular line. Rocco sat on the other side of the desk and leaned against the window, a cabinet filled with neatly arranged books behind him. However, the first thing that caught our attention upon stepping into the room was the enlarged sketch above the cabinet. A layout of the East Kowloon Cultural Centre took up almost half the area of the wall.

A few strokes on a sheet will often record inspiration at a specific moment in time. Rocco had always enjoyed painting, and even had thoughts of becoming a painter, but his dream was halted because he could not 'create something out of nothing'. In contrast to the unrestrained artistic creation of the imagination, he derives greater pleasure from the process of observing and sketching the surrounding objects. As such, the fusion of reality and visuality finds its closest resemblance in the realm of architecture.

Rocco graduated from the HKU Faculty of Architecture in 1976 and later started his apprenticeship at Spence Robinson Limited. After merely two years, he decided to start off his own business, which has now been running for more than forty years.

From libraries to universities, hotels to office buildings, and cultural centres to museums, Rocco's projects were increasing both in number and size. 'You ask me if an architect should have his own style? Yes, but not visually.'

Landmark architecture is a strong and glaring symbol. For better or worse, it can quickly become a focus of a party and a heated topic of discussion for everyone. Andy Warhol came up with the theory of 'Fifteen Minutes of Fame' half a century ago, but put that into today's context, fifteen minutes would be frowned upon for being too long. At the same time, this concept of landmark architecture often creates the illusion that this is where the value of architecture lies. Rocco has been in the architecture industry for more than forty years and has left many memorable works. However, they do not have the ostentatious and arrogant clothing of a landmark architecture, but rather a fair and justified existence.

How do you form a style without relying on visual effects? 'This is your attitude and the choices you make towards everything.' Rocco said in a steady and soft tone, with a hint of affirmation and confidence in his voice. 'Having a consistent attitude and approach towards everything will naturally develop into a style.'

The form of architecture is only one of the elements that contributes to the formation of a style, with the spirit playing a complementary role. In his book on architecture, *Presence*, 'the combination of form and spirit entails his understanding of architecture and the foremost value that he believes architecture should embody. In other words, if one were to pursue sincere architecture, its form must echo both its internal and external aspects.

Looking back at Rocco's debut work – the Jockey Club Mong Tung Wan Hostel – while it might not have been his most famous or proudest work, it was a creation that returned to the form that reflected his original ideals. Upon arrival at Mong Tung Wan on Lantau Island, the slight sea breeze brings a salty smell to our our noses, leaves rustle in the

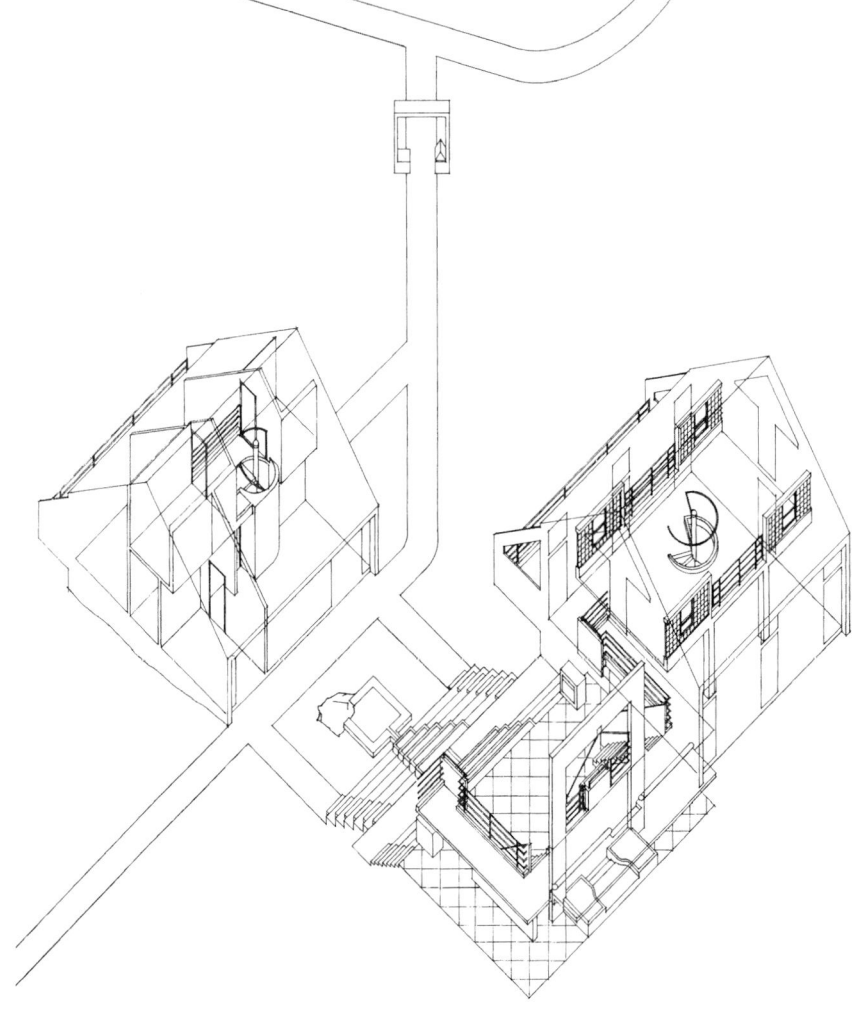

wind, and waves crash in the background. In such a serene and natural environment, what would be the nature of an architectural presence if it were to exist within it?

'I remember when Radio Television Hong Kong interviewed me. These were the words I said: "I want architecture in nature, and nature in architecture."' Although the interview was some thirty years ago, Rocco recalls his words perfectly.

His source of inspiration was, as usual, sketching. Carefully observing and feeling the surrounding environment and not taking the whimsical route. 'Architecture is not a self-centred individual. If its existence is inevitable, we should best think about establishing a good interaction with its surroundings.' Looking at the Jockey Club Mong Tung Wan Hostel, the structure gazes at the sea from the shelter of a mountainous backdrop; it is as if the hostel is merely stones scattered on the beach, echoing the sea in front of them. The texture and pattern of the architecture also echo the mountains behind, as if in a dialogue in the form of a duet.

What would you have done if you were to do it all over again? 'The idea hasn't changed. If possible, I would like to incorporate some environmental elements, such as solar power generation and natural ventilation systems.' In fact, whether it can be done again or not, the words 'The idea hasn't changed' act like a calming pill that allows him to stick to his belief while moving forward.

Unlike artists, architects are passive, but Rocco has been practising for many years and is still enthusiastic about participating in various architectural competitions, taking the initiative in the passive. When speaking on the topic of competitions, Rocco, who is usually gentle, suddenly seemed to be ignited with passion. 'Competition is a good thing. You can keep on taking on challenges.'

When faced with fluctuations in creativity, Rocco believes that only by keeping a sense of curiosity and a willingness to seek challenges can we constantly achieve personal breakthroughs. As Haruki Murakami writes in *Dance, Dance, Dance*, 'You gotta dance. As long as the music plays.'

1. The four independent buildings are in an enclosed layout, and the central garden is the activity centre of the hostel.
2. Looking at the dining hall building from the central garden.
3. The dormitory and the dining hall are connected by corridors to enhance the sense of enclosure in the central garden.

Outlying Islands

From the concept sketch, the buildings are located at the foot of the mountain slope, and their outlines echo the surrounding rocks and flow downwards.

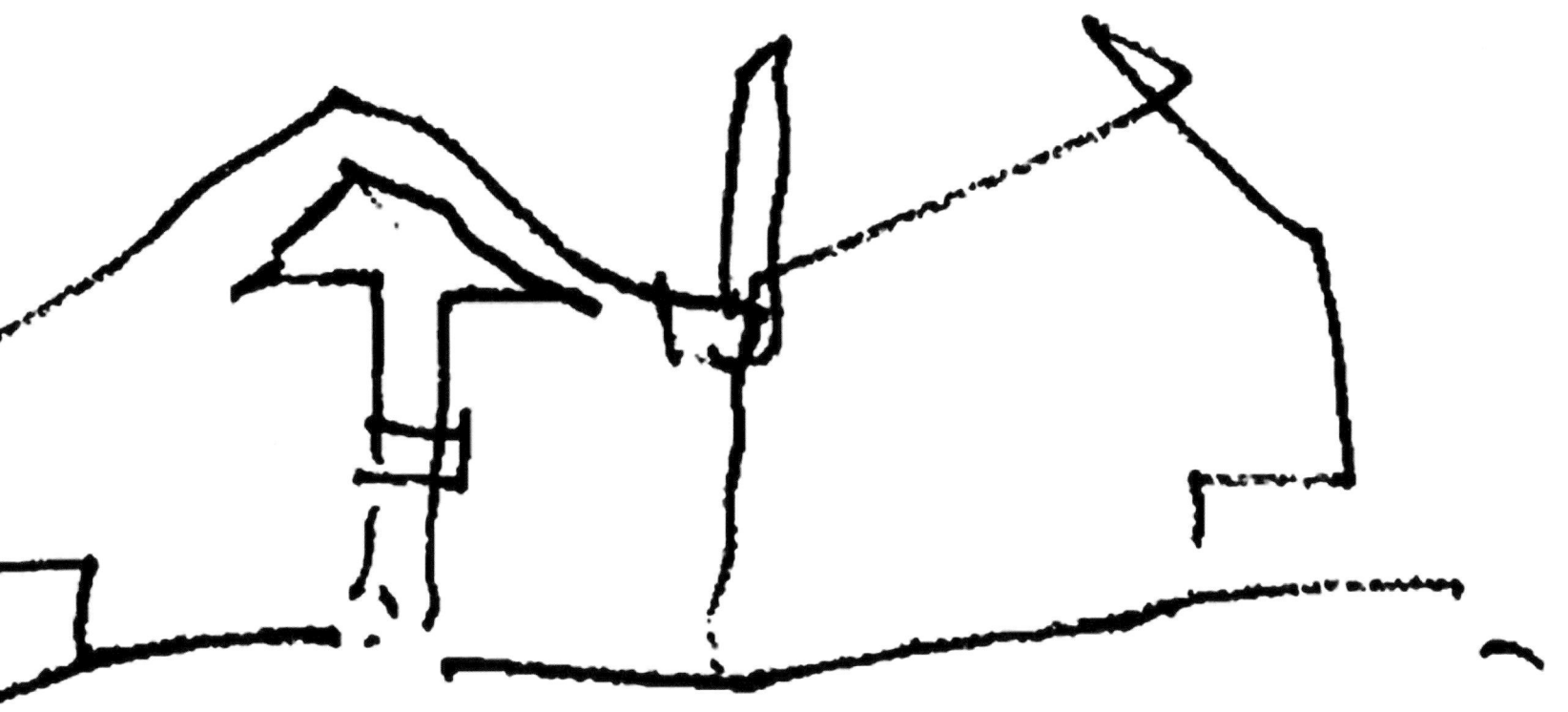

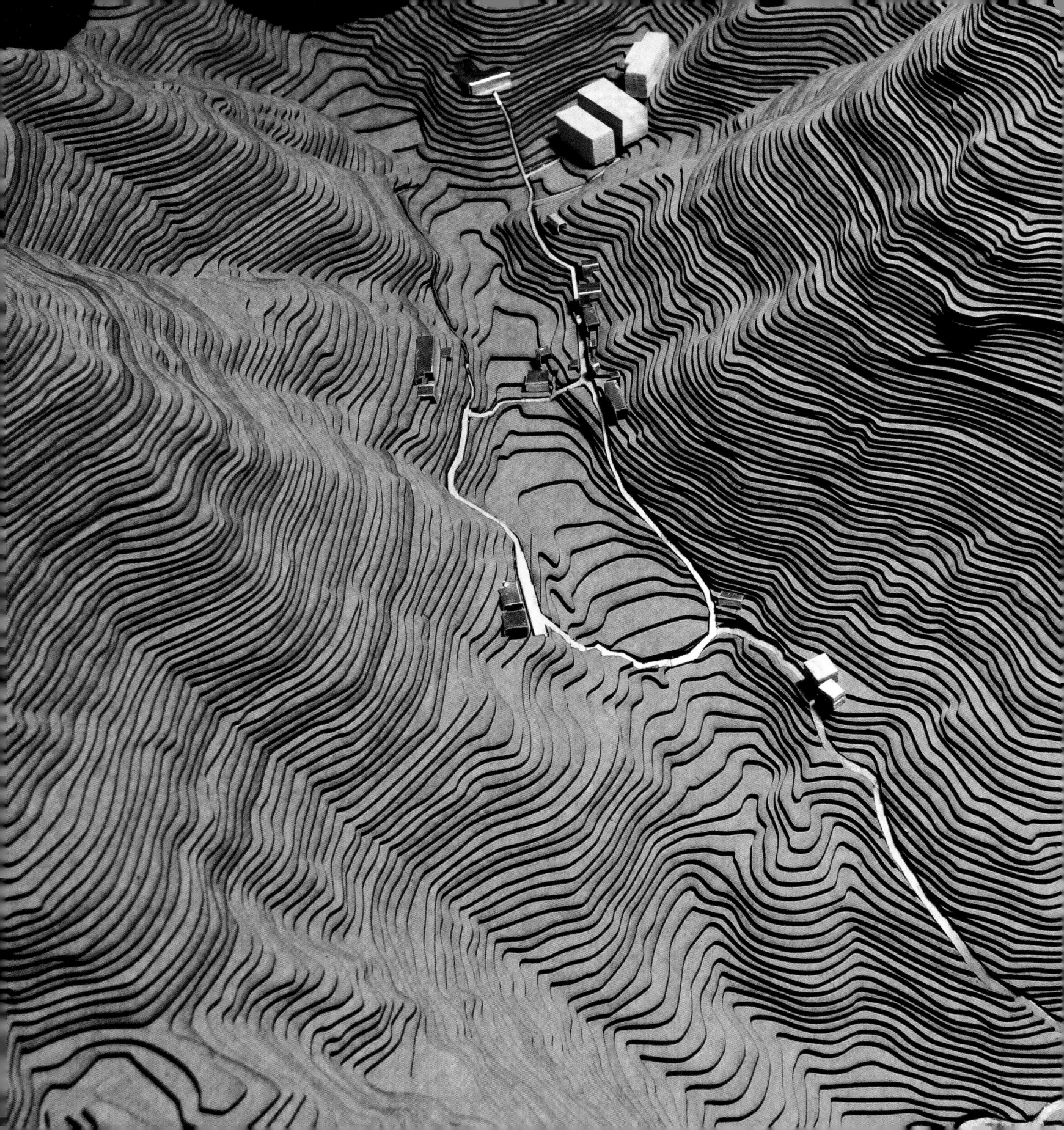

Christian Zheng Sheng College

The Path of Return is Always Longer

Prior to meeting with Mr Anderson Lee, I had already been through three interviews on that very same day. Arriving in Chai Wan in a slightly tired state, I walked through the loading bay and, as its doors opened slowly with a slight rumble, entered the elevator of this old-school factory building. Not needing to look left or right, I walked to the end of a corridor where there was a grey, fair-faced concrete wall with an engraving of the Modulor Man by Le Corbusier, the 'father of functionalism'.

As I pushed through the door, Chan Chan by the Cuban band Buena Vista Social Club was playing on the vinyl record player, and the air became lighter with its bright and spirited melody. The table next to the entrance was already set up with red wine and prosciutto. The warm light suggested the artistic atmosphere of New York's East Village, adorning the place with a relaxing vibe.

Anderson was wearing a plain white shirt with the sleeves rolled up to his elbows; with his swarthy, shoulder-length hair, and a beard grown from his sideburns to his chin, he spoke in a no-nonsense manner that exuded his unrestrained personality from head to toe.

Even at a very young age, Anderson had known what he wanted. After secondary school, he headed straight to the United States to read architecture. He graduated in 1992, but, according to him, it was a very bad year to graduate. 'I was knocking on the doors of many architecture firms with my résumé, but it was fruitless.' Recalling the situation some thirty years ago, Anderson said, 'I ended up at Steven Holl's, which was the last place I had wanted to be.' With his résumé and portfolio in hand, he lingered at the door for a while. 'Since I was there, I might as well give it a try.' Just as he was about to ring the doorbell, Steven opened the door. 'He asked me, "What are you doing here?"'

Once Anderson had given him his résumé and Steven had taken a look at his works, he simply asked him the question: When are you able to start work? 'Back then, including me, it was just a team of four, and Steven had just won the competition at the Kiasma Museum of Contemporary Art.' Exposure to projects of various sizes and types right out of school was a hugely influential experience for Anderson. 'Steven's influence on me was less about design and more about an attitude and him leading by example, which has directly influenced my design and level of professionalism.' He stayed there for seven years before bidding farewell to New York, where he had lived for ten years, returning to Hong Kong just as he was about to turn thirty.

Why did you choose to return when you were doing so well in New York? Did you get bored living there? 'I loved New York. Even now, I still love it.' Lee responded without any hesitation, and after a moment of silence, he said, 'After all, I am from Hong Kong, and it would feel something were amiss if I never made contributions towards my hometown.' Upon saying this, he jokingly remarked that it sounded more noble than it should. When a friend told him that the University of Hong Kong was hiring part-time teachers, he took the chance and submitted an application. 'And I've been teaching for almost twenty years now.' Apart from teaching, he also founded Index Architecture.

When chatting with Anderson, one could almost feel a spontaneous, casual vibe coming from him, while at other times, it was a feeling of 'let's cross that bridge when we come to it'. However, looking back at this project of his – The Christian Zheng Sheng College – no amount of red wine or Cuban melodies coming from the vinyl record player could hide the bittersweet hard work it entailed.

Christian Zheng Sheng College is located in a valley on the Chi Ma Wan Peninsula. Beginning with a ferry ride from Central to Cheung Chau, one has to then transfer via a different boat to another pier before walking up a steep path into the hills. The college is well hidden in the lush, forested mountains, isolated from the world. The place is as quiet as it is remote. To undertake construction in such a primitive environment is equivalent to starting from scratch, with the amount of time and money required being doubled at least.

Initially, the College had intended to relocate its campus to a vacant school premises in Mui Wo on Lantau Island, but the plan was met with unexpected opposition from local residents. 'Whenever people heard about Zheng Sheng College, they would naturally associate it with drug rehabilitation. But we didn't deal with drug rehabilitation; we were just dealing with various types of addictive behaviours and other underlying causes, but the parents just wouldn't believe us.' Anderson had always been concerned that such preconceived notions would override the true meaning of the College. The site in Mui Wo had been vacant for as long as Christian Zheng Sheng College had been in a see-saw struggle with various departments in the government. Anderson shook his head helplessly. 'The kids are actually very polite, they greet everyone in the morning and they are always upright and have never avoided the cameras.'

Perhaps Christian Zheng Sheng College was destined to embark on a difficult journey from the moment of its birth. Anderson knew from the first day he took on the project that it would be a long road ahead. From site selection to design, construction to completion, Anderson ran through the Narcotics Division, the Education Bureau, the Social Welfare Department, and also communicated, liaised and obtained permits from twelve different government departments such as the Water Supplies Department, the Buildings Department, the Architectural Services Department, the Planning Department and the Lands Department. The whole process had taken nearly seven years before actual work could even begin. 'Without consensus from everyone, it was difficult to implement and execute the plan. We had to resolve even the most basic issues such as water and electricity sources, infrastructure, roads and septic tanks; otherwise, even if you were to install lights, there would be no electricity. In addition, we also had to transport building materials up a steep eight-hundred metres mountain. How could all that be done without proper roads?'

The terrain of the valley was uneven, and so Anderson raised the platform using multiple pillars for the construction of the building. This approach not only minimized disruption to the natural landscape but also created an open and spacious environment by eliminating structural columns. But when the Buildings Department saw that the building would be elevated, they requested that space underneath be walled off with concrete to prevent future illegal construction. When I heard that, I thought, 'We are not speculating in real estate. If we need a bigger space in the future, we will request it, so why should we close off that space?'

On its design, Anderson went back to the basics, simplifying wherever possible and focusing on functionality. Beneath the clean façades are simple, black-painted steel columns without any extra decoration. The open space below the upper building is well-ventilated and well-lit, and, thus, suitable for group activities. From temporary use of a dilapidated building with a tin roof to a proper college building, the College did not have any air conditioning installed nor did it provide basic facilities such as hot water for bathing. 'The only place with air conditioning is where the computers are.' This was not done to save money; it was done at the principal's request. Mr Alman Chan Siu Cheuk once told Anderson that he did not want the school to be too luxurious. 'Because this is a place for students to practice asceticism and engage in life education.'

The College does not put its students into grades or employ the hierarchical distinctions typical of secondary schools. The principal and teachers were willing to take a pay cut to teach and live together with the students, setting an example for them. 'Don't think that the principal or teachers would be able to bathe in hot water or eat better food. Whatever the students cooked, they ate, too, and if it wasn't something tasty, they would just cook better the next time.'

Although it is uncommon for architectural projects to be completed in short time frames, what was Anderson thinking spending ten years of his life on one project? 'The craziest one wasn't me; it was the school director, Mr Lam Hay Sing, who initiated this project. He and Alman Chan have been here for as long as the College has been around.' And, thus, the 'three musketeers' finally came together. 'The principal asked me the same thing. "How could it have taken so long?" I said, "You, too?"' Surely, the two of them must have wished they'd met each other earlier. Their shared stubbornness on this project was clearly evident. It was as if the words of the Chinese saying was written on both of their foreheads: 'Venture forth into the mountain, even though that's where the tigers reside.'

I was suddenly reminded of the words of the poet Bei Do: 'Between the journey and the path of return, the path of return will always be longer.' For Anderson and the principal, and even the students, who were in the process of setting out on the right path, perhaps the long path of return was, in fact, their journey, and one of self-discovery at that. Anderson has never thought that one day he would be as deeply rooted in this place as Alman Chan. The project has now been completed, and Anderson has chosen to no longer be blind to the needs of others.

Under the blue sky and lush mountainous forest, Christian Zheng Sheng College appears particularly bright, and for Anderson, this has gone beyond the story told by bricks and tiles. 'This is something really close to my heart.' His words are frank and straightforward, yet deeply sentimental.

Careful design of the storey-to-storey height, the depth of the balconies and placement of the windows has contributed to natural cooling via the chimney effect, thus increasing circulation and avoiding excessive heating without the need for air conditioning.

1	3
2	

1   The spaces of the three main blocks have been laid out to enhance privacy and are staggered in sympathy with the topography of the site.
2   The building utilises slender and elongated pillars in place of traditional support columns, minimizing disruption to the natural landscape and enhancing spatial flexibility. The vertical design is accentuated through the façade's windows, rainwater collection pipes, and balcony railings.
3   Situated in a peaceful and picturesque valley on a small island, the architecture and its natural surroundings have a healing effect on the mind and soul.

Tai O Heritage Hotel

Big City, Small Scene

As I was travelling to Tai O, I came across a story in Ming Pao's *Sunday Life* written by the artist Ivy Ma. It was titled 'Vertical Bird, Horizontal Cat'. The short graphic story, illustrated with pictures, photos and words, was simple yet interesting. One caption read: 'It is said that some kinds of dinosaur were the ancestors of today's birds. Therefore, when we observe the birds of today, it is akin to witnessing the ancient past. Tigers are the largest felines in terms of size. Thus, when we see urban cats, we can easily imagine the wild plains and forests.' It seems that life requires a little more imagination to be truly captivating.

As the ferry sailed from Central to Ma Wan, the busy cityscape began to disappear behind me and a vista of blue sea and green islands began to open up in front of me. The occasional seagull flying overhead didn't detract from the peaceful journey. After rocking and swaying for forty-five minutes, the ferry arrived at the Mui Wo pier. I got off the ferry to catch Bus Service No. 1. Finally, I arrived at Tai O, about two hours after leaving Central. Arriving at this remote island was like entering a time warp and travelling back in time to the small fishing village that Hong Kong once was.

Tai O is surrounded by mountains on three sides with waterways snaking through the settlement. At the mouth of the river, sampans sway gently with the waves, while fishing nets hang on the sheds along the riverbanks, unintentionally depicting the memories of the water-dwellers. In such a calm and anachronistic setting, the island is adorned with historic buildings such as the Yeung Hau Temple, Shek Lun Kok, Wing Hing Petrol Station, the Tai O Charity Convenience Home, the Old Tai O Police Station and many more, silently recording the traces of Tai O's transformation from desolation to prosperity. Amongst them, the old Tai O Police Station was revitalised into the current Tai O Heritage Hotel, allowing it to continue to bear witness to the history of Tai O, albeit with a new identity.

The Tai O Police Station building was completed in 1902. When it was decommissioned in 1996, it fell into disrepair. In 2010, it was registered as a Grade II historic building by the Antiquities Advisory Board.

Following the revitalisation of the century-old Béthanie located in Pok Fu Lam, Mr Phillip Liao secured the Tai O Heritage Hotel project with a bold proposal under the Revitalising Historic Buildings Through Partnership Scheme. Transforming an abandoned police station into a boutique hotel required not only the preservation of valuable historical traces, but it was also about injecting a new soul to continue its local stories. As Philip remarked, 'Revitalisation is more difficult than rebuilding.'

Against the backdrop of a mountainous ridgeline, the Tai O Heritage Hotel gazes calmly at the sea, as its breeze caresses the landscape at sunset. Following revitalisation, the building still retains the charm of late nineteenth-century Hong Kong architecture. With views of the pale blue sky and the sea framed by the white arches of its exterior corridors, it brings to mind the stunning views of Santorini. In addition, the Chinese-style tiled roofs and wooden sash windows provide a quaint, traditional touch to the hotel. The hotel rooms are named after the various ranks of police and marine police during the British-governed period and have only undergone minor changes, mostly to revert spaces to their original configurations to enable natural ventilation and let in natural light.

1	2	1	The revitalised Tai O Heritage Hotel has British-styled architectural features with a Chinese tiled roof, gabled façades, wooden sash windows and fireplaces. The former police station's distinctive turrets, searchlights, corner towers and holding cells have all been restored and refurbished.
		2	The former report room was turned into a hotel reception and the old offices into hotel rooms. The roof of the building has been extended and transformed into a glass-roofed restaurant showcasing the creative work of Hong Kong artists.

Fireplaces have been retained in the rooms together with the inset tiles and iron fixtures of bygone days.

A glazed structure has been constructed on the roof to house a restaurant. During the day, it offers sunlight and a view of endless sea; at night, a gentle sea breeze and the vast, starry sky. If one embraces the peaceful ambience when sitting here, one can sense the stillness of time and the tranquillity of the years.

In relation to the revitalisation process, I specifically remember Phillip quietly remarking, 'Sometimes you have to hear what God has to say, smell the scent of the place and feel its breeze, they will tell you a lot about the place.' For him, architecture starts with humbling yourself and observing with an open mind the surrounding environment, climate, landscape, culture and customs. The greatest sense of success does not lie in winning an award, planting a flag somewhere or leaving behind an iconic building; it is about continuing the culture and story of the place and delighting its new users.

The Tai O of today remains quaint, yet unruly. It is a place that obviously does not care for the glitz and glamour of the city but only for the tranquillity of the years. The ongoing presence of people in the village testifies that the rare serenity of this place still remains precious.

Ham Tin Villas

An Immersive Moment

Mr William Liu is very soft-spoken, but he couldn't hide that shy smile of his in between his words. Even in moments of silence, his subtly arched eyebrows and crescent-shaped eyes create the impression of a perpetual smile. However, his architectural designs do not mirror his gentle demeanor; instead, they exude a touch of tension, expression, and unruliness.

William graduated with a degree in architecture from Greenwich University in 1986. He later moved to Hong Kong and worked for several architecture firms including Rocco Design Architects and OMA. In 2002, he founded his own firm, ARK Associate Architects Limited. 'The reason was very simple. I wanted to go my own way.'

His firm's name – a reference to Noah's ark – was chosen to symbolise a new beginning and hope. Shortly after he had founded the firm, William came across the story of the ark of the covenant – a symbol of God's omnipresence – when he was reading the Bible. He embarked on his journey of architecture and interior design with reverence and humility.

Many architects complain about Hong Kong's many building restrictions, especially those relating to market-driven architectural projects, and William agrees with them. 'However, finding breakthroughs in the midst of restrictions can be interesting.' Meanwhile, his preference has always been aligned with the concept of complete design – combining architecture and interior design – and, as an art lover, he also hopes to infuse a touch of aesthetics. Incorporating art into life is not just about hanging up a painting, so how can one truly integrate art and aesthetics into it? William's smile remained gentle, and he thought for a moment before saying calmly, 'For me, art expression has two aspects. One is form, like the form of sculpture; the other is space, and that is about creating interesting spaces.'

William likes expressive works of art, the V Point in Causeway Bay and Iceberg in Tsim Sha Tsui are two of his favourite projects. They are like giant sculptures, and they reflect the unruliness in his heart.

Another of William Liu's recent projects, Ham Tin Villas, is a far cry from V Point and Iceberg. Its characteristics seem to be more aligned with William's personality. The Ham Tin Villas are located on the southern coast of Lantau Island and adjacent to Pui O Beach. With ample views of the sea whilst being complemented by a mountainous backdrop, the villas are nestled amidst swaying, lush native trees and the soothing sound of flowing streams, creating an atmosphere of serenity and beauty that is a world away from the frenzy of the city.

For William, 'Every project has different restrictions and scope for expression.' Ham Tin Villas is located within nature itself with a minimalist design with its predominantly white exterior walls providing a hint of purity. Floor-to-ceiling windows penetrate the envelope of the structure sufficiently enough to make it look like a glass box from a distance. The two-and-a-half-storey building features a terrace garden that creates a direct dialogue with nature and provides a moment of solitude.

It has been more than two decades since the beginning of his entrepreneurial journey. William recalled that, in the 1990s when he first entered the industry, there was a prevalent emphasis on practicality in the public's understanding and pursuit of design. At times, interior design

	3	1	Inspired by the shape of an iceberg, the horizontally folded glass façade is composed of a white ceramic-coated cladding and reflective glass to create a multi-dimensional appearance.
1 2	4	2	This building's form is inspired by gemstones. The glass façade reflects its surroundings at different angles, creating a kaleidoscopic visual effect.
		3	Each villa is set within an extensive garden space, allowing nature to flow in and out of the living space and blurring the boundaries between inside and outside.
		4	The villas are designed with contrasting solid and glass walls. Transparent full-height glazing provides a centralised view and connection to the garden area.

took precedence over architectural form. However, as we entered the twenty-first century, William expressed that there is now a greater focus on a holistic experience. A simple phrase on ARK's website, 'Creating Experiences, Places and Lifestyles', encapsulates his understanding of architecture and design. Faced with this shift, he understands deeply the need to continuously pursue further education and growth as an architect, rather than remaining stagnant.

Giving Young Architects a Chance

In addition to interviews with individual architects, our team was fortunate enough to have organised a video symposium on the Sunday prior to the strict enforcement of social distancing measures due to the outbreak of Covid-19 in Hong Kong. The symposium focused on the entrepreneurial and growth opportunities for young architects and smaller firms. During this session, attendees were able to gain insights and enjoy valuable exchanges via speakers sharing their personal stories and experiences.

We also invited several senior architects who had long supported young architects as well as advocated architectural design competitions, including Mr Donald Choi, Ms Corrin Chan and Ms L.Q. Chan; with the younger architects being Mr Benny Lee, Mr Manfred Yuen, Mr Otto Ng, Mr Paul Tse, Mr Sarah Mui and Ms Kylie Chan. Other more experienced architects included Ms Lucia Cheung, Mr Frank Yu, Mr William Liu, Mr Au Fai and Mr Vincent Pang, who shared their experiences of success and failure. I also noticed that several of them who had taken on the path of alternative architecture were regular participants in public outdoor sculpture competitions. Also, many of those who had done well in architectural design competitions were later able to embark on smooth career paths.

Architects from different generations gathered at this forum, and everyone shared his or her personal experience, professional knowledge, earnest advice and generous dedication. These valuable exchanges have been recorded in the next chapter.

Corrin Chan: In order to survive, our architects have had to find different avenues through which to realise their creativity, including participating in competitions to put into practice their ideas so as to ensure that they can be more visible to the public.

Paul Tse: Competition for me is like an exploration, especially during my downtime, when I can put some effort and thought into it. At the same time, the benefit of a competition is that there is a very complete concept to support the design.

Frank Yu: I do occasionally participate in competitions in Hong Kong and the Mainland. However, generally speaking, they are few and far between. Nowadays, projects in both public and private sectors in the Mainland are often acquired through competitions, which is not a particularly healthy situation. There are many competitions where over a hundred architecture firms compete for a single private project, and even with the top three selected, the final decision on the design still rests with the developer. Imagine, they've got over one hundred designs in one go, and each one has been quite well thought out... Which is why we tend to commission our familiar clients directly.

Lucia Cheung: To a certain extent, competition is a waste of resources by selecting only one out of a hundred designs received.

L.Q. Chan: Actually, the choice to participate rests solely on those who are willing to take the bait, and it is purely an individual decision. It's not necessarily a waste even if you lose, for you might get something out of it.

Au Fai: In recent years, I have been a bit picky about competitions. Five or ten years ago, I would even participate in overseas competitions because they were interesting, and it was also easy to find inspirations and ideas. Later on, I found out that the chances of winning overseas competitions were rather low, but as William Liu put it, these design proposals are also resources. In recent years, there have been more local competitions in Hong Kong, which is a good thing.

Vincent Pang: Prior to taking part in competitions, my firm had actually been operational for five to six years mainly engaged with alteration, addition and interior design projects. In the past, most competitions in Hong Kong required invitations, so I didn't have many opportunities to participate in them. It was only when I knew that the West Kowloon Cultural District competition was open to local companies in Hong Kong that I became immediately interested.

Benny Lee: When I was studying in the UK, I often participated in competitions with my classmates. However, it was painful because even if we won, we were not able to implement our ideas. For instance, we once participated in the competition for the design of the Hong Kong-Zhuhai-Macau Bridge and won against Norman Foster and SOM to take first place. However, the project would not be given to such a young company.

Raymond Fung: In the past, winning a competition didn't guarantee the opportunity to put your ideas into practice. Eventually, when they did become a reality, it was actually the result of the collective hard work of many. Times have changed, though, and it is a good idea to start with small projects and build up gradually.

William Liu: Actually, an investment from a client equates to a form of great trust, but the premise of it is to first give customers enough confidence so that others will believe in you. For younger firms, while most of them do start off with smaller projects, it is still not easy.

Donald Choi: It would be a pity to label an architect as untrustworthy because he or she has entered into a competition and won but was not able to materialise that design, or because he or she hasn't had experience in dealing with large, complex projects. When we look back at Norman Foster, he had never even built more than a three-storey house before he built the HSBC Main Building in Hong Kong, yet he still managed to win the project along with the investment from his client. We have allowed the repeated occurrence of someone winning a competition yet not being able to realise their idea for so many years. This is indeed something we need to reflect on.

Corrin Chan: Actually, this matter of competition has yet to become an phenomenon or culture. For instance, the regulations in northern Europe stipulate that all public buildings are required to be put up for design competition, through which they are tendered. This approach may be surprising to Hong Kong architects. I once interviewed some young northern European architects, and I asked them this question: 'You are so young and yet you have won a competition of this scale. Is there any difficulty in implementing it?' It turns out that in northern Europe, these young architects receive a lot of support from their governments, and experienced architects provide background support in terms of division of labour, administration and implementation. The governments know that these young architects are gifted in creativity and innovation, and so they support them.

Manfred Yuen: Whether the outcome of a competition can eventually be implemented, it is a matter of results. We often say that good design comes from competition, but in fact, we live not in a binary society but a resource-integrated one. Therefore, in addition to improving ourselves through competition, I think there is one more idea worth exploring in the future – collaboration. I think that sometimes what we need is not competition but collaboration.

Benny Lee: Collaboration is the right way. Honestly, when we were reading architecture, we often had to criticise each other no matter how good the project was. We just had to pick out something bad to say, regardless; this seems to be in our nature. Now that I am over thirty, I have gradually realised the importance of appreciating the works of our fellow architects. Schools may not have been able to teach us about appreciating others; rather, they have taught us how to criticise the works of others. However, learning the art of appreciation towards others may actually be good for the industry.

Otto Ng: It has been said that the people here are often fettered by old conventions and are always on the lookout for model answers, but this assumption has been a far cry from the truth. In the past decade, people here have grown to be receptive and tolerant. They are beginning to believe that now is a suitable time to reform something that people have been afraid of: change. Just like our current colleagues, besides architects, there are also interior designers, sociologists and other professionals working together on architecture, and this is an undertaking suitable for a tiny place like Hong Kong.

Manfred Yuen: The world is different now from what it was twenty years ago. Sometimes, when a design has been completed and you are ready to build, you find out that many things are beyond the control of an architect. Apart from collaboration with other architects, you will also have to work with the suppliers and manufacturers. For instance, our client may not get the most out of our expertise if we do not know how to build or assemble a piece of architecture with new and updated methods. With regards to working with professionals of different disciplines to explore new methods of construction, or even more environmentally friendly ways of doing so, I believe that the architects of Hong Kong have been set on this path, but we have yet to reach an ideal level. Very often, we are still dealing with regulations within the framework or the relevant legal issues. Therefore, it is worth exploring how we can effectively promote collaboration with fellow professionals, contractors and large corporations.

Donald Choi: This book is about architecture, and I wonder if interior design is considered a part of architecture. We are still looking at architecture from a very narrow and barren point of view. We all have an aesthetic standard when we engage in our architectural works, but apart from placing the focus on its external aspect, we should also be concerned about creating an environment where people can live well. When we encounter a building on the street, its merits may not be solely evident in its outward appearance; the internal aspects are equally significant.

Raymond Fung: Architecture should be diverse, and interior design does not necessarily have a negative connotation, as both architecture and interior design are equally valuable.

L.Q. Chan: I agree that sometimes we have too narrow a view of architecture. Is it necessary for architecture to have a shape? Is the subway a form of architecture? When people first get into design, they are often afraid that said design cannot be visible enough, yet once they start to get into architecture, they become afraid that it will be too visible. In truth, we need to give thought to when we should be assertive and when we should be humble. For instance, if we are building next to someone else's landmark, do we have to compete to be conspicuous? Humble architecture comes in many different attitudes, even the small projects can be beautiful. If we focus only on exaggerated shapes, we simply cannot compete. Our strength, however, lies in our ability to create something special under such circumstances.

Manfred Yuen: It is important to ask what the architects of Hong Kong have been doing in the past two decades. Sometimes, setting the boundaries too wide can be a form of limitation. I feel that the architects of Hong Kong are in a disadvantaged position in Asia. In terms of hardware, unlike architects elsewhere, we may simply lack the space to build, so, instead, eighty per cent of architects in Hong Kong are interior designers. This world is much bigger than we can perceive, and we need to be clear about our position with respect to the whole of Asia.

Corrin Chan: We are underprivileged compared to architects elsewhere, and this is a wake-up call for the architectural community. This isn't only a problem of whether young architects are given the space to fully realise their potential but also a question of whether the entire profession has a future. Over a decade ago, since the era of Rocco Yim, there has been no soil for us to cultivate the next generation of young architects in Hong Kong, and this problem still persists.

Frank Yu: I started my business in 2003 during a time when the Mainland was developing at a relatively faster pace. However, most design firms weren't as experienced and meticulous as the architects in Hong Kong, and the experience referred to here relates to collaboration with foreign companies or the nature of projects encountered. Thus, we did have a relatively greater advantage back then. Of course, twenty years later, this no longer holds true. Design firms in the Mainland have become very impressive.

L.Q. Chan: In the 1980s, for instance, the people of Hong Kong were viewed as the cream of the crop by those in the Mainland. From what we have seen later, though, we may have this sense of inferiority in the face of others making progress at a much faster pace. However, there is no need to be afraid. What I'm trying to say is that even small-scale architectural projects can have great significance. The people of Hong Kong do not always have to compete with others to be interesting or stylish.

Otto Ng: Hong Kong is a very small place, but it's a good place for practice and it's easy to meet quirky people here. Just like we engage in many facilities and interior design, but we don't just focus on the architecture itself or its form. I think architecture includes everything from the inside and out.

Paul Tse: Hong Kong is very extreme in that things are either very small or very large, it's a very contrasting space, even when compared to Manhattan. In recent years, I have been focusing more on small buildings, because in these small spaces you can more directly perceive the relationship between architectural space and people.

Lucia Cheung: In the past, many decisions were made from the top down, but now we are seeing more opportunities for a bottom-up approach. Even if we don't necessarily get to own large-scale projects, we can still collaborate with large companies and engage in interior design for the entire project. Sometimes these opportunities allow us to start with interior design and then go back to architecture, so don't underestimate interior design. As L.Q. Chan said, the people of Hong Kong are amazingly good at finding ways to shine through the cracks.

Au Fai: I think many young architects are now finding their own way, such as LAAB Architects. Although they are not engaged in architectural practice in the traditional sense, they have nevertheless managed to carve out a niche market for themselves, given the multifaceted nature of architecture. Furthermore, as a professional discipline, how architecture can continue to evolve and thrive, I believe, lies in individuals finding their own path through their passion.

Corrin Chan: In this day and age, architecture as a profession is slowly changing. It is no longer just about the execution or the construction of a piece of architecture as it traditionally has been; it has expanded into considering the impact and change that a space can create. This innovative take can be said to have been forced out of the architects in Hong Kong given the environment in which they find themselves. We have to give thought to the question: 'What is the future of architecture?' We were on the topic of competition earlier, and I think that competition should go beyond the obvious and extend itself towards connecting the community and its residents, it should also be about the future of architecture, the future of our city, and should even be concerned with the next generation. The publication of Raymond's book at this particular moment is of great significance. The focus is not solely on admiring a few remarkable buildings but rather on whether we can cultivate a fertile ground for future architects of this place.

Raymond Fung: The purpose of this book is to bring awareness to the residents of Hong Kong that local architecture is very relevant to them; at the same time, architecture does not have to be very sophisticated; it can also be very grounded. This is why the book has been intended as a traveller's book, a light-hearted way to introduce the readers to the architecture of Hong Kong. Just like several of Sarah Mui's space-making projects, which help people here realise that good architecture does not necessarily come only from the world's most famous architects. Simply put, this book hopes to bring out the spiritual values of ordinary people and ordinary things.

Sarah Mui: I've been asking myself for the past two years, 'Are we ready? Ready to be ourselves?' I believe people like architecture because it has a constraint that comes from the city and the system, and the fun part has been how certain things can happen within it. I think I'm the most misunderstood architect amongst everyone here, but I try to tell myself that this is a process of discovery.

Manfred Yuen: Architecture has always been a profession, but these days it is becoming less so. Actually, we are a resource integrator. The problems we face today are no longer confined to just making sure that a building doesn't collapse; we now need to engage in a lot of research work for our customers and help them understand the market. If our clients are governments, then we will need to help them understand the needs of the public.

Sarah Mui: When it comes to architecture, we are so used to thinking about how to build 'our own' architecture that we tend to neglect the environment in which they are built. I often wonder, isn't an architect a facilitator? We shouldn't focus on celebrity architects, especially in education. Take my favourite, Bauhaus, for example; it is not just about building an architecture but also a future. Being an architect requires a forward-thinking mindset to think about this world and even to think about what life should be like. That's my view on architectural education.

Manfred Yuen: Many architects present have had experiences studying or working abroad. Does this underlying message explain the immaturity of Hong Kong's architectural education? My question is: everybody has been exposed to foreign cultures, wanting to transfer the foreign system to Hong Kong, which could influence the things that we do. As for the education system in Hong Kong, the teachers may be foreigners. I would begin to ponder, where do the problems of our education and training come from? Why do we have to experience so much foreign education and baptism to reach the present situation? The architecture education nowadays is not about doing something for the future; it is about how the world operated thirty or forty years ago – a system from foreign countries, not designed for Hong Kong. This is not necessarily a critical question, but an interesting phenomenon.

L.Q. Chan: I am a one hundred per cent born-and-bred local, and, to me, it might not necessarily be about a certain system producing a certain fixed outcome. During my time, no one was interested in competitions; without an adequate level of presentation skills, nothing could be done. However, I am proud that I have taken part in competitions and lost, as every unsuccessful attempt has given me room for self-reflection and cultivated my resilience.

Sarah Mui: A combination of Chinese and Western culture is actually the culture in which we grow up in. Finding our own distinctive features while integrating both cultures is something we have to face. As L.Q. Chan often says, 'Improvise!'

Donald Choi: Going back to doing things the way it was thirty years ago would, of course, spell failure. However, speaking of collaboration, regardless of technology or the environment, every generation has a different approach. In my opinion, there is no limit to designing and building, nor to creativity.

Paul Tse: It seems that architecture itself is a Western-oriented discipline. I have been abroad since high school, and when I returned to Hong Kong, I felt there was a need to reacquaint myself with this place, and so I started off a research project named 'Middle Man Hong Kong'. The project consisted mainly of twelve videos, each one sharing an important element of Hong Kong. 'Middle Man' is the namesake of Hong Kong's inherent characteristic. First, Hong Kong is a melting pot of Eastern and Western cultures. Secondly, Hong Kong plays a pivotal role as an intermediary in the realm of commerce. With little land, no industry chain and no natural resources, this city often relies on 'feasibility' to mobilise different endeavours. This concept is very similar to that of architecture, so I took on this theme to look at architecture in Hong Kong.

Sarah Mui: A lot of spaces are often ignored in our city. I remember when I had finished working on a basketball court located on a rooftop, I got a message from a friend saying, 'I have looked at basketball courts for over twenty years, and I never thought it would turn out this way.' Our city does not have as much space as those in other countries, and most households don't have a garden at home where you can socialise with others. However, our city does have a lot of shop houses, and some of our projects have been to turn these empty shop houses into limited community centres. The American sociologist Ray Oldenburg once said that every community should have a third space. So what is the 'third space' in our city? Are these shop houses the answer to that?

Kylie Chan: Growing up in Hong Kong, it was only after studying architecture that I came to understand the value that architecture or design can bring to a place, and it is difficult to quantify this value. For example, when we successfully secured a project for the Hong Kong Observatory through winning a competition, our role was to add value to the pier with a creative and well-designed concept. At the same time, I would also think about what a user could get out of the design. As for how the public will know if the design has brought added value to the place, they will have to experience it for themselves.

Sarah Mui: Speaking of users, we often hear that the people here do not know how to utilise space. I would counter that by asking, 'Have you told them how to? We haven't been encouraging users to ask questions, and so, naturally, when you ask them what they like, they may not be able to give you the answer, or their answer would be somewhere in between 'beautiful' and 'unattractive'. This relates to the question of education and culture. We have never applied architecture in public education. Is this something for us to reflect on?

Therefore, by involving the public in the design of an architecture, we can promote and facilitate the understanding of the architecture and make the design more relevant to the needs of the public. I once worked on a project that left a strong impression on me; it was a public lavatory project, and during the process we were given the advice of a wheelchair user. Usually, when we talk about disabled lavatories, we subconsciously think of them as having only one compartment and having a very long waiting time. What we didn't expect, though, was that a lady had actually asked us about the missing mirror and make-up station by the sink, as such users use make-up, as well. We cannot remain ignorant of the needs of others and naively believe that solving the issue of space is all there is to it. Instead, we should be thinking about utilising design to cause behavioural change and, thus, improving the quality of life for everyone. The problems of this world are all interconnected. For instance, it is not enough to appoint a non-profit organisation to operate a historic building; there is much more to it than that.

Lucia Cheung: This is the key to continuity for architecture.

Donald Choi: This involves caring for the lifecycle of architecture. Our architects often say, 'Let's finish up and move on.' However, if it is so difficult finding new projects and there is already a customer on hand, and since the architecture surely has its own lifecycle, then why don't we keep this relationship? Why don't we turn the relationship with each customer into a long-term service? This is a fatal flaw of ours.

Epilogue

The Whys and Wherefores of this Book

Ever since my retirement from the Department of Architecture at the Chinese University of Hong Kong, I have had the intention of publishing this book. Subsequently, due to my teaching commitments of ink painting and frequent exhibitions, the project was put on hold…

On a Sunday in 2020, I came across a report in Ming Pao on local public architecture, and I was overwhelmed with mixed feelings.

I lamented the news that an outstanding architect was retiring soon, then I thought of the many unknown, many excellent but unknown architects in Hong Kong who had yet to have their stories told, and just who was going to do that? To complete this book would be a huge endeavour and would require assistants who have had experience in conducting interviews. I am very thankful for the two young volunteers who joined the team with great enthusiasm: Ms Karen Tsui and Ms Helena Hau, who together have visited dozens of local architecture offices and shared the heaviest responsibility of recording the interviews and the subsequent writing. I would also like to express my gratitude towards Mr Kelvin Li and Mr Joseph Ting Sun Pao, who were willing to act as consultants, Ms Ida Sze and Mr Samuel Chan, who took care of the graphic design and Mr Jeff Tung, who shared with us his photography collection for the cover page, making the book more complete and beautiful. This long-held wish of mine was finally realised with its Chinese publication in 2022, followed by the English edition in 2023, which coincided with my seventieth birthday.

I am also grateful for a home-grown Hong Kong-based not-for-profit initiative, together with the Jury Committee, for supporting us with a generous grant fund to further propel my writing and works into an English edition for international audiences. DESIGN TRUST, founded in 2014 as a granting and community platform, is led by Marisa Yiu, who is the Co-Founder/Executive Director of this registered charity initiative. It is particularly meaningful, as I have known of Marisa's work since the 2009 Bi-City Biennale of Architecture & Urbanism on the West Kowloon waterfront promenade, for which she was also the Chief Curator. Since then, she has been leading and supporting many micro-park projects, to foster emerging scholars and designers with this NGO. I am thrilled to widen the reach with this publication on Hong Kong local architecture values and its relevance to the global stage.

The Architects of this Generation

This book has been inspired by the Hong Kong Institute of Architects' publications of 熱戀建築：與拾伍香港資深建築師的對話 (ISBN 9789627732099) and 筆生建築 29 位資深建築師的香港建築 (ISBN 9789620440496), both of which are monographs on Hong Kong's master architects. This book, *Untold Stories: Hong Kong Architecture*, serves as an introduction to Hong Kong's new generations of architects that focuses on the middle and younger generation. Using their designs as a form of introduction, this book seeks to explore and analyse the heartfelt stories of these architects.

Writing this book required personal interviews with various architects. In addition to visiting dozens of architects' offices, we also had to wait patiently for the results of the various open architecture competitions to come in so that we could interview the winning architects. A severe pandemic in the middle of the process meant that the last part of the interview was compressed into a round table format or conducted in a video group, involving conversations with sixty architects. Specifically, the interview chapters pertaining to my works were conducted by Ms Helena Hau. These included the sections for the Victoria Peak Garden, Tsim Sha Tsui Promenade, Archivilla, The Flower Box and the Sai Kung Visual Corridor. On the whole, it took a year to complete the book for the original Chinese edition, followed by another year for its English edition to come to fruition.

Through these interviews, I have come to appreciate the passion of fellow architects who continue to fulfil their architectural missions even after many years in the industry; and I am grateful for the valuable advice given by our enthusiastic fellow architects. The studio of each architect interviewed was distinctive in its design and decor, reflecting individual preferences and tastes. One of the studios, for example, was located in a common factory building in Chai Wan, with an ordinary, if not a little grimy, appearance. However, on stepping through the door, one was met by uplifting music with a Latin flair, red wine and white wine, salmon, and the romantic recklessness of Bohemia, reminiscent of the post-apocalyptic sentiment of the East Village in New York years ago. The owner and I were both former visitors to New York, and during our four-hour interview, we shared a moment of mutual empathy; reminiscing about times gone by and the swift passage of time, as well as the bittersweet memories of both struggles and triumphs.

Four Gains

It has been a labour of love completing this book, and I am pleased to have achieved four objectives with its publication:

(1) To document the untold stories of architects in Hong Kong;

(2) To understand the lives of individual architects and appreciate the ideas behind their architecture;

(3) To spread positive energy; and

(4) To develop and maintain priceless friendships.

Last, but not least, my sincere gratitude for the support offered by Unicorn Publishing Group LLP, without whom these stories would not have been told.

Acknowledgements

Untold Stories: Hong Kong Architecture is a publication supported by the Design Trust Seed Grant.

Design Trust provides funding support to the project only and does not otherwise take part in the project. Any opinions, findings, conclusions or recommendations expressed in these materials/events (or by members of the project team) are those of the project organisers only and do not reflect the views of Design Trust.

DESIGNTRUST
信言設計大使
AN INITIATIVE OF THE
HONG KONG AMBASSADORS
OF DESIGN

Ms Marisa Yiu

Mr Billy Chan

Mr Kelvin Li

Ms Ida Sze

Mr Charlie Xue

Mr Joseph Ting Sun Pao

Mr Jeff Tung

Mr Wong Fook-yee

Mr Daniel Wong

Ms Phyllis Wong

Ms Salome Yip

Raymond W.K. Fung, JP
FHKIA, HonAIA (HK)

Raymond is a renowned architect, artist and designer. He is Adjunct Professor of the School of Architecture, Chinese University of Hong Kong; former Visiting Professor of the Central Academy of Fine Arts, Beijing; Board Member of the Hong Kong Palace Museum, Honorary Advisor of Museums, Leisure & Cultural Services Department. He has also written seven books on art and architecture.

Helena W.Y. Hau
BSS (Hons) in Media and social communication, B.A. in fine arts

Graduated from Hong Kong Baptist University and RMIT University/Hong Kong Art School, Helena is currently the assistant managing content editor in Etnet, and was a hostess of the Etnet ArtInvest channel.

Karen C.C. Tsui
M.A., Ph.D. in Art Theory

Dr. Karen Tsui is an independent curator and Chinese Art specialist graduated from the Central Academy of Fine Arts. Her academic research focuses on Song and Yuan Chinese painting, history of collecting and museum management.

Christopher S.H. Hau
LLB (Hons)

Christopher is a culturally fluent writer and translator with a deep understanding of the English and Chinese languages. He has a diverse educational background, having been educated in Hong Kong, Singapore, and the United Kingdom, which allows him to bring a unique and nuanced perspective to his work. His expertise in cultural representation allows him to deliver precise and impactful translations.

List of Interviewed and Mentioned Architects

1	乙增志	T.C. Yuet	26	林偉明	Lam Wai Ming	51	景國祥	K.C. King	76	蕭國健	Stanley Siu
2	丁慧中	Evelyn Ting	27	林雲峯	Bernard V. Lim	52	曾永璋	Anson Tsang	77	謝怡邦	Paul Tse
3	王安華	Edward Wong	28	施琪珊	Ida Sze	53	曾偉倫	William Tsang	77	謝錦榮	Kenneth Tse
4	王維仁	Wei Jen Wang	29	徐莊德	Ray Zee	54	馮永基	Raymond Fung	79	藍兆偉	Andrew Nam
5	朱珮汶	Annette Chu	30	高文安	Kenneth Ko	55	馮奕萍	Sherry Fung	80	羅建中	Chris Law
6	朱國勇	Steven Chu	31	區佩瑁	Selah Au	56	馮慧雯	Vivien Fung	81	羅發禮	James Law
7	何文堯	Ivan Ho	32	張智強	Gary Chang	57	黃德明	Humphrey Wong	82	譚士偉	Kenneth Tam
8	何永賢	Winnie Ho	33	張豔芬	Lucia Cheung	58	黃錦星	K.S. Wong	83	譚秉榮	Bing Thom
9	何宗憲	Joey Ho	34	梁文傑	M.K. Leung	59	溫灼均	Thomas Wan	84	譚漢華	Billy Tam
10	余嘯峰	Frank Yu	35	梁志天	Steve Leung	60	葉晉亨	Yip Chun Hang	85	嚴迅奇	Rocco Yim
11	吳永順	Vincent Ng	36	梅冬景	Tony Mui	61	葉華明	Ray Yip	86	蘇陽彪	S.O. Yeung Piu
12	吳享洪	Anthony Ng	37	梅詩華	Sarah Mui	62	葉頌文	Tony Ip	87	鍾鳴昌	M.C. Chung
13	吳家健	Gary Ng	38	梅鉅川	Paul Mui	63	廖宜康	Philip Liao	88	梁建航	Donald Leung
14	吳偉滔	Michael Ng	39	陳志偉	Edwin Chan	64	廖偉廉	William Liu	89	李美茵	Jacqueline Lee
15	吳偉麟	Norman Ung	40	陳健華	Eric Chan	65	劉天行	Peter Lau	90	李百怡	Tuesday Li
16	吳鎮麟	Otto Ng	41	陳嘉麗	Kylie Chan	66	劉振宇	C.Y. Lau	91	盧智恒	Boris Lo
17	呂達文	Frankie Lui	42	陳維正	Billy Chan	67	劉偉健	Tony Lau	92	甄孟仁	Francis Yan
18	李亮聰	Anderson Lee	43	陳翠兒	Corrin Chan	68	劉達楹	T.Y. Lau	93	周安遠	Daniel Chow
19	李昭明	Benny Lee	44	陳樂文	Norman Chan	69	劉蔚茵	Sofia Lau	94	姚嘉珊	Marisa Yiu
20	李培基	Kevin Li	45	陳麗喬	L.K. Chan	70	歐暉	Au Fai	95	黎雋維	Charles Lai
21	李翹彥	Michael Li	46	陸忠霖	Patrick Luk	71	練偉東	Ryan Lin	96	胡燦森	Roger Wu
22	阮文韜	Manfred Yuen	47	麥尚青	Michael Mak	72	蔡宏興	Donald Choi	97	劉柏堅	Joshua Lau
23	周德年	Thomas Chow	48	勞志成	Jacen Lo	73	鄧文彬	Stephen Tang	98	朱海山	Paul Chu
24	周蕙禮	Wailee Chow	49	彭一欣	Angela Pang	74	鄧可欣	Elva Tang	99	李少穎	Ivy Lee
25	林偉而	William Lim	50	彭耀輝	Vincent Pang	75	鄭炳鴻	Wallace Chang	100	何周禮	Barrie Ho

Citation

余震宇：《上半山．下中環：一個城區的蛻變》(香港：中華書局, 2017)。
Jacky Yu:《上半山．下中環：一個城區的蛻變》(Hong Kong: Chung Hwa Book Co., 2017) (ISBN: 9789888463954)

林中偉：《建築保育與本土文化》(香港：中華書局, 2015)。
Tony Lam:《建築保育與本土文化》(Hong Kong: Chung Hwa Book Co., 2017) (ISBN: 9789888310920)

建築遊人：《築覺：閱讀香港建築》(香港：三聯書店, 2013)。
Archtraveler:《築覺：閱讀香港建築》(Hong Kong: Joint Publishing (H.K.), 2013) (ISBN: 9789620433832)

香港建築中心：《筆講建築：當城市、人文、自然遇上建築》(香港：三聯書店, 2021)。
Hong Kong Architecture Centre:《筆講建築：當城市、人文、自然遇上建築》(Hong Kong: Joint Publishing (H.K.), 2021) (ISBN: 9789620447501)

香港建築師學會：《建築宏圖》(香港：香港建築師學會, 2006)。
The Hong Kong Institute of Architects: Architectural Blueprint : HKIA 50th anniversary commemorative book (Hong Kong: The Hong Kong Institute of Architects, 2006) (ISBN: 9627732087, 9789627732082)

香港建築師學會：《筆生建築：29 位資深建築師的香港建築》(香港：三聯書店, 2016)。
The Hong Kong Institute of Architects:《筆生建築：29 位資深建築師的香港建築》(Hong Kong: Joint Publishing (H.K.), 2016) (ISBN: 9789620440496)

香港設計中心：《香港城區設計散步》(香港：商務印書館, 2012)。
Hong Kong Design Centre:《香港城區設計散步》(Hong Kong: Commercial Press, 2012) (ISBN: 9789620756016)

高馬可：《香港簡史》(香港：中華書局, 2013)。
John Mark Carroll: A Concise History of Hong Kong (Hong Kong, Chung Hwa Book Co., 2013)

高添強：《香港今昔》(香港：三聯書店, 1994)。
Ko Tim-keung:《香港今昔》(Hong Kong, Joint Publishing (H.K.), 1994)

陳翠兒、蔡宏興：《空間之旅：香港建築百年》(香港：三聯書店, 2005)。
Corrin Chan, Donald Choi:《空間之旅：香港建築百年》(Hong Kong: Joint Publishing (H.K.), 2005) (ISBN: 9789620424953)

單霽翔：《宅茲香港：活化歷史建築》(香港：中華書局, 2022)。
Shan Jixiang:《宅茲香港：活化歷史建築》(Hong Kong: Chung Hwa Book Co., 2022) (ISBN: 9789888807383)

馮永基：《誰把爛泥扶上壁：你所不知的香港建築故事》(香港：中華書店, 2016)。
Raymond Fung:《誰把爛泥扶上壁：你所不知的香港建築故事》(Hong Kong: Chung Hwa Book Co., 2016) (ISBN: 9789888420223)

魯金：《九龍城寨史話》(香港：三聯書店, 1988)。
Jin Lu:《九龍城寨史話》(Hong Kong: Joint Publishing (H.K.), 1988)

劉智鵬：《香港早期華人菁英》(香港：中華書局, 2011)。
Lau Chi-pang:《香港早期華人菁英》(Hong Kong: Chung Hwa Book Co., 2011) (ISBN: 9789888104963)

龍炳頤：《香港古今建築》(香港：三聯書店, 1992)。
David Ping-yee LUNG:《香港古今建築》(Hong Kong: Joint Publishing (H.K.), 1992) (ISBN: 9620410203)

薛求理：《城景：香港建築1946-2011》(香港：商務印書館, 2014)。
Mr Charlie Xue:《城景：香港建築1946-2011》(Hong Kong: Commercial Press, 2014) (ISBN: 9789620756313)

饒久才、王福義：《香港林業及自然護理：回顧與前瞻》(香港：郊野公園之友會, 2021)。
Rao Jiucai, Wong Fook-yee:《香港林業及自然護理：回顧與前瞻》(Hong Kong: Friends of the Country Parks, 2021) (ISBN: 9789882196155)

饒久才：《香港的地名與地方歷史》上 (香港：天地圖書, 2011)。
Rao Jiucai:《香港的地名與地方歷史》上 (Hong Kong: Cosmos Books, 2011) (ISBN: 9789882193512)

饒久才：《香港的地名與地方歷史》下 (香港：天地圖書, 2012)。
Rao Jiucai: 香港的地名與地方歷史》下 (Hong Kong: Cosmos Books, 2012) (ISBN: 9789882194618)

Bing Thom Architects, *Bing Thom Works* (New York: Princeton Architectural Press, 2011).

Chris van Uffelen, *China: The New Creative Power in Architecture* (Switzerland: Braun Publishing, 2019).

James Saywell, *Presence: the architecture of Rocco Design* (Hong Kong: MCCM Creations, 2012).

Ulf Meyer, *Architectural Guide 2021* Hong Kong (Berlin: DOM publishers, 2013).

Citation

Untold Stories: Hong Kong Architecture

Author	Raymond Fung
Co-writers	Helena Hau Karen Tsui
Translator	Christopher Hau
Responsible Editor	Lucie Skilton

First English Edition published by

Unicorn Publishing Group
Charleston Studio
Meadow Business Centre
Lewes
United Kingdom
BN8 5RW
www.unicornpublishing.org

Text copyright © 2023 Raymond Fung

All rights reserved. No part of the contents of this book may be reproduced, stored in or introduced into a retrieval system, or transmitted, in any form or by any means (electronic, mechanical, photocopying, recording or otherwise), without the prior written permission of the copyright holder and the above publisher of this book.

Every effort has been made to trace copyright holders and to obtain their permission for the use of copyrighted material. The publisher apologises for any errors or omissions and would be grateful to be notified of any corrections that should be incorporated in future reprints or editions of this book.

ISBN: 978-1-911397-33-5

Printer

Fine Tone Ltd

First published in Hong Kong, China by

Chung Hwa Book Company (Hong Kong) Limited

ISBN: 978-1-988-8807-44-4

Editor's Note

'Translation is not a matter of words only: it is a matter of making intelligible a whole culture' – Anthony Burgess

The utmost care has been given to accurately convey the messages and meaning of this book, originally written by Raymond Fung in Chinese. It is a celebration of collaboration between a great number of people: author, interviewers, interviewees, translators, editors and publisher. Mindful that Raymond is not only an architect but also an artist who specialises in Chinese ink painting, every attempt has been made to not only convey the literal translation of his words but to show respect for his original vison for this book. Some phrases might appear slightly different to the native English reader, but take a moment to consider them and they will reveal a new appreciation for the beauty and artistry of the original language and culture and all their subtle complexities.

Translator's Note

Within the realm of communication, the spoken word may occasionally deviate from our true intentions. However, the written word serves as a vessel that delves deep into the profound emotions we wish to express. In undertaking this translation, my objective has been to meticulously capture not only the literal words, but also the profound sentiments that reside within them. Translation itself is a nuanced interplay of languages and cultures, embodying the profound realisation that despite our diverse origins, our souls naturally yearn for mutual understanding and connection.

Publisher's Note

UK English has been used as much as possible. However, many names of organisations, projects and quotes from individuals utilise US English and these have been deliberately left in their original form.